Lesbian Friendships

THE CUTTING EDGE
Lesbian Life and Literature

THE CUTTING EDGE
Lesbian Life and Literature

Series Editor: *Karla Jay*
Professor of English and Women's Studies
PACE UNIVERSITY

EDITORIAL BOARD

Leila J. Rupp
History
OHIO STATE UNIVERSITY

Ann Allen Shockley
Librarian
FISK UNIVERSITY

Elizabeth Wood
Musicologist and Writer
Committee on Theory and Culture
NEW YORK UNIVERSITY

Bonnie Zimmerman
Women's Studies
SAN DIEGO STATE UNIVERSITY

THE CUTTING EDGE
Lesbian Life and Literature

Series Editor: Karla Jay

The Cook and the Carpenter: A Novel by the Carpenter
by June Arnold
with an introduction by Bonnie Zimmerman

Ladies Almanack
by Djuna Barnes
with an introduction by Susan Sniader Lanser

Adventures of the Mind:
The Memoirs of Natalie Clifford Barney
translated by John Spalding Gatton
with an introduction by Karla Jay

Sophia Parnok: The Life and Work of Russia's Sappho
by Diana Burgin

Paint It Today by H.D. (Hilda Doolittle)
edited and with an introduction by
Cassandra Laity

The Angel and the Perverts
by Lucie Delarue-Mardrus
translated and with an introduction by Anna Livia

Heterosexual Plots and Lesbian Narratives
Marilyn R. Farwell

Spinsters and Lesbians: Independent Womanhood
in the United States, 1890–1930 and 1950–1980
by Trisha Franzen

Diana: A Strange Autobiography
by Diana Frederics
with an introduction by Julie L. Abraham

Lover
by Bertha Harris

Elizabeth Bowen: A Reputation in Writing
by renée c. hoogland

Lesbian Erotics
edited by Karla Jay

Changing Our Minds: Lesbian Feminism and Psychology
by Celia Kitzinger and Rachel Perkins

(Sem)Erotics: Theorizing Lesbian : Writing
by Elizabeth A. Meese

*Bisexuality and the Challenge to Lesbian Politics:
Sex, Loyalty, and Revolution*
by Paula C. Rust

The Search for a Woman-Centered Spirituality
by Annette J. Van Dyke

Lesbian Friendships: For Ourselves and Each Other
edited by Jacqueline S. Weinstock and Esther D. Rothblum

*I Know My Own Heart: The Diaries of Anne Lister,
1791–1840*
edited by Helena Whitbread

*No Priest but Love: The Journals of Anne Lister,
1824–26*
edited by Helena Whitbread

Lesbian Friendships

For Ourselves and Each Other

EDITED BY

Jacqueline S. Weinstock and
Esther D. Rothblum

NEW YORK UNIVERSITY PRESS
New York and London

NEW YORK UNIVERSITY PRESS
New York and London

Library of Congress Cataloging-in-Publication Data
Lesbian friendships : for ourselves and each other / edited by
Jacqueline S. Weinstock and Esther D. Rothblum.
p.   cm. — (Cutting edge)
Includes bibliographical references and index.
ISBN 0-8147-7473-3 (pb : alk. paper). — ISBN 0-8147-7472-5 (hc :
alk. paper)
1. Lesbians — United States.   2. Lesbian couples — United States.
3. Female friendship — United States.   4. Friendship — United States.
I. Weinstock, Jacqueline S., 1961-   . II. Rothblum, Esther D.
III. Series: Cutting edge (New York, N.Y.)
HQ75.6.U5L375   1996
305.48'9664—dc20   96-10114
CIP

New York University Press books are printed on acid-free
paper, and their binding materials are chosen for strength
and durability.

Manufactured in the United States of America
10 9 8 7 6 5 4 3 2 1

To our friends . . .
present, past, and future
And to our friends' friends . . .

Contents

PART IV. Fixed Points in a Changing World:
Personal and Political Dimensions of Friendship

PART V. Afterword

Foreword

KARLA JAY

Despite the efforts of lesbian and feminist publishing houses and a few university presses, the bulk of the most important lesbian works has traditionally been available only from rare-book dealers, in a few university libraries, or in gay and lesbian archives. This series intends, in the first place, to make representative examples of this neglected and insufficiently known literature available to a broader audience by reissuing selected classics and by putting into print for the first time lesbian novels, diaries, letters, and memoirs that are of special interest and significance, but which have moldered in libraries and private collections for decades or even for centuries, known only to the few scholars who had the courage and financial wherewithal to track them down.

Their names have been known for a long time—Sappho, the Amazons of North Africa, the Beguines, Aphra Behn, Queen Christina, Emily Dickinson, the Ladies of Llangollen, Radclyffe Hall, Natalie Clifford Barney, H.D., and so many others from every nation, race, and era. But government and religious officials burned their writings, historians and literary scholars denied they were lesbians, powerful men kept their books out of print, and influential archivists locked up their ideas far from sympathetic eyes. Yet some dedicated scholars and readers still knew who they were, made pilgrimages to the cities and villages where they had lived and to the graveyards where they rested. They passed around tattered volumes of letters, diaries, and biographies, in which they had underlined what seemed to be telltale hints of a secret or different kind of life. Where no hard facts existed, legends were invented. The few precious and often available pre-Stonewall lesbian classics, such as *The Well of Loneliness* by Radclyffe Hall, *The Price of Salt* by Claire Morgan (Patricia Highsmith), and *Desert of the Heart* by Jane Rule, were cherished. Lesbian pulp was devoured. One of the primary goals of this series is to give the more neglected works, which constitute the vast majority of lesbian writing, the attention they deserve.

A second but no less important aim of this series is to present the "cutting edge" of contemporary lesbian scholarship and theory across a wide range of disciplines. Practitioners of lesbian studies have not adopted a uniform approach to literary theory, history, sociology, or any other discipline, nor should they. This series intends to present an array of voices that truly reflects the diversity of the lesbian community. To help me in this task, I am lucky enough to be assisted by a distinguished editorial board that reflects various professional, class, racial, ethnic, and religious backgrounds as well as a spectrum of interests and sexual preferences.

At present the field of lesbian studies occupies a small, precarious, and somewhat contested pied-à-terre between gay studies and women's studies. The former is still in its infancy, especially if one compares it to other disciplines that have been part of the core curriculum of every child and adolescent for several decades or even centuries. However, although it is one of the newest disciplines, gay studies may also be the fastest-growing one—at least in North America. Lesbian, gay, and bisexual studies conferences are doubling and tripling their attendance. Although only a handful of degree-granting programs currently exists, that number is also apt to multiply quickly during the next decade.

In comparison, women's studies is a well-established and burgeoning discipline with hundreds of minors, majors, and graduate programs throughout the United States. Lesbian studies occupies a peripheral place in the discourse in such programs, characteristically restricted to one lesbian-centered course, usually literary or historical in nature. In the many women's studies series that are now offered by university presses, generally only one or two books on a lesbian subject or issue are included, and lesbian voices are restricted to writing on those topics considered of special interest to gay people. We are not called upon to offer opinions on motherhood, war, education, or on the lives of women not publicly identified as lesbians. As a result, lesbian experience is too often marginalized and restricted.

In contrast, this series will prioritize, centralize, and celebrate lesbian visions of literature, art, philosophy, love, religion, ethics, history, and a myriad of other topics. In "The Cutting Edge," readers can find authoritative versions of important lesbian texts that have been carefully prepared and introduced by scholars. Readers can also find the work of academics and independent scholars who write about other aspects of life from a distinctly lesbian viewpoint. These visions are not only various but intentionally contradictory, for lesbians speak from differing class, racial, ethnic, and religious perspectives. Each author also speaks from and about a certain moment of time, and few would argue that being a lesbian today is the same as it was for Sappho or Anne Lister. Thus no attempt has been made to homogenize that diversity, and no agenda exists to attempt to carve out a "politically correct" lesbian studies perspective at this juncture in history or to pinpoint the "real" lesbians in history. It seems more important for all the voices to be heard before those with the blessings of aftersight lay the mantle of authenticity on any one vision of the world, or on any particular set of women.

What each work in this series does share, however, is a common realization that gay women are the "Other" and that one's perception of culture and literature is filtered by sexual behaviors and preferences. Those perceptions are not the same as those of gay men or of nongay women, whether the writers speak of gay or feminist issues or whether the writers choose to look at nongay figures from a lesbian perspective. The role of this series is to create space and give a voice to those interested in lesbian studies. This series speaks to any person who is interested in gender studies, literary criticism, biography, or important literary works, whether she or he is a student, professor, or serious reader, for the series is neither for lesbians only nor even by lesbians only. Instead, "The Cutting Edge" attempts to share some of the best of lesbian literature and lesbian studies with anyone willing to look at the world through lesbians' eyes. The series is proactive in that it will help to formulate and foreground the very discipline on which it focuses. Finally, this series has answered the call to make lesbian theory, lesbian experience, lesbian lives, lesbian literature, and lesbian visions the heart and nucleus, the weighty planet around which for once other viewpoints will swirl as moons to our earth. We invite readers of all persuasions to join us by venturing into this and other books in the series.

We are very pleased to include an anthology on friendship in "The Cutting Edge" series. Friendship plays a special role in the lives of lesbians and gay men as some of us are cut off by our families of origin and many more are not treated as equals of their heterosexual siblings. As a result, lesbians in general rely heavily on friendship networks that may include former lovers, lesbian friends, heterosexual women, and both heterosexual and homosexual men. *Lesbian Friendships* is the first collection to explore and celebrate the diversity and richness of lesbian friendships.

Acknowledgments

This has been a deeply personal project at the same time that it has been a part of our professional work. There are many people to thank who have helped us move this book from an idea to a reality. Among these, none are more important than the authors of the chapters in this collection; without them, we could not tell the stories of lesbians' friendships.

We also wish to thank Timothy Bartlett, Despina Papazoglou Gimbel, and their staff at New York University Press, as well as Karla Jay, editor of the Cutting Edge series. Jackie Weinstock would like to thank the Methodology Center at the Pennsylvania State University, the National Institute on Aging Postdoctoral Training Program, and the University of Washington Tacoma for their support during the preparation of this book. Esther Rothblum would like to thank the Department of Psychology at the University of Vermont for continuing support of and enthusiasm for her work. This book was completed while she was a Visiting Scholar at the Institute for Research on Women and Gender at Stanford University.

At a more personal level, we wish to thank our friends who have inspired and reaffirmed our commitment to friendship. There are many to thank: friends of the present and of the past, those that are just becoming friends and those that have been with us a long, long time, and friends linked to us in all sorts of friendship. To adequately thank all these friends would require a book in and of itself. We hope that they know what they mean to us through our actions, including the action of editing this book on friendships. Here, in these acknowledgments, then, we select out only a few of the many ways we wish to thank and honor our friends.

Jackie would especially like to thank her close friends for their love and support and for the many conversations shared about so many different things, including all the themes that run through these pages and much, much more. She would also like to express her deep appreciation for the commitment to friendships felt and acted upon among her friends and within lesbian communities more generally. It has been her friendships that have inspired and sustained her adolescent and adult life.

Esther would like to thank the close friends from her childhood to the present who have shaped and shared her life, both those in the United States and those overseas, and especially those who are still in her life. Her family of friends are the backbone of her life.

We dedicate this book to our friends, who have inspired this book as they have inspired our lives.

PART I

An Introduction to Lesbians' Friendships

Jackie Weinstock (right) and Betsy Hinden (left) enjoying each other's company and friendship at another friend's birthday celebration on a beautiful Vermont evening in September 1992. Surrounded by many of her other most special friends, including Josie, Dorothy, Lynn, Eileen, Diane, and Golda, Jackie couldn't be happier, though admittedly part of the moment's laughter is due to Jackie just having been teased by Betsy about her shy interest in another party-goer. Photo by Josie Juhasz and Dorothy Forsyth.

The Bad Girls—from left to right, Connie Chan, Linda Garnets, and Esther Rothblum—get together annually to practice being bad and outrageous. Photo by Barrie Levy.

ONE

What We Can Be Together: Contemplating Lesbians' Friendships

JACQUELINE S. WEINSTOCK AND ESTHER D. ROTHBLUM

Friends as lovers; lovers as friends; ex-lovers as friends; ex-lovers as family; friends as family; families of friends; families of creation; communities of friends; lesbian community. These are just a few of the phrases we hear often in the daily discourse of lesbian life. We suspect these phrases will be familiar and personally meaningful to many lesbians reading this book. But what meanings do they have for us? How many of us view our friends as family? What do we really mean when we consider friends to be "family"? Who comprises these families of friends? How often are ex-lovers part of our families of friends? How common is it to establish or sustain friendships with ex-lovers? How often do our ex-lovers become friends with each other? How often do we become lovers with our friends? And why are there some among us who choose not to use the language of family to identify the importance of our friendships?

While some of the questions above have been explored through research, fiction, and/or personal conversations among friends, most have not been deeply examined in public discourse. There are many other types of questions that have not been examined as well: questions that compare lesbian and nonlesbian patterns of friendship. How do our conceptions and experiences of friendship compare with those of heterosexual women, for example, or with gay men? How often do lesbians pursue friendships with men, with bisexual or heterosexual women, with heterosexual married couples? And what kinds of friendships develop when they are pursued? In what ways do these friendships differ from, and in what ways do they resemble friendships between lesbians?

Most of the academic literature on women's friendships has not included much attention to lesbians' friendships with each other nor to friendships between lesbians and nonlesbians. We have been particularly struck by the absence of explorations into conceptions of friendship as they relate to conceptions of family. Perhaps this is in part because such questions may be less crucial to heterosexual women and men. The legal definition of "family" consists of biological relatives, relatives acquired through a legal marriage ceremony (e.g., in-laws), or relatives acquired through legal adoption. Friends, in contrast, are people with whom there are no biological or legal ties. In this traditional view of families versus friends, a "family of friends" is a contradiction in terms.

Our motivation for this book emerged from these circumstances, as well as from our personal experiences and political commitments. Each of us has been profoundly influenced by and grateful for our friendships, from childhood through to our current life circumstances. We have participated in as well as observed friendships in lesbian communities that differ from mainstream accounts of friendships. This collection of stories and research reports is our way of beginning to address this gap. It is also our way of celebrating lesbians' friendships and lesbian communities.

We began this endeavor in 1994 with the following statement:

Jackie Weinstock and Esther Rothblum are interested in editing a book that focuses on lesbians' experiences of friendship. We are particularly interested in hearing from lesbians and their friends about the ways in which being lesbian affects friendships. The book's focus will be on actual accounts of friendships involving lesbians, with particular attention to friendships that portray a diversity of ages, ethnicities, genders, nationalities, physical abilities, races, sexualities, etc.

We welcome submissions that rely on diverse formats, such as letters exchanged between friends, dialogues, poems, jointly constructed accounts of a friendship or separate accounts of the same friendship by its members, as well as single-authored accounts.

This announcement was sent to lesbian and feminist newsletters and to colleagues and friends. It was published in a wide variety of academic, social, and political publications across the United States (and a few international settings). We also wrote directly to several researchers and theorists whose work has addressed lesbian friendships. This book is the result of the submissions we received and accepted.

The majority of chapters in this collection are personal narratives of friendship. Because we are both social scientists, we have also included a few chapters that describe research studies and present research findings. While there are hundreds of published articles and books about women's friendships, only a handful have focused on friendships among lesbians.

Lack of Attention to Lesbian Friendships

As a developmental and clinical psychologist, respectively, we have seen firsthand how important friendships can be in supporting the health and development of adults, their families, and their communities. There has also been a recent and growing interest in the development of women's friendships. Still, in comparison with other forms of interpersonal relationships in adulthood, we know little about the role of friendships. Family relationships (as traditionally conceptualized) tend to garner much greater attention than friendships.

This greater attention to family than friendship is observable in research that focuses on lesbians as well as in that which focuses on nonlesbians. Indeed, most of the research in psychology (and, we believe, other fields) that is concerned with the lesbian experience continues to focus on the causes of sexual or gender identity/orientation, the "normalcy" of being a lesbian in comparison with being a heterosexual, or the consequences of being a lesbian in a heterosexist and gender-dichotomous society. More recently, there has been greater attention to the strengths of our communities (see Morin and Rothblum, 1991, for a review of the changes since "homosexuality" was removed from the second edition of the *Diagnostic and Statistical Manual of Mental Disorders* as a mental illness in 1973), but little of this focus has been on the role of friendships. Yet even with so little attention, the few existing references indicate to us that friendships and friendship networks are central to community development, political organizing, and the healthy development of the individual. As such they require our greater attention.

Much of what we do know about lesbian life comes to us more through personal writings and stories (historical and fictional) than through theory or research. Some writers have collected the stories of women, including lesbians, who have constructed diverse families of friends. Others have sought, through their work, to reignite and recenter lesbian attention to lesbian communities. In doing so, they highlight the importance of lesbian friendships. As Audre Lorde phrased it (1984, p. 167) "[t]he question of lesbian friendship is central to the building of lesbian community and realizing a lesbian vision."

We understand the invisibility of lesbian friendships as one example of how mainstream theories have preference over theories that emerge directly from lesbian experiences and communities. We also see it as an example of the privileged place some forms of relationships have in both lesbian and mainstream cultures. That is, despite some personal, fictional, research, and theoretical evidence to the contrary, friendships appear to hold as unprivileged a place in lesbian writing as they do in heterosexual writing. This is particularly true when we compare attention to friendships with attention to family relationships (as traditionally defined). We hope that this collection encourages more attention to an understanding of lesbian friendships.

Lesbians' Families of Friends

This book is an attempt to focus greater attention on the functions and meanings of friendships among lesbians. This includes the role of friendships in the personal lives of lesbians as well as in our theoretical and political discourse. There is a need to value and respect the sharing of our personal experiences of friendship with each other. At the same time, we need to be concerned about the extent to which this private discourse remains separate from, yet potentially shaped by, dominant conceptions of friendship, family, and politics. We are concerned about the absence of lesbians' perspectives on friendship in the public discourse, but we are also concerned about the ways in which that public discourse has affected lesbians' experiences with and conceptions of friendship. To what extent have we lesbians ourselves examined our notions of friendships and our roles within them? How aware are we of the many uncontested assumptions about friendship that pervade the mainstream discourse? Relatedly, what are the intended and unintended consequences of our adoption of family terms to describe our friendships? These, we believe, are central questions, yet ones we have not yet deeply considered.

There is clearly a need both for personal and political explorations of lesbians' friendships and lesbians' families, and the interrelationships between the two. One important aspect of lesbians' friendships is the tendency for lesbians to remain friends with ex-lovers, evidenced in several of the chapters that follow (see also Becker, 1988). This does not seem to be the case among heterosexual women's relationships with ex-spouses and ex-partners. Yet with only a few exceptions, there is little available written evidence exploring the extent to which lesbian, gay, or heterosexual ex-partners become or remain friends, especially when there are no children involved. For example, a study by Constance Ahrons (1981) on relationships among heterosexual ex-partners centered on the coparental aspects of these relationships. Interactions that did not focus on the children were termed "nonparental" and were not further investigated. Additionally, it has been argued that the best postdivorce arrangements are ones that involve little interaction between former spouses except as coparents who are not also friends (see, e.g., Ahrons and Wallisch, 1987; Durst, Wedemeyer and Zurcher, 1985).

Along with an image of lesbians as being likely to form and/or sustain friendships with ex-lovers, there is also much talk about the creation of alternative families comprised of friends within the lesbian and gay communities. While there has been some exploration of these notions (see, e.g., Weston, 1991), we still know hardly anything about the forms and functions of these families of friends. It is also unclear to what extent we purposefully discuss and formally create these friendship families with those we consider family members.

While friendship families may in fact reflect a unique family and/ or friendship form, the use of a family discourse to describe our friendships may also reflect the adoption of mainstream assumptions about the privileged role of family in relation to friends. Describing our friends as family may confer greater importance and/or status on our friendships, but so too does it appear to reinforce the hegemony of the family. For example, developmental psychologists have found that persons in young and middle adulthood tend to spend less time with and focus less attention on friends than do adolescents; more time is spent dealing with work and/or family demands. However, these theories have assumed a typical heterosexual life course that includes a marriage or marital-type relationship and children. We do not know whether lesbians make a similar shift from friends to family in early and middle adulthood. Perhaps we are more likely to remain focused on friends and less on family, or perhaps we balance these multiple commitments and focus our attention equally on both forms of relationship. The notion of friends as family that is salient among many lesbians seems to suggest an attempt to more fully integrate these diverse close relationship forms.

Whether or not lesbians negotiate friends and family differently, we need to understand the reasons for our choices and outcomes. There is evidence to suggest that lesbians follow different patterns from heterosexual women into and through adulthood. For example, women may delay identification (or construction of an identity) as a lesbian until late adolescence, early adulthood, or even middle and later adulthood or may have restricted opportunities throughout the life course to express these identities. There is limited familial and societal support for lesbian couple relationships and families, as well as limited economic resources. The personal and political beliefs and choices of lesbians may also affect our life patterns.

Given these factors, we must ask to what extent lesbians "choose" families of friends: perhaps this "choice" is simply one of the very few available to us. When we talk about friends as family, are we striving to create for ourselves that which has been denied us in the traditional fashion, or are we purposefully critiquing and expanding society's notion of family? When we use the language of family to describe our friendships, are we attempting to assimilate to or radically depart from the politically charged and publicly accepted conception of family? Kath Weston (1991) explores this question in *Families We Choose*; so too did Karen Lindsay (1981) a decade earlier in *Friends as Family*. Similarly, Carol Stack examined the notion of family—and fictive kin—back in 1974 in relation to a community of African-Americans living in a poor, urban neighborhood. These works describe the ways in which various groups that typically hold limited power and resources relative to dominant groups create and sustain kinship ties. The question we must ask ourselves, we believe, is what we mean by kin and what motivates our use of kin terms to describe our connections with friends.

Additionally, we must ask ourselves whether our adoption of family terms to describe our friendships actually enters us into—and indeed contributes to—a family discourse that is at once heterosexist, racist, and classist (see, e.g., Popenoe, 1993). The family debates in the United States of the 1990s, as we hear them, rarely use the term "family" as a shorthand for a relational context involving mutual love and respect among all the participants. Instead, the discourse we hear reinforces the privileged status of lifelong, middle- to upper-class, heterosexual marriage and the biological children that result from this union. Additionally, it is the reduction of families that reflect this form—symbolized in the popular and political discourse as the decay of family values—that is viewed as the cause of most of our current social problems (Stacey, 1994).

Within conservative as well as liberal political (and some feminist) discourse, and in our own disciplines of developmental and clinical psychology, social scientific research findings are (mis)interpreted and misapplied as indicating support for the argument that traditional families are "normal." We know comparatively less about what it means to live in families without access to heterosexual, gender, class, and race privileges. Indeed, in both politics and academia, there has been too little attention to the ways families function and too much attention to the particular forms that families take. Similarly, there has been too little attention to the match between individuals (their preferences, capacities, and needs) and their families (in terms, for example, of composition, division of labor, and relational processes). For example, among heterosexual, married couples with children, McHale and Crouter (1992) found that spouses who differed in their attitudes toward sex roles and their ideas about an appropriate division of labor were more dissatisfied with their marriage than those with similar attitudes about sex roles. In lesbian families, where equality is a frequently espoused value and ideal for the couple relationship (Kurdek, 1995a), children are also more well adjusted (and parents more satisfied) when the parents share equally in child care (Patterson, 1995a). Taken together, these diverse findings highlight the importance of attending not simply to particular family forms or processes but to the match between family members' personal beliefs, capacities, and preferences, and their actual family practices. The debate over family, however, rarely addresses such issues of matches and mismatches; the central concern seems to be family structure and, in particular, a two-parent, heterosexual family structure.

The discourse on the family rarely—if ever—acknowledges lesbian and gay relationships and families; it ignores as well those families that are single-parent by choice, as well as many other family forms. Indeed, even lesbians' own discourse on the family—when we enter the political arena—focuses on those family forms that most reflect the privileged two-parent, heterosexual family form. In such a context, then, we wonder whether family politics are dangerous for lesbian friendships. We recognize and indeed value the great efforts of members of our communities toward garnering equal rights and benefits for lesbian and gay partners and families, including the efforts of researchers to document the similarities between lesbian and gay couples and their heterosexual counterparts (Kurdek, 1995b) and the outcomes to children growing up in lesbian and gay families (e.g., Flaks, Ficher, Masterpasqua, and Joseph, 1995; Patterson, 1995a, 1995b).

Yet we worry too that the legitimation of relationship and family forms that are most similar to heterosexual relationships will ultimately result in a continued privileging of some forms of family (e.g., committed, partner relationships) above others (e.g., single parenthood, friendship families) and, indeed, of individuals in couples above single individuals (see also Weston, 1991). Why, for example, should some of us—because of the similarity of our relationships to heterosexual norms—receive the right to include another adult under our health benefits, while single adults with the same jobs do not receive that right? Such a policy clearly privileges romantic partners over friends. Relying on the discourse of the family to describe our friends, we believe, only covers up these kinds of inequities. Clearly we must directly examine the ways in which we may be replicating in our own communities the unequal distribution of privileges within heterosexual society.

There are other elements to consider before endorsing the language of family to represent the importance of our friendships. As Bev Jo's essay "Lesbian Friendships Create Lesbian Community" (this volume) suggests, the concept of the family as sacred and private has enabled physical, sexual, and emotional abuses of family members, especially women, children, and the elderly, to go on without acknowledgment or retribution. Many of us have been the recipients of abuse from our families upon identifying ourselves (or being identified) as lesbian. Certainly for many of us, our experiences in our families of origin highlight just how chosen these families truly are— for despite the rhetoric of indissoluble blood ties, we have seen too many of us disowned and cut off from these supposedly permanent bonds. Indeed, as Weston (1991, p. 74) put it, "coming out tended to bring 'choice' to the center of awareness and make it explicit as a significant facet of kinship relations that are ostensibly given in biology and nature." Given the pain that families of origin may have caused us, do we want to adopt the term "family" to honor our friendships?

On the other hand, for those of us who grew up in and continue to experience loving, accepting, and respectful relationships with our families of origin, the idea of claiming this term to describe our friendships is a positive one. So too for those of us who may not have experienced loving and accepting relationships in our families of origin but who grew up craving these relationships. Perhaps by creating close friendships and naming them as family, we give ourselves something we were unable to find in our families of origin.

We wish to note a few final issues to consider in our choice of language and our efforts to express the importance of our friendships. We worry that describing friends as family will lead us to overlook some of the real differences that may exist between the two. Perhaps there are aspects of our friendship relationships that are unique and uncaptured by the notion of family. Perhaps as well the association of these concepts leads us to overlook some of the tensions we may experience between the two. Despite the extent to which we lesbians seem to value our friendships, so too do we, like many heterosexuals, struggle to sustain them, to find time for them, to figure out their place in our lives in relation to partners and/or to children, to our families of origin, and to our work and community commitments and choices.

It is only through asking and addressing our actual ways of being friends and doing friendship with each other that we may be able to uncover the hidden assumptions in the current debates over the family and the fight for domestic partnership and family rights for lesbians. This debate will also enable us to explore what we really want to choose in and for our friendships and our families. Only then will we be able to expand the public discourse and lesbian political agendas, as well as our possibilities for friendship and family forms.

Still, despite all that we have said thus far, we, the editors, continue to speak and to think about our friendships in family terms. While we do not want to see friendships subsumed under family relationships, nor to ignore the unique elements of friendships in comparison with other forms of close relationship, we know what it feels like to experience intimate friendships and to find in these friendships a sense of place, of family. We hope that further explorations among lesbians into the meanings and functions of our friendships and our families will enable us all to better create the kinds of friendships — and families — we desire with and for each other. We offer the chapters that follow, then, as an opening up and a beginning of this important conversation.

Overall Framework of *Lesbian Friendships*

We have organized the contributions to this collection into four main sections: (1) An Introduction to Lesbians' Friendships; (2) Exploring the Continuum: Friends, Lovers, and the Places in Between; (3) Friendships across Difference; and (4) Fixed Points in a Changing World: Personal and Political Dimensions of Friendship, followed by a brief afterword. These are not, however, comfortable divisions. Many other organizational schemes could have been used, and many contributions easily fit into multiple sections. Our organizational framework does not imply rigid boundaries between one set of issues and another; it only reflects the themes we thought were most salient or telling about lesbians' experiences of friendship in each set of writings. As much as possible, however, we sought to honor the themes the authors themselves wished to emphasize. Yet throughout the editing process we were also guided by our own personal and professional interests. For example, our personal interest in the ways women negotiate conflicts in their friendships led us to pick up on any friendship struggles authors noted in initial drafts; conflict is a particularly central focus of much of Weinstock's research (see, e.g., Belenky, Bond, and Weinstock, in press; Weinstock, 1993). Subsequently, we asked these authors to more fully explore their friendship struggles and their processes for dealing with the conflicts.

We were also interested in highlighting both what we believe are distinct themes in lesbian friendships and themes that highlight the personally/politically uplifting potential of these friendships. Finally, we sought to maintain our original focus, as expressed in our initial announcement and call for contributions, on how being a lesbian affects our friendships. As a consequence, there are many important aspects of friendships in general and of the friendships explored in these pages that have been omitted or only briefly attended to, because they do not directly or uniquely bear on friendships in which at least one participant is a lesbian.

I. An Introduction to Lesbians' Friendships

There has been little available writing that explores the friendship experiences and perspectives of lesbians. After our own introduction, we begin this book with a piece by Terri de la Peña entitled "Eco de una Amistad/Echo of a Friendship," that highlights both the joys and the pains that may be a part of close friendships. The particular friendship Terri describes is one that many lesbians might desire. It begins in an experience of instant sisterhood with a woman who is also, like herself, a Latina, a lesbian, and a writer. "We were linked by an instinctual sisterhood, sharing religious and cultural upbringings, bilingual abilities," Terri writes. Yet the friendship ends in disagreement and betrayal; by sharing with us the friendship's movements from beginning to end, this selection signifies as well as honors close friendship in all its complexities.

We also wanted to begin this book of mostly personal accounts with a more general analysis of themes that lesbians may experience in our friendships. Through her focus group research exploring lesbians' own thoughts about and experiences with friendships, Jeanne Stanley has been able to identify many of the salient themes in lesbians' friendships, particularly the themes that arise in lesbians' friendships with each other. Her chapter, "The Lesbian's Experience of Friendship," reviews the workings and dynamics of lesbians' friendships, among ex-lovers, between lesbian couples, and between partnered and single lesbians. It serves well, then, along with the current chapter and de la Peña's piece, as an introduction to the chapters that follow.

II. Exploring the Continuum: Friends, Lovers, and the Places in Between

Sheila Jeffreys (1985) suggests in "Women's Friendships and Lesbianism," a chapter in her book *The Spinster and Her Enemies: Feminism and Sexuality 1880-1930* that self-identified lesbians today may be freer to have and express intimate friendships with each other than are heterosexual women. For the latter, there are still too many pressures to sustain distance from other women so as to continually prove and maintain their appearance of heterosexuality/normalcy.

Yet homophobia also interferes with and limits lesbians' and gay men's as well as heterosexuals' same-sex friendships. This is especially true for adolescents and adults who are just beginning to self-identify as lesbian or gay and who are in contexts that are particularly dangerous for them to express these identifications. It is also likely to be especially true in terms of physical and emotional expressiveness in friendships (e.g., Faderman, 1991; Hetrick and Martin, 1987.) In the discussion here, however, we are speaking of self-identified lesbians who are not concerned with the appearance of lesbianism, at least not within their own lesbian friendship networks and communities.

This very freedom may open up for self-identified lesbians unique opportunities to question definitions and choices regarding intimacy and sex, friendship, and lover relationships. In contrast with heterosexual women, lesbians tend to form lover relationships as well as close friendships with women. Thus, for lesbians, neither sexual identity nor gender sustain the boundary between friends and lovers, regardless of other factors that may sustain it. How, then, do lesbians negotiate between friendships and lover relationships? What distinguishes between our intimate friendships and our intimate romantic partnerships? Most often, the presence of current sexual activity is viewed as a key distinguishing factor between these two forms of relationship. Indeed, sex has been noted as a threat to lesbians' friendships (Raymond, 1986). Yet Rothblum and Brehony (1993) have described partnered relationships that are asexual, and Card (1995) argues that lesbian lovers can also be considered friends. Similarly, some friends may be sexual with each other but not consider themselves lovers or choose to be a romantic couple. Others may share erotic feelings yet choose not to express these feelings in a sexual manner. All these patterns blur the sexual boundaries between lesbian friendship and lesbian lover relationships.

Several chapters in our second section explore this boundary. Some examine the fluidity of movement from friends to lovers and back to friends that many lesbians have experienced; others highlight the struggles, strains, and sometimes impasses that occur in these attempted shifts between friends and lovers. Still others reject the need for movement between the two and create and describe friendships that hold places inbetween what many of us may see as a boundary separating lover and friend.

We have combined these diverse works into one section, although with two parts: (1) "From Friends to Lovers and/or Lovers to Friends; and (2) "Erotics in Friendship." In the first of these two subsections, we sought to highlight for the reader what was highlighted for us in the course of gathering stories for this book: the great many women who explore the movement from friends to lovers and/or lovers to friends. We sought also to highlight the unique patterns of movement that lesbians often evidence as they make these transitions. While there is not a large literature on lesbians' experiences of friendship, several theorists and researchers have noted the tendency among many lesbians—in contrast to the pattern prevalent among heterosexual women—to move from friends to lovers (e.g., Rose, Zand, and Cini, 1993; Vetere, 1982) and lovers to friends (e.g., Becker, 1988). The stories we have placed in the lover/friend section of our book explore the experiences of women who have made—or attempted to make—these kinds of movements in their friendships.

The first piece we include is a chapter by Jane Futcher and Catherine Hopkins entitled "Heart like a Wheel: A Friendship in Two Voices." The authors, writing in middle age, take us from the beginnings of their meeting twenty years earlier through various phases of adapting—and reacting—to their own and each other's life events, including a lover relationship between them that endured for several years. Next, Hilary Lapsley reports on the multiply dimensioned relationship between Margaret Mead and Ruth Benedict, in a chapter entitled "Ruth Benedict and Margaret Mead: Portrait of an Extraordinary Friendship." The relationship between the two women was sexual for a time, and negotiations surrounding this aspect of their relationship seemed quite central. But we might also include it as an example of a friendship across different sexualities (as Lapsley interprets it, lesbian for Benedict and bisexual for Mead) or as a lifelong friendship that serves as a fixed point through life's changes (the same may be said for Futcher and Hopkins's chapter).

Next is Lauren Crux's chapter "Namasté," which begins with a poem written for Lauren's best friend, at a time when the two women were just moving from friends to lovers. "Namasté" is a short story that expands upon this poem and lets us deeper into the decision-making process the friends went through when thinking about becoming lovers. It also takes us through this transition to an outcome of loss of the friendship. While there are many who make the transition from friends to lovers, and/or from lovers to friends, with positive consequences, Crux's chapter demonstrates other possibilities. Yet even through the pain of an estrangement, Crux honors the friendship they did share together and offers the hope of a new ending to be reached in the future.

The second subsection, "Erotics in Friendship," explores friendships in which erotic and/or sexual feelings are experienced within the context of a friendship, whether or not the feelings are shared or expressed in that friendship. In any of these cases, though, the relationship continues to be experienced as a friendship, rather than (or in addition to) a romantic, lover/partner relationship. It is this that best distinguishes all these entries from those in the first subsection. The chapters we group together here are stories of friendship that explore erotic feelings, with or without physical or sexual expression as part of the friendship.

First, Carey Kaplan and Ellen Cronan Rose explore the erotics of their friendship, with particular attention to others' reactions to these erotics. Their chapter, "On the Other Side of Silence," is also about a professional collaboration, as well as a friendship between a lesbian and a heterosexual woman, but we put it here to help highlight eros in friendship—and the ambivalent reactions to this from lesbians and nonlesbians alike. The next piece, "Guided Journey: The Road to Myself," is, as the title suggests, a personal exploration of identity and self-development. As part of this story, Kathleen Jones recognizes and honors the role of a straight, white woman professor with whom Kathleen (herself black and beginning to identify as a lesbian) becomes friends. During part of Kathleen's journey, she falls in love with this friend. Through a letter to this friend that Kathleen shares with us, she explores and moves through the various phases of their friendship.

Marcia Munson's story, entitled "Celebrating Wild Erotic Friendship: Martha and Marcia," describes two friends' celebration of "twenty-one years of open love, uncommitted sex, firm friendship, and wild adventure." The anniversary party they throw for themselves is a rare event in the annals of friendship. Yet it is one which raises questions regarding the different ways we celebrate and honor friendships in comparison with other relationships and life events. It is also a story that raises questions about friends and lovers, sex and commitment. The final piece in this subsection is "Going against the Fold," by Shelagh Robinson. Here Shelagh shares with us the story of three women, all in their twenties, who become friends and share passion with each other. Two of the three friends become lovers, and this is a central theme in the story. Yet it is also about each woman's personal development and life changes and her love and friendship with the other two.

III. Friendships across Difference

In addition to the challenges and changes that erotic feelings or romantic relationships present to friendships (and vice versa), other challenges to friendship may arise. Differences in past experiences may lead to differing conceptions of and desires for friendship. This may be especially likely when lesbians reach for friendships across boundaries of race, ethnicity, age, class, religion, political belief, or physicality. Locations within each of these boundaries are associated not only with differential access to power but also with different expectations of what a friendship can—or is likely to—be like, as well as what it must offer/provide if it is even to come to be.

Two chapters in this section explore friendships among women who share (at least by the end of the story) a lesbian identity yet whose identities and individualities are diverse in other ways. In the chapter entitled "Lesbian-Meets-Christian-Heterosexual-Woman-in-the-Midwest-and-They-Become-Lifelong-Friends," Kris Morgan and

Rebecca Nerison describe their friendship and the differences between them that made each ponder the feasibility of ever establishing a friendship. As with several other stories in this collection, the authors take us with them through the many processes of self- and other-discovery that affect and are affected by their growing and continuing friendship.

Ruth Hall and Suzanna Rose report on the findings of an interview study that explored interracial friendships among lesbians. This chapter, entitled "Friendships between African-American and White Lesbians," was motivated by the authors' own interracial friendship as well as their feminist and antiracist politics. Their explorations into interracial friendships raise important questions about race relations as they play out in the development of interracial friendships. Despite the presumably free choice involved in friendships and the absence of any formal structures to shape or restrict them, Hall and Rose's work clearly point out ways in which racism and race politics pervade lesbians' preliminary ponderings about whether to pursue a friendship with a lesbian of another race. This work also highlights some of the ways friendships that are formed across these racial boundaries may differ from those friendships we form within such boundaries.

In addition to forming friendships across the kinds of differences noted above, lesbians also form friendships with others with whom they do not share a lesbian identity or even, perhaps, a gender identity. Interesting and unique questions and issues may arise in friendships between lesbians and heterosexual women and between lesbians and heterosexual men, as compared with lesbians' friendships with each other. For example, how does a shared gender identity yet differing sexual identities/orientations shape the kinds of friendships women form with each other? What are the boundaries that are established between the friends, and how are they experienced by each woman? Much of what we know about women's friendships may very well be shaped more by heterosexuality than by gender; this remains an issue that is largely unexplored. Similarly, what kinds of dynamics arise in friendships between lesbians and heterosexual men? Are they the same as those that arise in friendships between heterosexual men, or between heterosexual women and men, or do they reflect most closely lesbians' friendships with each other, or with gay men?

So many of the above questions presume a centrality of sex and sexual feelings in friendship. Indeed, most of the research that has explored cross-sex friendships has focused on the issue of sex between friends. Our own questions about these kinds of friendships — and the issues the writers of the following chapters raise and address — are, however, much broader than the question of sex and/or sexual tension. Exploring friendships across what are often perceived — and experienced — as enemy lines can highlight the potentials and problems of allegiances across these differences. We may also learn more about what lesbian identity and community mean to those both in and outside lesbian communities, as well as how our meanings may differ across diverse backgrounds and contexts. These are the themes that the subsequent chapters gathered in this section address.

In her chapter entitled "Well-Worn Conversations," Diane Felicio describes her own development of a lesbian identity and a friendship with Eileen, a self-identified heterosexual woman. She explores these developments from their early beginnings. She also explores the implications of her and Eileen's differing identities as well as of her own assumption, held at various times over the course of their friendship, that Eileen must be a lesbian. Her story raises many important questions about the influence of differing identities on a friendship marked by a long history of honest communications.

The next selection is entitled "Negotiating Difference: The Friendship of a Lesbian-Identified Woman and a Heterosexual Man," coauthored by Karen Conner and Mark Cohan. Through their own example, Karen and Mark share with the reader some of the realities of, as well as the possibilities for, such friendships. The main themes they address include others' perceptions of their friendship, their own differing perspectives and politics in relation to the lesbian, gay, and bisexual communities, and their own growing sexual attraction to each other. By presenting their story in conversational form, they also allow us a glimpse at "the flavor and the substance" of their everyday interactions.

Anndee Hochman's story "Uncommon Kin" is next; it explores Anndee's friendship with a heterosexual woman named Rachael that, over time, comes to include Rachael's partner, John. Indeed, together, the three come to create a kind of family that is not well understood by most outsiders. Anndee's experiences in this nontraditional family composition leave her with a deep "faith in the unnamed and the untried"; so too, we believe, will readers broaden their own belief in new possibilities for friendships and family.

The final piece in this section is the research report of Cherie O'Boyle and Marie Thomas, "Friendships between Lesbian and Heterosexual Women." Emerging from their own experience of friendship with each other, these psychologists decided to conduct focus group sessions with primarily white, middle-class, young and middle-adult lesbians and heterosexual women. Their work provides us with important insights into the ways heterosexism and homophobia serve as barriers to friendships between heterosexual women and lesbians.

IV. Fixed Points in a Changing World: Personal and Political Dimensions of Friendship

In the final section of this collection, we present seven chapters that represent lesbians' friendships with others—lesbian or not, of the same or different races and class backgrounds, etc.—as they shape and are shaped by lesbian culture and experience in a currently heterosexist and homophobic world. These pieces highlight, honor, and celebrate lesbian friendships and lesbian culture. Indeed, all the stories in this collection do. We have selected these particular pieces for the final section because they specifically present powerful images of what we are—and what we can be—to each other through the building, sustaining, and honoring of our friendships. The title of this section is drawn from a quote by Rachel Perkins (1993, pp. ix–x), about how she was "extra special best friends" with Margo Jane Lidstone, who was recently killed in a cycling accident. Rachel writes:

"Critical of each other, but at the same time loyal, we valued our friendship: we strove to be each other's fixed point in what could often be a changing world. And we succeeded."

The first piece in this section is Pat Schmatz's "Pat T. Bunny Meets Lynnepig," which tells the tale of Pat's friendship with "Lynnepig" through the means of a children's story. The themes addressed in this story convey the fun of discovery as well as the fear of closeness that many of us experience when we begin to let someone new into our lives and hearts. The story also conveys a lesson of growth and change through love and friendship.

The second piece is a short story, "Deeper than Biology," by Gail Dottin, in which the lifeline of support offered between friends is powerfully portrayed.

"Portrait of Skinny and Me," by Nancy Davidson, explores the coming of age of two young women during the mid-1970s, when lesbian and gay rights were themselves coming of age. The reader is then moved through twenty years of life and friendship, built on fun, conversations, pain and change. Overall, the story of these two women and their friendship is a story of the possibilities for lesbian lives that opened up in the years following the Stonewall riots. It is also a story of the possibilities we women create for ourselves, with the help of each other, for living rich and gratifying lives full of love for and attention to the larger society, ourselves as old women, and our friendships.

Following Davidson's story are two pieces that reflect upon and honor the memory of a friendship and a friend. In "Cindy," Connie Chan stresses the importance of shared ethnicity, gender, and sexuality in the friendships of those who must struggle against the multiple oppressions of racism, sexism, and heterosexism. Indeed, as Connie puts it, "If Cindy hadn't been my friend, I would have had to invent her." The excitement and power of this long-term friendship are matched only by the pain of its loss. Similarly, in "A Significant Friend," Joyce Warshow portrays her friendship with Adrienne Smith, a woman whose commitment to overcoming sexism, racism, hetero-sexism, and ageism serves as an example for us all. So too, Joyce tells us, should Adrienne's gift for and commitment to friendship.

Finally, we close this section with two stories of lesbian friendship and community, written by two women who have been best friends for over twenty years. Both these women identify as working-class Lesbian Separatists; both struggle with chronic illnesses. In separate pieces, they write about the central and essential roles lesbian friendships have played in their lives. Linda Strega's "A Lesbian Love Story" is her way of publicly thanking the networks of lesbian friends that provided lifesaving support to her as she struggled with cancer, in addition to multiple chronic illnesses. Bev Jo's "Lesbian Friendships Create Lesbian Community" also examines the power and potential of lesbian friendships. But she addresses, as well, some of the forces that can and do limit our friendships; some of these forces are external, while some are more directly under our own control. By highlighting the limits of friendships as we enact them, Bev pushes us to reexamine our very commitment to each other and to our friendships, especially when we are sick or disabled or struggling financially to make ends meet. This reexamination of friendships as they are and as they can be reflects the hopes we as the editors have for this collection.

V. Afterword

In "Toward a Politics of Lesbian Friendship," Celia Kitzinger reflects upon this book from a radical lesbian feminist perspective. She also critiques many of the personal and political assumptions that often underlie research and thinking about lesbians' friendships and at the same time challenges us to move beyond these assumptions to focus more deeply on the power and potential of lesbian friendships.

Two Caveats

Before turning to the chapters themselves, we wish to highlight two areas of concern with regard to the current collection: (1) the question of definition—of lesbian identity/orientation, of friendship, and of sex/sexual activity and its place in friendship; and (2) the dimensions, types, and forms of friendship that do not appear in these pages.

Definitions of Lesbian Identity, Friendship, and Sex/Sexuality

Through the course of editing this book on lesbian friendships, we have continually pondered, yet left largely unaddressed, many questions of definition. In one way, we have sidestepped the need for definitions by accepting those of the individual writer. Thus we have used whatever labels authors used to identify themselves, the characters in their stories, or the participants in their research; and we have accepted their own identification of various relationships as friendships. Yet this is not a fully adequate stance, nor does it reflect accurately on the editorial process. First, in accepting authors' current definitions of sexual identity/orientation and of friendship, we have also treated identity and friendship both as "real" and permanent. We have not addressed the passage of time and alterations of contexts, both of which influence our identities and relationships. Indeed, many authors have addressed changes in identities and relationships that occurred prior to the time in which their stories are set. Yet we have ignored the question of changes in identities and friendships that may occur in the future (see Kitzinger, 1987, 1995; Kitzinger and Wilkinson, 1995, however, for more on the social construction of lesbian identity). Additionally, by the very nature of this book—an edited volume in which lesbians' experiences of friendship are the focus—we have clearly emphasized one particular aspect of identity (being a lesbian), though that aspect varies in meaning and salience from one author to the next.

What we are most uncomfortable about, however, is not this acceptance of individuals' self-definitions and descriptions but the times that we interfered in these self-definitions. As this most often arose in the context of friendship, and the relationship between sex/sexual activity and friendship, we wish to explore this issue further here. Specifically, we chose not to invite some writers to participate in this collection based on their submissions of abstracts that, to us, appeared to focus more on romantic relationships than on friendships. That is, we distinguished between stories that centered on lovers who were also friends and stories of friends who were also lovers; and we excluded the first, while accepting the second. Yet we have included stories of friendship that involve sexual activity or erotic feelings, as well as stories of friendships with ex-lovers, where sexual activity or erotic feelings have been and may continue to be a part of the relationship. Our ability to make this distinction, however, is questionable; relationships and story constructions are time-bound. We cannot know whether particular friendships will be sustained over time or the ways in which they may change; the same is true for lover relationships.

Throughout the editorial process, we have pondered the question of inclusion and of the definition of friendship. Despite becoming aware of Card's (1995) argument for the inclusion of lovers in conceptions of friendship in the final stages of the book's preparation, we remain, for now, committed to our choice of materials. We realize, however, that readers may disagree. Definitions and conceptions of friendship and lover relationships vary just as much as the meanings we place on sexual identities. Lesbians differ in what we view as constituting a close friendship, as opposed to a casual one. We differ in the importance of friendships in relation to other aspects of our lives. And, as can be seen by reading this collection, we lesbians differ in the degree of eroticism we experience and choose to accept as part of friendship, and in our definitions of sex and eros.

One of us has explored in writing the question of just what constitutes sex or sexual activity (Rothblum, 1994; Rothblum and Brehony, 1993). Because this issue arose throughout the process of working on this book, and appears as well in so many of the stories included within it, we think it important to consider this question again, now most specifically in relation to friendship. Most definitions of sexual activity—whether they be oriented toward or developed by heterosexuals, bisexuals, gay men, or lesbians—focus on genital activity (Rothblum, 1994; see also Loulan, 1993). But what about nongenital sexual experiences? If we consider that nongenital physical contact or perhaps even nongenital and nonphysical contact (i.e., contact that is more emotional, psychological, spiritual, or intellectual in form, without also being physical) may constitute sexual experience for the participants, then the line between friends and lovers is no longer easily or clearly drawn; it is certainly not a "straight" line.

Still, we believe there is a line, and that the stories included here hold to it—because of the authors' own constructions of the relationships they wrote about more than because of the feelings or even sexual activities that characterize those relationships. The stories we did not include, we believe, crossed this line in that the authors neither currently nor predominantly constructed the relationships as friendships. Certainly many of the stories in this collection involved a phase of romance and/or coupledness. But the phase was in the past, and the stories themselves focused on the current friendship and how it came to be this friendship, rather than on a current romantic, lover relationship. We excluded pieces that focused on the latter because our goal in this book was to highlight lesbians' friendships. We wanted as well to take a stand against a culture—among both lesbians and nonlesbians alike—that emphasizes romantic and sexual relationships to the exclusion of friendship. Indeed, we have available to us, through research and fiction, stories of lesbian romance and lesbian partner relationships; while not enough, it is more than we have available about our friendships.

We realize, however, that our decision to exclude stories of lovers who are also friends itself assumes that relationships between lesbians are primarily either romantic partnerships or friendships. We can be both to each other, but one still predominates. This may or may not be true for all readers; it is, however, a line we uncomfortably yet decidedly constructed as we planned the book.

Still, we believe the stories in this collection break through this separation and call into question notions of love and primacy, import and commitment, as they relate to both lovers and friends. Yet they do so in a way that sustains the focus on friendships. A recent mainstream movie, *Boys on the Side,* modeled after *Thelma and Louise,* also examines the line between friends and lovers. Whereas in *Thelma and Louise* each woman is explicitly identified as heterosexual and issues of attraction between them are left unexplored, *Boys on the Side* directly examines the line between friends and lovers, although it does so predominantly (though not exclusively) through the one identified lesbian character. While stories about a current "romance" or "couple" relationship would have also contributed to breaking through these artificial distinctions, they would have shifted us away from the focus we chose for this book: friendship.

Limited Diversity

Most of the chapters in this collection focus on close friendships in young or middle adulthood. The absence of younger writers is not surprising, given that we advertised in academic and lesbian community publications that may not be easily accessible to adolescents. Similarly, the absence of old women may reflect our advertising procedures as well as historical factors: older women have had to be more closeted to survive in past decades.

Indeed, while many of the stories included in this collection reflect upon some of the negative effects of heterosexism on our friendships, some of these effects are invisible. For example, one woman had to withdraw her accepted project upon the request of her friend, who was afraid of experiencing homophobic backlash if their story was made public. The focus on close friendships and on positive outcomes for friendships that experienced diverse struggles is also not surprising. It is likely that those who have had positive as well as powerful and challenging experiences in close friendships are more likely to want to write about them.

Additionally, of the personal stories, most are by and about lesbians' friendships with other lesbians, and most involve friendships where the individuals are quite similar on multiple dimensions. This may not be surprising given that similarities across a diversity of dimensions, including gender, age, marital status, and political beliefs, have been found to affect friendship formation and continuation among heterosexuals (see, e.g., Rose and Roades, 1987; Weston, 1991).

Indeed, one of the insights O'Boyle and Thomas (this volume) gained from their focus groups with lesbians and with heterosexual women was that lesbians described a shared bond with other lesbians that they did not have with heterosexual women, and that homophobia and heterosexism are clearly obstacles to friendships between these two groups. The National Lesbian Health Care Survey (Bradford, Ryan, and Rothblum, 1994) found that most of the 1,925 respondents indicated having more lesbian friends than any other type of friend. Lesbians were also more out to lesbian and gay friends than to straight friends.

Still, future collections would benefit from including the voices of heterosexual women and men, as well as bisexual women and men, and gay men, reflecting upon their friendships with lesbians. How does the nonlesbian friend interpret the friendship and what are the salient themes? Future collections would also benefit from greater representation of friendships where the participants are markedly diverse in age, race, class, and physical health/abilities. In general we hear more about and from lesbians who are white, middle-class, nonmothers, and formally educated through and beyond college than about and from lesbians with other backgrounds and experiences. This collection continues to reflect and perpetuate this multiply privileged discourse. That we, the editors, can also be described as white, middle-class, nonmothers, and college educated undoubtedly contributed to this outcome.

We remain hopeful, however, that the variety of contributions that are included here offer an important beginning: by expanding the discourse on friendship to include lesbians' voices and the discourse on lesbians to more fully include friendships. We also hope these chapters do for you, the reader, what they continue to do for us: make us laugh as well as cry, proud and happy as well as sometimes sad and angry. But most of all, we hope they serve to motivate us all to seriously think about and reflect upon our own friendships and to further attend to the strengths and struggles, power and potential, of lesbian friendships in our personal lives, professional endeavors, and political activities.

REFERENCES

Ahrons, C. 1981. The continuing coparental relationship between divorced spouses. *American Journal of Orthopsychiatry* 51: 415–28.

Ahrons, C. R., and L. S. Wallisch. 1987. The relationship between former spouses. In D. Perlman and S. Duck, eds., *Intimate relationships: Development, dynamics, and deterioration*, pp. 269–96. Beverly Hills, CA: Sage.

American Psychological Association. 1972. *Diagnostic and statistical manual of mental disorders.* 2nd ed. Washington, DC: American Psychological Association.

Becker, C. S. 1988. *Unbroken ties: Lesbian ex-lovers.* Boston: Alyson.

Belenky, M. F., L. A. Bond, and J. S. Weinstock. In press. *A tradition that has no name: Public homeplaces and the development of women, families, and communities.* New York: Basic Books.

Bradford, J., C. Ryan, and E. D. Rothblum. 1994. National Lesbian Health Care Survey: Implications for mental health care. *Journal of Consulting and Clinical Psychology* 62: 228–42.

Card, C. 1995. *Lesbian choices.* New York: Columbia University Press.

Durst, P. L., N. V. Wedemeyer, and L. A. Zurcher. 1985. Parenting partnerships after divorce: Implications for practice. *Social Work,* September/October, 423–28.

Faderman, L. 1991. *Odd girls and twilight lovers: A history of lesbian life in twentieth-century America.* New York: Penguin Books.

Flaks, D. K., I. Ficher, F. Masterpasqua, and G. Joseph. 1995. Lesbians choosing motherhood: A comparative study of lesbian and heterosexual parents and their children. *Developmental Psychology* 31: 105–14.

Hetrick, E. S., and A. D. Martin. 1987. Developmental issues and their resolution for gay and lesbian adolescents. *Journal of Homosexuality* 14: 25–44.

Jeffreys, S. 1985. *The spinster and her enemies: Feminism and sexuality 1880-1930.* London: Pandora Press.

Kitzinger, C. 1987. *The social construction of lesbianism.* Newbury Park: Sage.

———. 1995. Social constructionism: Implications for lesbian and gay psychology. In A. R. D'Augelli and C. J. Patterson, eds., *Lesbian, gay, and bisexual identities over the lifespan: Psychological perspectives,* pp. 136–61. New York: Oxford University Press.

Kitzinger, C., and S. Wilkinson. 1995. Transitions from heterosexuality to lesbianism: The discursive production of lesbian identities. *Developmental Psychology* 31: 95–104.

Kurdek, L. A. 1995a. Developmental changes in relationship quality in gay and lesbian cohabiting couples. *Developmental Psychology* 31: 86–94.

———. 1995b. Lesbian and gay couples. In A. R. D'Augelli and C. J. Patterson, eds., *Lesbian, gay, and bisexual identities over the lifespan: Psychological perspectives,* pp. 243–61. New York: Oxford University Press.

Lindsay, K. 1981. *Friends as family.* Boston: Beacon Press.

Lorde, A. 1984. *Sister outsider: Essays and speeches.* Freedom, CA: Crossing Press.

Loulan, J. 1993. Celibacy. In E. D. Rothblum and K. A. Brehony, eds., *Boston marriages: Romantic but asexual relationships among contemporary lesbians,* pp. 62–69. Amherst: University of Massachusetts Press.

McHale, S. M., and A. C. Crouter. 1992. You can't always get what you want: Incongruence between sex-role attitudes and family work roles and its implications for marriage. *Journal of Marriage and the Family* 54: 537–47.

Morin, S. F., and E. D. Rothblum. 1991. Removing the stigma: Fifteen years of progress. *American Psychologist* 46: 947–49.

Patterson, C. J. 1995a. Families of the lesbian baby boom: Parents' division of labor and children's adjustment. *Developmental Psychology* 31: 115–23.

———. 1995b. Lesbian mothers, gay fathers, and their children. In A. R. D'Augelli and C. J. Patterson, eds., *Lesbian, gay, and bisexual identities over the lifespan: Psychological perspectives,* pp. 262–90. New York: Oxford University Press.

Perkins, R. 1993. For Margot, in thanks for years of love and friendship. Dedication in M. J. Lidstone, *Sir—To Begin with Sappho,* pp. ix–xii. London: Onlywomen Press.

Popenoe, D. 1993. American family decline, 1960–1990: A review and appraisal. *Journal of Marriage and the Family* 55: 527–44.

Raymond, J. G. 1986. *A passion for friends: Towards a philosophy of female affection.* Boston: Beacon Press.

Rose, S., and L. Roades. 1987. Feminism and women's friendships. *Psychology of Women Quarterly* 11: 243–54.

Rose, S., D. Zand, and M. A. Cini. 1993. Lesbian courtship scripts. In E. D. Rothblum and K. A. Brehony, eds., *Boston marriages: Romantic but asexual relationships among contemporary lesbians,* pp. 70–85. Amherst: University of Massachusetts Press.

Rothblum, E. D. 1994. Transforming lesbian sexuality. *Psychology of Women Quarterly,* 18: 627–41.

Rothblum, E. D., and K. A. Brehony. 1993. *Boston marriages: Romantic but asexual relationships among contemporary lesbians.* Amherst: University of Massachusetts Press.

Stacey, J. 1994. Dan Quayle's revenge: The new family values crusaders. *The Nation,* July/August, 119–22.

Stack, C. 1974. *All our kin.* New York: Harper and Row.

Vetere, V. A. 1982. The role of friendship in the development and maintenance of lesbian love relationships. *Journal of Homosexuality* 8 (2): 51–65.

Weinstock, J. S. 1993. College women's conceptions of close friendship, conceptions of conflicts with close friends, and epistemological perspectives. Doctoral dissertation, University of Vermont, Burlington.

Weston, K. 1991. *Families we choose: Lesbians, gays, kinship.* New York: Columbia University Press.

TWO

Eco de una Amistad/Echo of a Friendship

TERRI DE LA PEÑA

On the slate-grey carpet, I sit cross-legged beside my oak desk. I have rummaged through its files, determined to get rid of accumulated junk. My intention is to replace the discards with heaps of newer materials crouched nearby, waiting for a home. My obsessive house-cleaning is in preparation for the visit of a writer friend.

Surrounded by untidy piles of birthday and holiday cards, fading envelopes containing undated letters, and the yellowing pages of unfinished stories, I inspect each, tempted to toss the nostalgic mess into the trash. Yet something prevents me. Sentimentality perhaps? A misconceived notion of transforming the unlikely treasure into the basis for creative work? A likelier reason is this: a decade of the most climactic period of my life lies splintered in that haphazard collection of memorabilia. Those silly cards, those half-forgotten letters—even those incomplete stories—are proof that I was not alone during my first ten years as an "out" lesbian. Though I recall being mostly solitary then, I *did* have friends—one in particular.

I call her Elisa here, though that is not her real name. I do not remember ever cleaning my apartment for one of *her* visits. We were close enough to each other that neatness—or the lack of it—did not matter.

Elisa was fair-skinned and plump with mesquite-brown hair and cholla-green eyes, a Latina who could "pass" for white if so inclined.

31

Yet she was Nueva Mexicana to the core, from the striped tip of the hawk's feather in her straw cowboy hat to the scuffed heels of her leather-tooled boots, and proud of it. Her wide grin lit her face like a glowing luminaria.

In May 1983 we met at Sisterhood Bookstore in west Los Angeles. We had gone there for the same reason: to see and listen to local Latina writers read from their work. Like me, Elisa remained to converse, eager to join their group. We began a tentative conversation while waiting. Our bonding congealed on learning we were both unpublished but hopeful. Up to that point, neither of us had ever met another Latina writer, much less another Latina *lesbian* writer. We continued to huddle, whisper and joke between ourselves. Finally, the friendliest of the writers suggested we submit samples of our work. We agreed and excitedly exchanged phone numbers. Within weeks, Elisa and I were members of that envied group.

Then our *real* friendship began. Elisa and I were the only fiction writers at the semimonthly meetings. We supported and defended each other, listened to and critiqued our stories, argued about technique, discussed developing characters and their foibles. We shared our writing outside the group, too, between ourselves only. She had several plays to show me; I had a few chapters of a novel-in-progress.

We grew close, even more so because she lived a few blocks away. I was four years older, but she had been "out" longer. We learned each other's family dynamics—we both were middle children and commiserated about being dutiful Catholic-raised Latina lesbian daughters. We laughed and cried over coming out issues. With characteristic humor, she taught me about the details of dyke life, from pinkie rings to vulva-inspired pottery. Her spontaneous warmth and cheerfulness even won over my skeptical parents.

Elisa introduced me to the works of many lesbian writers, initially to Barbara Wilson's collection *Walking on the Moon*. I read Elisa's copy over and over, marveling at those intricate stories, wondering if mine would ever be printed. We went to numerous bookstore readings, confessed to liking Katherine V. Forrest's mysteries, adoring Eloise Klein Healy's poetry. We wanted to see and hear as many lesbian writers as possible.

My New Hampshire-born lover was more than a bit jealous of Elisa. In her New England accent, my lover sometimes expressed a desire to write fiction, and perhaps for that reason, felt threatened that Elisa and I were creative types already, not to mention Latinas, too. With that plain-spoken Yankee, I often had to translate my mother's Spanish phrases and interpret cultural traditions; with Elisa, I rarely had to explain *anything*. We were linked by an instinctual sisterhood, sharing religious and cultural upbringings, bilingual abilities. Otherwise, my lover had no reason to be jealous. I never was sexually attracted to Elisa. I considered her una hermana, a sister. We did not always agree, but respected our differences. For instance, Elisa seemed to believe that falling in love would solve anything; I tended to be more realistic than that. And I did not realize that beyond her cactus-colored eyes, her almost habitual smile, lay a restless yearning, an unexpressed sadness.

Elisa fell in love often and passionately, with women who would not or could not reciprocate. Most of the time, I failed to comprehend her attraction to them. Some were closeted and determined to remain so; others drank or smoked too much. None seemed to appreciate Elisa enough. I kept mum, mindful of her feelings. Elisa would weep with bitterness over those losses, yet always seemed resilient enough to redirect her energies into reworking a story, starting a screenplay. My pragmatic lover pegged her as an unstable, hopeless romantic, while I began to sense the simmering turbulence beneath Elisa's wreath of smiles. Sometimes she would be inexplicably moody. Though she came from a big family, she wanted to live alone to have writing space without the distraction of roommates.

As soon as a vacancy was available in the apartment building my parents owned, they offered it to me. Though I was tempted, I was unwilling to live that close to them. I knew Elisa was apartment-hunting and mentioned that to my parents. She was ecstatic about the opportunity to live in a rent-controlled Santa Monica building. The arrangement seemed to suit everyone. Elisa had her own home, my elderly parents had a trustworthy tenant, and I did not have to go far to visit any of them.

Though she had a bachelor's degree in film, Elisa only talked and dreamed about doing studio work. Perhaps she realized the chances of a Latina's breaking Hollywood's sexual-racial barriers were slim. Instead, she took temporary positions as a legal secretary. Between assignments, she would return to her family homestead in New Mexico for weeks at a time, and fall in love there, too.

In that stifling small town in the northern part of the state, lesbian life lay mostly underground. There was no feminist bookstore, no Sunday afternoon readings, no sister-writers. Elisa's companions there were old-time dykes, with little or no knowledge of feminism and the lesbian literature she loved to read and strove to write. She sent me wrenching letters describing her lovers' inevitable betrayals. Elisa would bemoan the women's infidelities, vowing to forget about them, to come back soon.

On reading her letters, I would recall how often I confided in her about my own troubled, long-distance relationship. That realization encouraged me to refrain from being judgmental. My closeted lover lived in another county and held a demanding administrative position in the educational field. We saw each other only on weekends or during school vacations. When she and Elisa were both out of town, I felt particularly vulnerable and alone.

That intensified during the summer of 1985. My lover went East to spend time with friends and family while the "Night Stalker" serial murderer terrorized Los Angeles. Frightened out of my wits when a "copycat" killing occurred a few blocks from my apartment, I stayed overnight with Elisa, and she, in turn, came to stay with me. We were too scared to sleep much, whispering and giggling like nervous schoolgirls.

Though I often relied on her good-humored company while my lover was gone, I did not take into account her growing unhappiness. The writers' group disintegrated, and neither of us remained disciplined writers. More and more frequently, she would quit a job and leave town. Her extended absences eventually resulted in her becoming delinquent with her rent. My parents would complain to *me* first. Irked, I would write to Elisa about the dilemma. Sometimes she would apologize, send a partial payment, sometimes not.

In the summer of 1986, my father phoned to tell me the front upstairs apartment was available. Never one for direct communication, Daddy knew its west-facing windows and private deck appealed to me. The fact that he phoned me himself led me to glean his underlying message: he wanted me home. He had been diagnosed with diabetes a few months before, and due to his sudden weight loss, I suspected cancer. He apologized for not feeling well enough to paint the apartment or to help me move. I assured him that was unnecessary. Without delay, I gave notice to my landlord. My lover and I hurriedly painted before leaving for a Hawaiian vacation.

When Elisa helped with the move, she was excited that I would be living upstairs. She joked about the likelihood of our future "Lucy and Ethel" adventures. However, I was not as lighthearted about my change of address.

Two months later, Daddy was diagnosed with pancreatic cancer. The tumor had not shown up on the first ultrasound; the delay made it inoperable. He chose to die at home. Having Elisa downstairs during those sad days made them a bit more bearable; she bolstered me, cried with me, agreed that I had made the right decision to accept his invitation to live in the building.

Daddy died within a few weeks, and Elisa took it very hard, further endearing her to me. Soon after, she returned to the desert, saying "things were not the same without him." Her departure intensified my grief. During the next months, while she came and went, my depression deepened.

Nearly a year went by. Elisa was gone again when my relationship ended. My lover had grown impatient with my extended mourning; she had expected me to be more resilient. In previous bad times, I had turned to writing to ward off the blues. I saw that as an avenue to escape the depression, while she opposed it vigorously. She viewed my decision to write book reviews for the local lesbian newspaper as a threat to her closeted status, my refusal to use a pseudonym a form of disloyalty. She broke up with me.

Elisa's letters and phone calls became a lifeline during that wrenching period. She had been through similar ordeals and understood the depths of my grief. Eventually, I revealed via letter that I had begun to rework my long-neglected novel. I sent Elisa early chapters to critique; she offered insights as well as praise.

In the times she stayed away, she began to revert to previous patterns. Without steady income, she had no way to meet her monthly obligations to my widowed mother. I chided Elisa by phone and mail, demanding that she show consideration and pay the accumulated rent.

"I wouldn't do this to *your* mother. How can you do this to *mine?*" I once asked in total frustration. As tactfully as possible, I even suggested that she alleviate the situation by moving out.

My entreaties had no effect. Elisa seemed to have every intention of maintaining two residences, unrealistic as that seemed; her debt grew larger. Many months later, my mother consulted an attorney. I was too tired, too betrayed by Elisa's erratic behavior, to convince my mother otherwise.

By then, my novel had been accepted for publication. In January 1991, Barbara Wilson, my editor at Seal Press, came to Los Angeles for a bookstore reading. She was my houseguest the same weekend Elisa arrived to move out. Barbara and I were on our way downstairs when Elisa appeared, laden with boxes to pack her possessions. We had not seen each other in several months. Blushing, she gazed at us from the foot of the stairs, embarrassed yet astonished to be introduced to Barbara, whose fiction Elisa had revealed to *me* years before. What should have been a proud occasion—a time for celebration—proved awkward. That winter morning was the last time I saw, or heard from, Elisa.

In the years since, I have met many other writers. With most of them, Latinas and lesbians in particular, I have felt an incipient sisterhood. However, the instant chemistry, the outright affection, the sense of being sister-writers, is missing from many of those relationships. With some, there is even a spark of competition which Elisa and I never experienced. I recall her friendship as vital during my struggle to merge my identities as Chicana, lesbian, writer. I have no doubt that together we learned so much—as Latinas, as lesbians, as writers—during those turbulent years. And, though I long to recreate that caliber of friendship, I know I have changed dramatically since that time. Nowadays I often wind up being a mentor, a guide, or a workshop leader for other writers, rather than una hermana, una amiga.

What saddens me most about Elisa's departure is the loss of that common trust, that precious hermanidad, we once shared. Years later, I still feel betrayed by her lack of respect and consideration for my mother, even more so by her failure to explain her reasons — or strive for reconciliation. Perhaps she felt the time had come to simply vanish, unanswered questions and all. Despite that, I could not bring myself to exclude her from the acknowledgments page of my first novel; she belonged there, in print, if nowhere else. Sometimes I wonder if she has ever seen or read that book.

With memories and musings, my housecleaning has become melancholy. I sift through more crumpled papers and find a typewritten poem. Elisa once sent it to me from New Mexico. My eyes moisten on reading its title: "Missing Terri."

> In the early morning light
> shadows
> those timid moths
> trying to escape one's vision
> but captured all the same
> out of the corner of my eye.
> Those little echoes cannot escape me
> and though thoughts of you
> attempt to get by
> they are cajoled into staying.
> They are so needed, here
> where I, the foreigner, am longing for home
> and being with you again.

Wiping my eyes, I fold that cherished page. It joins the growing pile of items I will keep.

NOTE

A shorter version of "Eco de una Amistad/Echo of a Friendship" was published in the newsmagazine *Frontiers* (Los Angeles), December 2, 1994, p. 57.

Pictured from left to right are Ro, Adrian, Julia, Jeanne, Ellen, and Barb. These "Ogunquit Gals" are a group of friends who have been renting the same house in Ogunquit, Maine, every summer for over thirteen years.

THREE

The Lesbian's Experience of Friendship

JEANNE L. STANLEY

When I proposed the topic of lesbian friendships for my research, I met with support as well as hesitation from colleagues: even though I believed lesbian friendship was a fascinating topic, did there indeed exist interest among other lesbians about the role of friendship in their lives? This question was clearly answered on the first warm day of May 1991. As part of my research, I set about running a focus group (a method used to gather information from a group of individuals by listening to them discuss a certain topic) at a popular lesbian festival in southern Pennsylvania called "Campfest." This is a four-day event that draws approximately nine hundred women together at a summer camp facility in the woods. The site has two pools, a lake, a craft area, an outdoor main stage, indoor stages and dance halls, a cafeteria, and over twenty cabins. Once a year this children's summer camp is transformed into a sea of tents and cabins (some equipped with electric blankets, coffeepots, and blow dryers, no less) and lesbians of all ages. It is for many the one time of the year they can feel completely free to be themselves.

There is an excitement in the air as women walk hand in hand, and friends who have not seen each other for a year hug, catch up on their lives, and reminisce. During the day the pool area becomes a scene where hundreds of women are splashing, floating, playing volleyball, and basking in the sun. At night musicians and comedians draw many of the women to the main stage. Other activities throughout the long weekend include movies, dances, sporting events, and workshops.

I took the opportunity to talk with lesbians about their friendships by leading a workshop entitled "Lesbian Friendships: A Discussion Group." The workshop was described as an opportunity to discuss the role of friendship in the lives of lesbians. I hoped that at least eight women would be interested enough to leave the pool, the warm sun, and the other events to offer their opinions and experiences, which would eventually become an integral part of my research findings. Noon came, and I eagerly awaited the start of my workshop. Three women arrived, then two more, then four, for a total of nine women; I was so grateful that enough women had chosen to participate. Ten minutes into the focus group one woman interrupted to say that there had been some confusion regarding the location of this workshop—even more women were waiting for the workshop at another site over the hill. I asked her to invite those women to come join our group. A few of them began trickling over the hill. Then, to my elation, a hoard of women came pouring over the hill, until more than one hundred were sitting in front of me, wanting to discuss lesbian friendships. The feeling I had at that moment, standing in front of all those women who were so eager for a means to share and discuss friendships, was overwhelming. Needless to say, when I reported the enormous amount of interest to my colleagues the following week, I was told not to hesitate and to move ahead.

This chapter is based upon research consisting of qualitative information I gathered from the Campfest focus group and from another focus group conducted at the National Lesbian Conference (NLC), both held in 1991. I also draw upon my secondary analyses of the quantitative data from Dr. Natalie Eldridge's 1987 study that consisted of 550 lesbians' responses to a questionnaire in which there was a section addressing friendship. No results can be representative of all lesbians, yet the findings addressed in this chapter provide a foundation for understanding the lesbian's experience of friendship.

The themes that will be presented include the importance of friendship for lesbians, the benefits as well as potential drawbacks of friendships, distinctive aspects of lesbian friendships, and the ways friendships may differ for single and partnered lesbians. But first I provide an overview of the research project and my approach to data analysis.

In setting out to understand lesbian friendships, I wanted to gather both quantitative and qualitative information in order to gain a broader perspective. (For a detailed description of the design, analysis, and results of this study, see Stanley, 1993.) I began to comb existing data sets to find a study that had tapped the subject of lesbian friendship but had not primarily focused on this aspect in analyses and writings.

Through the Henry A. Murray Research Center at Radcliffe College, I located Eldridge's (1987) study which examined the psychological correlates of relationship satisfaction and role conflict in dual-career lesbian couples. (For a more detailed description of the design, analysis, and results of this study, see Eldridge, 1987).

Eldridge's study was based on the responses of 550 partnered lesbians (275 couples) to a thirty-page questionnaire. The questionnaire included sections that measured the participant's degree of social intimacy/friendship, self-esteem, and relationship satisfaction.

Both members of each couple completed the questionnaire separately. The duration of the partnerships ranged from six months to twenty-two years, with an average of five years. Eighty-two percent of the sample were employed full-time; the other 28 percent reported that they were working part-time or were currently unemployed. Participants were from thirty-nine states, the District of Columbia, Canada, and Israel, and ranged in age from twenty to fifty-nine, with an average age of thirty-five. Most of the participants were Caucasian; less than 10 percent were women of color. All of the participants had graduated high school, and over half held a bachelor's degree or higher.

I performed secondary analyses on the scales of the Eldridge questionnaire that measured self-esteem, relationship satisfaction, and social intimacy/friendship. Self-esteem was measured in the Eldridge study with the Rosenberg Self-Esteem Scale (Robinson and Shaver, 1973), a self-report scale that measures the self-acceptance aspect of self-esteem. The scale consists of ten items and responses on a five-point scale ranging from *strongly disagree* (1) to *strongly agree* (5). Higher scores indicate a higher degree of self-esteem. An example of the items in the scale is "I feel that I have a number of good qualities."

Relationship satisfaction was measured by Eldridge using ten questions from Spanier's Dyadic Adjustment Scale (Spanier, 1976). The scale consists of behavioral, as well as global, measures of the quality of the relationship. The ten items are ranked on a five-point scale ranging from *all the time* (0) to *never* (5). An example of an item on this scale is "How often do you and your partner quarrel?"

The Social Intimacy Scale of the Personal Assessment of Intimacy in Relationships Inventory (PAIR) by Schaefer and Olson (1981) was also included in the Eldridge study. It assesses the extent to which one has friends in common with one's partner and similar or overlapping social networks. It consists of six items that are rated on a seven-point Likert scale, from *not at all true* (1) to *very true* (7). An example of the items of the Social Intimacy Scale is "We have very few friends in common."

I examined the relationships among participants' ratings of friendship, their self-esteem, and their relationship satisfaction. The results of these correlational analyses indicated a significantly positive relationship between friendships and both the partnered lesbian's self-esteem and relationship satisfaction.

The qualitative portion of the study was implemented in order to capture a more detailed understanding of the thoughts and feelings of lesbians regarding their friendships and thereby expand the meaning of the quantitative findings. The qualitative data was drawn from the two focus groups conducted in 1991; written statements in the comment section of the Eldridge questionnaire were also reviewed.

The first focus group was held at the National Lesbian Conference in Atlanta, Georgia, attended by over three thousand women. Fourteen women attended the focus group. These women came from throughout the United States and ranged in age from twenty-eight to fifty-eight, with an average age of thirty-eight. Almost all of the women reported themselves as Caucasian, and the majority reported holding a bachelor's degree or higher.

The focus group at Campfest is more difficult to describe in detail because over one hundred lesbians, out of the nine hundred attending the weekend gathering, participated in the focus group. The focus group consisted predominantly of Caucasian lesbians from the Northeast and Mid-Atlantic states ranging in age from the mid-twenties to the late sixties.

The qualitative data from the focus groups and the comment section of the Eldridge questionnaire were analyzed for similar themes and areas of interest. Both the quantitative and qualitative findings yielded the results I now discuss.

Why Is Friendship So Important in the Lesbian Community?

Friendships, regardless of one's sexual orientation, are one of several sources of support, affirmation, and love in an individual's life. Friendships for lesbians, however, are often the main, if not sole, source of these feelings. Lesbians may experience rejection from traditional sources of support such as parents, siblings, relatives, or coworkers. Friends therefore take on even greater importance than usual in that they offer not only acceptance but affirmation for the lesbian; they often become "surrogate families" or "family networks." Indeed, friends are at the focal point of life celebrations and milestones for lesbians, such as anniversaries, birthdays, weddings, and childbirth. For example, friends "give away the bride (or brides)" or act as the aunt for a lesbian friend's child.

Friendships with other lesbians, bisexuals, or gay men may also become a means for lesbians to develop and affirm their lesbian identity and gain power through their shared experiences (Ettorre, 1980; Gartrell, 1981; Sophie, 1982). The unity that lesbian friends in particular may offer can serve as a buffer against the socially devalued status of lesbians. Participants in both focus groups supported these ideas as they discussed how important it was to have friendships with other lesbians and create a community of support and affirmation for themselves as women and as lesbians.

Another essential aspect of support that lesbian friendships provide is role modeling. Friends are one of the few sources of information and guidance concerning aspects of being a lesbian, since society often treats lesbians as invisible or nonexistent. There are consequently few outwardly accessible lesbian role models who can pass on knowledge in such basic areas, for example, as how to ask another woman out on a date, plan a marriage/commitment ceremony, or create a family. As one participant wrote in her questionnaire, "Friends enable me to work through things for which I have no other models or guidelines."

Another way in which lesbian friends exchange valuable information is by providing each other with a historical perspective. A friend who has known one well for a period of time is able to point out one's progress, significant changes, stalled status, or regression. A participant in the focus group at Campfest commented that "some friends, just because of time, know things about me that others don't know." She went on to describe how this has helped her understand and appreciate herself better. Friendships may also have an effect on the lesbian's self-esteem. As friends listen to each other, discuss their thoughts and feelings, and offer feedback, a more realistic understanding of oneself may develop. One woman from NLC found the feedback she received from her friends was invaluable because it provided her with "a reality check about myself."

For lesbians who are less open about their sexual orientation, lesbian, bisexual, and gay friends provide one of the few opportunities to express this and other related aspects of their lives. Some women in the focus groups described their friends (in many cases their lesbian/gay/bisexual friends) as the only people who knew that they were lesbians and could share in their everyday lives.

Friendships are also important for lesbians who are in a lover relationship. Partnered lesbians may experience stress related to the lack of recognition as a valid couple, internalized homophobia, and isolation (Slater and Mencher, 1991). Lesbian couples cannot acquire legalized sanctions of marriage, nor are their relationships recognized and supported by society in other ways. Slater and Mencher (1991) cite social networks in the lesbian community as perhaps the couple's only source of positive support. One of the Eldridge study respondents wrote:

My partner and I were married by an Episcopalian minister (female of course!) two years ago in the presence of about 30 friends and relatives. We are committed in this relationship and chose to publicly profess our commitment to one another. We feel by doing this we have gained much support from the people (our community) who were there and we feel we have a strong commitment to hold us together through rough times!

Another respondent from the Eldridge study commented on the importance of friends at her and her partner's commitment ceremony:

One of the most important aspects of our development as a couple was our wedding three and a half years ago. Since we are both Jewish, we had a traditional Jewish wedding with a twist. All our friends (gay, lesbian and straight; Jewish and Gentile) attended and participated in the ceremony.

Her partner also commented on the important role of friends:

Three and a half years ago we had a marriage ceremony (Jewish), had a wonderful wedding night with all of our close friends, and I feel that it was a real turning point in our lives together.

Friends may also offer the partnered lesbian a reminder of the history and progress of her relationship. Without societal or family-of-origin recognition of the couple via traditional means such as weddings and anniversaries, friends' acknowledgments and celebrations for the couple take on even greater importance. Maintaining a friendship with an ex-lover also provides the opportunity for historical perspective. A former partner may point out old relationship patterns and/or progress in her ex-lover's current relationship. A friend's knowledge of one's history can also be beneficial to the partnered lesbian who is beginning a new romantic relationship. A number of women at NLC described their friends as resources who shared insights about them to the new partner, which increased the intimacy shared between the couple.

Friends also support the couple's relationship by providing the lesbian with an outlet, other than her partner, for confidences. One participant at Campfest said, "I can share things with my friend that I cannot with my lover because they may be about her." Friendships avert the stifling drawbacks associated with a closed or isolated relationship. As one woman in the Eldridge study wrote:

> My lover and I started this relationship when we were 14 years old, and isolated ourselves for years. We have been very open about being lesbian yet depended on each other almost exclusively for support, companionship, etc. We have used couples therapy to work on issues of dependency/enmeshment and are now beginning to explore separate interests and friendships with others.

These benefits of lesbian friendship do not mean that there may not also be potential problems. Tensions in friendships are inevitable. They may best be understood through exploring the impact of general social factors related to sexual orientation (e.g., homophobia, heterosexism, and the importance of community) as well as individual factors (e.g., age, relationship status) on lesbians and their friends.

The Impact of Sexual Orientation on Lesbian Friendships

While there are many similarities in the friendship experiences of lesbians and heterosexual women, there are also some telling differences. Many of these differences spring from the impact of sexual orientation on friendships in terms of homophobia, heterosexism, and the importance of community.

The Impact of Homophobia and Heterosexism on Lesbian Friendships

Lesbians face varying degrees of condemnation for their sexual orientation. Homophobia and heterosexism impact their friendships as well. At times homophobia and heterosexism may pull friends together. A sense of unity develops as friends manage similar oppression and provide each other with support and understanding. The opposite, however, may occur: friends may disconnect because of homophobia and heterosexism. Some lesbians fear the risks are too great, in terms of losing their family, careers, children, or heterosexual friends, to remain anything but silent about their sexual orientation. This may limit the degree of closeness and honesty a closeted lesbian can have with her heterosexual friends, since she is hiding such a large part of her identity and her life (Ettorre, 1980). Yet self-disclosing to heterosexual friends may at times result in losing friendships, as many participants in both the focus groups and the Eldridge questionnaire experienced. For example, one woman in the Eldridge study wrote:

> A number of long-term straight friends initially were very positive-sounding but then became strikingly avoidant. I think they preferred to think of me as straight, still, and they couldn't deal with my coming-out in my thirties.

A national survey on American sexual norms conducted in 1970 with over three thousand participants shows that a lesbian may indeed lose friends by disclosing her sexual orientation (Klassen, Williams, and Levitt, 1989). In response to the question, "What would you do if you found out that a good friend who is female had homosexual sex?" 51 percent reported that they would no longer be friends, while another 28 percent said that they would remain friends, but that doing so would be a problem. Only 19 percent said that remaining friends would *not* be a problem. Klassen, Williams, and Levitt (1989) conclude that homosexuality takes a great toll on friendship, but it seems more appropriate to say that homophobia and heterosexism are the culprits that undermine friendships between lesbians and heterosexuals.

In terms of lesbians and their homosexual or bisexual friends, homophobia may lead some lesbians to avoid lesbian/gay/bisexual friends altogether, fearing guilt by association. Homophobia can keep lesbians isolated from other lesbian friends, as reported by two different lesbians in the Eldridge questionnaire:

> I myself have just accepted my lifestyle and am comfortable with it. I wish I could be more open about it—I want to feel free. I'd like to develop friendships outside our relationship, but I think my fear of others finding out keeps me from reaching out.
>
> The only part of our relationship that I am at all unhappy with is the inability (our lacking strength?) to live totally openly—to be able to share the true extent of our love and joy with more than a few friends.

Some closeted lesbians have begun to find less direct ways to connect with other lesbians and create friendships that help combat the isolation fostered by homophobia. For example, one member of a couple in the Eldridge survey wrote:

> We live in a very isolated community where there is only one person who is out to any great extent. . . . [W]e do miss being with others but have recently found lesbian couples to talk to through our computer and that helps a lot.

And her partner wrote:

> Our support group is our women friends on the computer. We live in a *very* isolated area—small town—and aren't "out" to people.

Homophobia may also lead to choosing friends on the basis of sexual orientation. Lesbians may be less willing to pursue friendships with heterosexual women, for example, to reduce the risk of rejection. They may also prefer other lesbians as friends because of the shared identity as lesbian. Women in the focus groups reported having heterosexual and bisexual female friends, but the majority of the participants said that their friends, particularly their closest friends, were lesbians. As one woman in the NLC focus group said, "I am much closer to lesbians because of our shared lifestyle." This supports Rubin's (1985) findings that lesbians often prefer friendships with other lesbians, who share their homosexual identity. Lesbians do not have to explain themselves to other lesbians, as they might to heterosexual friends, because sexual orientation ceases to be a difference between the friends (Rubin, 1985). Shared identity may also influence why participants in the focus group reported having gay male friends, while only a small number reported being friends with heterosexual men.

The Impact of Community on Lesbian Friendships

Another factor related to the impact of sexual orientation on lesbian friendships is the importance of community. One unique aspect of the lesbian community is that lesbians come together to create a community across differences in history and culture, unlike those in other oppressed groups (Faderman, 1991; Pearlman, 1987). Other oppressed groups use family or religious gatherings to create support in their community and to pass on traditions. Lesbians, however, gain the traditions and norms of lesbianism, almost exclusively, from lesbian friendship networks (Rainone, 1987).

Friendships among lesbians support the defining elements of lesbians' existence—as women who love other women. Their commonality in living as lesbians and thereby challenging the expectations of their families and society affords lesbians a basic common experience that stands as a foundation for their lesbian identity as well as the formation and maintenance of their friendships.

Communities of lesbian friendship networks are found either within lesbians' everyday social surroundings or through specific events which create community for lesbians, such as women's gatherings at music festivals or Gay Pride events. The women at the National Lesbian Conference and Campfest, the Women's Weekend, spoke openly of the importance of having such gatherings of lesbians in which they could be open about themselves and connect and make friends without the varying degrees of fear many experience on a daily basis as a lesbian.

The Impact of Descriptive Factors on Lesbian Friendships

The lesbian's own descriptive factors, such as age, race, ethnicity, or relationship status, also have an impact on the dynamics of the friendships. Due to the participants' lack of diversity in race, ethnicity, and education, the impact of these variables could not be examined. Participants' variations in the descriptive factors of age and relationship status, however, could be examined and are described below.

The Impact of Age on Lesbian Friendships

One factor that continually surfaced in both the quantitative and qualitative data was the impact of age on friendships. The results from the questionnaire showed a significant relationship between the lesbian's age and friendship, suggesting that as the lesbian grows older, she is more likely to utilize her friendships, and, if partnered, have more friends in common with her partner.

Both heterosexual and homosexual women utilize their friendships more as they grow older (Raymond, 1986). As children grow up and as partners pass away, women have more time, and need, for friends. A lesbian may have grown accustomed to the disconnection from her family of origin or to a life without children, but she may not be prepared for the death of her partner, and therefore reaches out and connects even more with her friends. A participant in the NLC focus group said, "My fear is that as I grow older, I will never have a lover, but I know I can look to my friends to be there for me."

With age, lesbians also tend to value their friendships more (Blumenfeld and Raymond, 1988). One is less likely to take friends for granted and is able to be more appreciative of their strengths and accepting of their limitations. As one woman from the NLC focus group commented, "With age I have become more demanding but also more accepting of who [my] friends are."

The Impact of Relationship Status on Lesbian Friendships

The other important factor that emerged in this study was that relationship status has an impact on lesbian friendships. Single and partnered lesbians share some similar experiences with friends but also report differing patterns and experiences.

A number of single lesbians in the focus groups reported being more comfortable with friends who were also single, because of their shared status. These women said that it was at times painful to spend time with their coupled friends, because of the constant reminder this provided of their own lack of a partner. Other women, who preferred to be single, said it was easier having single friends, because they had more free time and flexibility in their schedules, which meant they were more likely to have time to get together.

Many single lesbians in the focus groups also reported a common experience of feeling "abandoned, expendable, or replaced" when friends entered a new relationship. They discussed the sense of being displaced by their friend's new partner as the friend gave less time and attention to the friendship. One woman at Campfest referred to this as her friend's "honeymoon stage," in which she knew her friend would rarely initiate contact. Many women described feeling hurt as well as resentful toward friends who gave new lovers immediate priority over longtime friends. West (1989) supports these sentiments when she describes the beginning of many lesbian relationships as a "universe for two" in which friends are "shamefully neglected" and feel abandoned (p. 95).

The participants in the focus groups discussed the importance of maintaining a balance in the development of a new romantic relationship while continuing the emotional, intimate ties to friends. Participants offered suggestions for how to deal with a friend's tendency to "go on sabbatical" from her friendships when she enters a new relationship. The general consensus was that one must acknowledge and allow for a friend's excitement and preoccupation in the early stage of a romantic interest and meet the new situation with tolerance and flexibility. One participant commented that she knows to give her friend "space" whenever she enters a new relationship.

The second suggestion was to make an effort to set specific times to get together with a friend and her new partner as well as times when only the two friends get together. If one is still feeling neglected, it was suggested that being honest about missing the friend, while showing an understanding of the excitement of a new relationship, may facilitate reconnection.

The participants also discussed the importance of keeping in mind how they felt set aside, so as they themselves became involved in a new relationship, they would avoid neglecting their own friends. Other women stated that it was also important to examine what really lies behind the anger and jealousy one feels at being replaced by a new lover: Is the friend simply upset about the neglect of the friendship, or is it there an unacknowledged romantic interest in that friend?

As single lesbians reported a preference for single friends, so partnered lesbians reported having more partnered than single friends. The high value that the lesbian community in general places on being in a relationship may often lead lesbian couples to associate more with other couples than with friends who are single (Boston Lesbian Psychologies Collective, 1987). Participants in the focus groups also believed lesbian couples spend more time with other couples because they find it beneficial to be with others who can share and relate to similar experiences and ideas as a couple.

Regardless of whether the women in the couple have single or partnered friends, a number of participants felt it was important to have friends in common as well as separate friendships. This allows both women in the relationship to have shared experiences with friends, while each also has other connections outside the relationship.

Like the single lesbians in this study, partnered lesbians also addressed concerns, frustrations, and negative experiences in their friendships. Some partnered lesbians struggled with the difficulty of finding time and energy for both friends and lovers. Pearlman (1987) stated that partnered lesbians are less socially available because of their relationships. Consequently, tension sometimes arises with friends. Participants at NLC said that some friends were too "emotionally draining" and that at times it becomes "almost impossible to work around friends, commitments, and jobs and fit in a relationship." Therefore, a balance is needed and boundaries must be established, so that friends are neither neglected nor allowed to invade the partnered lesbian's personal time or time with her partner.

Another difficulty for partnered lesbians was related to differences that arise between the couple when the two women have differing friendship styles (Clunis and Green, 1988). For example, introverted versus extroverted friendship styles may lead to disagreements within the relationship. A woman in Eldridge's study wrote:

> We are basically different people. I'm very outgoing and like to be social, whereas she likes to stay home and other than myself her best friend would be her mother. I can't understand her lack of need for friends when I cherish the relationships with my friends.

Focus group members brought up the importance of couples discussing each other's style of interacting with friends in order to gain a better understanding of each other and to develop strategies and compromises to deal with their differences.

A negative experience that a few couples reported having with friends was the feeling that some friends seemed more interested in the couple's relationship ending than having the couple remain together. Johnson (1990), in her research on long-term lesbian couples, found that although friendships provide many important sources of support, some couples felt at times that members of the lesbian community were "hostile to the idea of long, committed relationships." One woman who had been with her partner for almost twenty years wrote in the questionnaire:

> We have lived together so long, we have outgrown, outlived our coupled friends. They're all broken up and gone. We have difficulty finding friends who will accept our relationship—most try to break us up!

Participants in the focus groups felt the best way to handle this situation was to be honest and speak directly to the friend about their concerns.

The most frequently addressed concern regarding couples and their friends was the potential threat of a friend becoming romantically involved with one member of the couple. For all individuals—regardless of their sexual orientation, gender, or relationship status—there is always the potential of becoming attracted to and involved with a friend. Since our culture places such a strong value on people being part of a romantic couple, all those who are significant to a person are potential partners, including friends (Kolbenschlag, 1979).

It may be argued, however, that this phenomenon is particularly exacerbated for lesbians and their friends. In her research on lesbians, Vetere (1982) found that "almost all the women interviewed had at some time felt feelings of attraction toward female friends, and a large majority had at some point acted on them" (p. 64). There are several reasons why lesbians may have a higher potential for becoming romantically involved with their friends than heterosexuals.

First, lesbians, because of their lack of societal acceptance, have fewer venues in which to interact with other lesbians. This limits the circle of individuals with whom one can form friendships or romantic attachments.

Second, as stated earlier, lesbians lack social norms for dating and therefore rely instead on the more ambiguous conversion from friend to partner. An initial experience of progressing from a friendship into a romantic relationship may set a precedent or a familiar pattern that is emulated in future situations since few other roads to partnership have been experienced.

Lastly, lesbians who are already in a committed relationship are not immune to the danger of one partner becoming romantically involved with a friend. In fact, it can be argued that they are more at risk than their heterosexual counterparts; lesbian couples cannot take advantage of the boundaries that go along with having recognized, structured formats or societally recognized markers acknowledging and sanctioning their relationship. Legalized marriage, though by no means guaranteeing a lifelong commitment, does set some degree of precedence for the couple and for others to respect.

It is common at some point, whether you are single or in a relationship, to be attracted to a friend. It is what you do or do not do with the attraction that will affect you and your existing romantic relationship (if you are already in one). Participants in the focus groups discussed specific points to take into account when one finds oneself romantically attracted to a friend.

Many women in the focus groups felt that the ambiguity surrounding the distinction between friend and lover in the lesbian community is considerable. If a friendship is to remain a friendship rather than move into a romantic relationship, it is important to establish and maintain clear boundaries with one's friends. It may also be helpful to speak directly with a friend about these boundaries, to make it clear that the connection is and will always be a friendship and is not going to be transformed into a romantic involvement.

It is also important to be honest with oneself. Following through on an attraction to a friend is likely to change your connection with that person. This may sound obvious, but when one feels such an attraction, it is often difficult to be rational and to think through the possible repercussions of one's actions. How may the friendship change? Talk with the other person involved. Confer with other friends. And think through the situation yourself.

For the partnered lesbian, the potential for friends becoming lovers may affect how she reacts to her partner's friends. It is not uncommon for a partnered lesbian at times to view her lover's friend as a possible threat to the primary relationship. Feelings of jealousy, mistrust, and doubt toward a partner's platonic interest in a friend may become detrimental to the romantic relationship. For example, a participant in the Eldridge study wrote:

> There is only one area where we have any major conflicts, and that is that my partner is jealous of a few (not most) of my friendships, particularly with people who seem to want a friendship with me that doesn't include her very much (these are non-sexual friendships—I am totally committed to monogamy). We argue bitterly occasionally over these friendships.

A partner's feelings of jealousy or one's own feelings of guilt motivate some lesbians to relinquish their friendships in order to maintain serenity in their relationship (Rubin, 1985). One woman from the Eldridge study wrote, "*I* want friendships outside the relationship but feel fear and guilt—though I'm not wanting a physical relationship." Jealousy may particularly arise if one of the partners remains friends with an ex-lover, and the friendship may be relinquished because of it. Some women at Campfest described losing their ex-lovers as friends because their current partners were jealous and disapproving of these friendships. Women in both focus groups stressed the importance of establishing boundaries for the current relationship with the ex-lover, thus providing guidelines for everyone to be aware of and to respect.

Although there was talk in the focus groups about some of the difficulties related to friendships between partnered lesbians and their ex-lovers, there was even more discussion about the tendency to stay connected with ex-lovers because of the positive experiences associated with remaining friends. The degree and way in which ex-lovers relate as friends varies tremendously; indeed, Carol Becker, in *Unbroken Ties: Lesbian Ex-Lovers* (1988), presents a detailed description of the broad range of friendships through which ex-partners may connect.

"How many lesbian friends does it take to change a lightbulb? It depends on how well your ex-lovers get along." A weak joke, but one that speaks to the tendency of lesbians to remain friends with their ex-lovers. Mencher and Slater (1991) believe that within the lesbian community the incorporation of ex-lovers into one's friendship network is normative. This supports the results of the Hite Report, a national survey of forty-five hundred women, which indicated that over 60 percent of lesbians remain friends with their ex-lovers (Hite, 1987).

There are various reasons why lesbians remain connected to their ex-lovers as friends. Some stay linked because of the limited size of their lesbian community and the need to remain close to existing connections. This may be particularly important for lesbians who are closeted and have few connections with friends who know of their sexual orientation.

Additionally, the intense closeness and intimacy shared between two ex-lovers does not necessarily end with the disbandment of their relationship. Clunis and Green (1988) cite the effort that was put forth into the relationship and the value set upon it as a substantial reason why lesbians work hard to make the transition from lover to friend following a break-up. This is apparent for a participant in the Eldridge study who wrote: "We both came off of rather long-term relationships when we became a couple. . . . [W]e both are intensely loyal to our immediate ex's and consider them intimate friends."

The early stages of the transition from being lovers to friends are not always easy or smooth. In some cases one or both women have no interest in maintaining a friendship or harbor too many negative emotions to want to remain connected. Participants in the focus group, however, who had gone through the transition process offered insight into facilitating the reconnection.

Many women at Campfest agreed that the first step was to clearly terminate the romantic relationship and establish closure on the two women's former view of themselves as a couple. This may be accomplished in a number of stages and ways, such as getting separate living quarters, dividing shared properties, telling others that the relationship has ended, and most importantly, stating verbally to oneself and to one's partner that the relationship has ended.

The next essential step, according to the Campfest participants, was to allow some time to pass before trying to reconnect. A hiatus from contact, according to Becker (1988), is an essential part of the "ex-lover transition"; it works toward resolving the end of one kind of relationship and moving on to another. The Campfest participants suggested waiting periods of six months to two years, with many agreeing on somewhere between one to two years, before attempting to reconnect with an ex-lover. One woman said that the time following her break-up helped to create a "mental boundary" that confirmed to her that the former relationship had ended and that a friendship with her ex-lover would now be possible. Besides time, participants cited other factors such as amiable break-ups, geographic distance, and involvement in a new relationship as facilitating the transition from lover to friend.

Participants also commented on the importance of discussing with one's current partner the role that each wants ex-lovers to play in their lives. Women said it was particularly helpful to discuss any fears, whether warranted or not, that a friendship with an ex-partner may arouse in one's current partner.

Conclusion

I still smile when I think back to that day in May when all those women came walking over the hill and sat down on the grass, eager to discuss, understand, and share their experiences regarding their friends. I am grateful to all these women whose impressions, stories, and wisdom provided such a vivid portrayal of the role of friendship in lesbians' lives.

The most important theme to emerge in this research came near the end of both focus groups. Participants stated that lesbians need to value friends and publicly acknowledge the importance of friendships in our lives. Our society has no institutionalized rituals for celebrating friendships and publicly affirming them (Allan, 1989). Thank goodness lesbians do not always follow the institutional norms of society. It's time to give friends unsolicited thanks and praise for everything they do for us and to celebrate our friendships. Enjoy!

REFERENCES

Allan, G. 1989. *Friendship: Developing a sociological perspective.* Boulder, CO: Westview Press.

Becker, C. S. 1988. *Unbroken ties: Lesbian ex-lovers.* Boston: Alyson.

Blumenfeld, W. J., and D. Raymond. 1988. *Looking at gay and lesbian life.* Boston: Beacon Press.

Boston Lesbian Psychologies Collective. 1987. Introduction. In Boston Lesbian Psychologies Collective, eds., *Lesbian psychologies: Explorations and challenges,* pp. 1–16. Chicago: University of Illinois Press.

Clunis, D. M., and G. D. Green. 1988. *Lesbian couples.* Seattle: Seal Press.

Eldridge, N. S. 1987. Correlates of relationship satisfaction and role conflict in dual-career lesbian couples. Doctoral dissertation, University of Texas, Austin.

Ettorre, E. M. 1980. *Lesbians, women and society.* Boston: Routledge and Kegan Paul.

Faderman, L. 1991. *Odd girls and twilight lovers: A history of lesbian life in twentieth-century America.* New York: Columbia University Press.

Gartrell, N. 1981. The lesbian as a "single woman." *American Journal of Psychotherapy* 4: 502–9.

Hite, S. 1987. *Women and love: A cultural revolution in progress.* New York: Alfred A. Knopf.

Johnson, S. E. 1990. *Staying power: Long term lesbian couples.* Tallahassee, FL: Naiad Press.

Klassen, A. D., C. J. Williams, and E. E. Levitt. 1989. *Sex and morality in the U.S.* Middletown, CT: Wesleyan University Press.

Kolbenschlag, M. 1979. *Kiss Sleeping Beauty good-bye: Breaking the spell of feminine myths and models.* New York: Doubleday.

Mencher, J., and S. Slater. 1991. New perspectives on the lesbian family experience. Paper presented at the annual meeting of the Association for Women in Psychology, March, Hartford, CT.

Pearlman, S. F. 1987. The saga of continuing clash in lesbian community, or will an army of ex-lovers fail? In Boston Lesbian Psychologies Collective, eds., *Lesbian psychologies: Explorations and challenges,* pp. 313–26. Chicago: University of Illinois Press.

Rainone, L. F. 1987. Beyond community: Politics and spirituality. In Boston Lesbian Psychologies Collective, eds., *Lesbian psychologies: Explorations and challenges,* pp. 344–54. Chicago: University of Illinois Press.

Raymond, J. 1986. *A passion for friends: Toward a philosophy of female affection.* Boston: Beacon Press.

Robinson, J. P., and P. R. Shaver. 1973. *Measures of social psychological attitudes.* Ann Arbor: Institute for Social Research, University of Michigan.

Rubin, L. 1985. *Just friends: The role of friendship in our lives.* New York: Harper and Row.

Schaefer, M. T., and D. H. Olson. 1981. Assessing intimacy: The PAIR Inventory. *Journal of Marital and Family Therapy* 7: 47–60.

Slater, S., and J. Mencher. 1991. The lesbian family life cycle: A contextual approach. *American Journal of Orthopsychiatry* 61: 372–82.

Sophie, J. 1982. Counseling lesbians. *Personnel and Guidance Journal* 60: 341–45.

Spanier, G. B. 1976. Measuring dyadic adjustment: New scales for assessing the quality of marriage and similar dyads. *Journal of Marriage and the Family* 38: 15–28.

Stanley, J. L. 1993. The partnered lesbian and her friends: The impact of friendship on self-esteem and relationship satisfaction. Doctoral dissertation, University of Pennsylvania, Philadelphia.

Vetere, V. A. 1982. The role of friendship in the development and maintenance of lesbian love relationships. *Journal of Homosexuality* 8: 51–66.

West, C. 1989. *A lesbian love advisor.* Pittsburgh: Cleis Press.

PART II

Exploring the Continuum: Friends, Lovers, and the Places in Between

A. From Friends to Lovers and/or Lovers to Friends

Catherine Hopkins (left) and Jane Futcher (right), November 1992, in Catskill, New York. Photo by Erin Carney.

FOUR

Heart like a Wheel:
A Friendship in Two Voices

JANE FUTCHER AND
CATHERINE HOPKINS

Catherine Judith Hopkins died on January 4, 1996, in
Catskill, New York. She was fifty-four years old.

New York, 1973-77

JANE: I was twenty-six in 1973, the year you and I met. I'd had sex
with two women — Jill Johnston and my boyfriend's sister — and I
wanted more. But I was scared, and I was lonely, and Philadelphia,
where I lived seven blocks from my parents' house, didn't feel like
a place where I could come out as a lesbian. So in June, when
Harper & Row offered me a job in New York, I jumped at the
chance. By July, I had met Lynne, and by September, Lynne and I
were lovers.

Lynne told me all about you: that you were a lesbian and were
beautiful and witty and fun and lived in the Village and were the
art director of the paperback department, where she worked. But
it wasn't until I walked into 459 Hudson Street late that fall that I
realized how extraordinary you were. You had gone to Europe
with Patricia and asked Lynne to housesit for Augusta, a.k.a.
"Snouty," your dachshund. Your apartment was a universe of
beauty and sense, nothing like the transient, mix-and-match crash
pads I'd lived in. You had walls of books, a deep red oriental
carpet and a brown velour couch, cane chairs, a brick fireplace, an
art studio, and a bedroom, cool and spare, with only an oak
dresser and the iron bed, painted white. And of course, there was

65

Augusta, who befriended strangers and burrowed down under the sheets at night and licked your face in the morning and barked until you took her for a walk. By the time you returned from Tuscany, I was in love.

"Can we go see Catherine?" I used to say to Lynne on weekends, when we'd wander around the Village. We'd knock bashfully on your door and wait, as you stopped whatever you were doing, flicked back your long brown-silver hair, and opened the door, winking at us with those clear blue eyes, as if you had all the time in the world. You were so exciting to be around that I always spilled something, like a full glass of Harvey's Bristol Cream. You never complained, just teased me for being clumsy and wiped up after me.

In the spring of 1974, Lynne decided to go back to men. In July I met Mary Lou at the Duchess, and in August, although you and I didn't know each other well, you helped me move into my apartment on Eleventh Street, in the Village. It was November '74, I think, the night you and I went out with friends to dinner at Mother Courage, stopped in at the Duchess for a drink, then found ourselves returning to 459 Hudson . . . together. I waited shivering in your bed, on those crisp red sheets with the little white squares and black dots, while you finished a paste-up job you owed an art director in the morning. What a night. What a turning. You opened your home and your heart, and your touch opened *my* heart. Augusta smiled and wagged her tail and snuggled down beneath the sheets.

Before we met, I felt like an orphan, moving from apartment to apartment, from city to city, scared of men and attracted to women who rejected me. Always, in the end, I was alone, watching people's lives from a distance, always an outsider. You opened your door and welcomed me, introducing me to your friends, sharing your home. You had created a lesbian family, and I became part of that family. After a great wringing of (my) hands, I moved in with you, and we were very, very happy. I remember nights lying together on the couch as Linda Ronstadt sang "Heart like a Wheel," about love that never ends, just grows and bends. We had dinner parties with friends and spent two weeks in a cabin in Nantucket. We took taxis to work each morning and came home together on the F train, stopping to buy London broil at Gristede's. We explored the city on weekends, ate scrambled eggs at the Bagel on West Fourth Street, borrowed Diane's red VW and drove to Bear Mountain to hike with Augusta. In the months and years we were together, you were infinitely patient with my crushes, with my anxiety about being a lesbian, with my writer's struggles for money and recognition. I felt incredibly lucky, as if I'd narrowly escaped hell and found someone to show me what heaven could be like.

CATHERINE: After hearing much about you from our friend Lynne, we finally met outside our office building one noontime. Lynne introduced us in the darkened arcade; my immediate response and bright memory are the same: I love that face! I got to love all of you, but your open and honest face really delighted me. I did not at all sense romance, and we made a friendship. Months later, dancing at a bar, I looked at you and all at once fell in love. It was really that uncomplicated for me. But I'd never been romantically attracted to someone I'd first had a friendship with—before you.

From that first night we stayed together every night with few exceptions. You still had your apartment, "in case." You let it go after a year, but it was the idea of moving to San Francisco that equaled commitment. This was before most of our community had rituals and rites of passage to recognize and celebrate our partnerships and secure our places with each other and society at large.

We spent time with your parents in Philadelphia while we still lived in New York. You loved visiting with them, and I liked to see you all together, listening to your lives and learning about family customs. And I enjoyed being included. It's a bond that continues. I just missed meeting your only sibling, a sister; Marge said good-bye to her family about the time I met you. I think I filled up some space Marge would have occupied in your life.

San Francisco, 1977-83

JANE: The decision to move to San Francisco seemed right at the time. It was Fall 1976, and Harper & Row was about to lay me off. I wanted to write a novel, and you, having lived in New York most of your life, were tired of the city and eager to take the job as art director of the West Coast office. But as moving day approached—February 26, 1977 (I remember because the next day was my thirtieth birthday)—my anxiety set in. How could we leave New York, our families, and the community of lesbian and gay friends who supported, reflected, and enriched our lives? Would we ever be able to create such a life in San Francisco?

As always, you talked me through my fears, comforted me, stayed upbeat and optimistic. I felt better when we found our beautiful flat on Webster Street, just a few blocks from San Francisco Bay. I started my novel, and you started your job. We bought a new yellow Honda Civic that we called Rubber Ducky. We used to say that Rubber Ducky was our marriage license, because the loan—the most money either of us had ever borrowed—was in both our names.

CATHERINE: We were thrilled with the beauty of California. But going from the dark interiors of New York to the expansive light of San Francisco exaggerated the isolation we felt, bereft of people we felt close to and saw often. We had to create a new life and relied upon each other for emotional sustenance. I had an office to go to with many people in it, but you worked alone at home, writing, with no interaction. Evenings I was too tired for emotional stimulation and wanted less talk. Some of our needs were very different, and we didn't have the means yet to overcome the obstacles. We'd become great friends but had lost our romantic partnership.

Jane's Affair

JANE: In retrospect, I think the six-year difference in our ages became more problematic after our move to San Francisco, where we no longer had our network of friends and the stimulation of New York. I had only been "out" for a year when you and I became lovers. I'd spent most of my life fighting my lesbianism, and we met just as I was beginning to know myself and enjoy my sexual and emotional freedom. I was about as mature as a late-blooming fifteen-year-old, while you, at thirty-seven, had been a lesbian for much longer, had had many affairs and several serious relationships, and were ready for a monogamous, committed partnership.

Despite the onslaught of houseguests—beloved friends from New York—I was terribly lonely. I began to take for granted, even find irritating, the predictability of our life together. From an outsider looking in, I'd become an insider pining to get out.

"Make some friends," you used to say. "Call people. Join a club. *Do* something." So I did. I became a member of the Feminist Writers' Guild, and through that group I met a woman with seven cats and three dogs and a male lover.

Just a few weeks after my affair started, you came home from work one night, kissed me, then stared at me oddly. "Who did you see today?"

"No one," I said nervously.

"Did you sleep with her?"

"Don't be silly."

"I'm not being silly," you said, your face going pale. "I smell her on your clothes. You slept with her."

"Yes," I said guiltily. I was no good at lying. "Twice."

"Then it's over with us," you said quietly.

It was May 1, 1979. The next day I flew, as planned, to Arkansas, for a family reunion.

The Break-Up

CATHERINE: It was a hard blow when I learned of your love for someone else. It was a shock, but I hadn't been paying good attention to our relationship. We both put up a brief struggle, but we knew that the relationship was gone, and sexuality was badly

desired on your part. I'd been drinking too much and was probably depressed, too. I hated us to separate, but I knew our sexual
partnership was over, and I still wanted you in my life. So I had to
let go of the idea I'd fixed in my mind and heart for so long, and
get onto a new way of being with you. We'd always enjoyed each
other's company a great deal, and our sense of familiarity and
basic trust was not diminished. Your friendship helped me so
much in my life, and I didn't believe that was to be over. And it's
not.

JANE: As the one being left, you suffered more, I guess. But I'm not
sure. I remember many days, after we made the decision that I
would move out, lying on the floor of our living room, listening to
Cris Williamson singing "Fillin' Up and Spillin' Over," wailing,
pounding my fists, clutching Augusta, who would lick my face and
smile anxiously. Our break-up was extraordinarily painful. I was
losing my best friend, the kindest lover, the most loyal and generous person I'd ever known, to be with a wild woman who lived in
Marin in a ramshackle house with a man. The new relationship
was doomed. You and I both knew that. And yet I could not break
it off, could not stop it, could not go back to our old life. It was a
nightmare for both of us. I was rejecting the only security, the only
family, the only real happiness I had ever known in adulthood.
What was wrong with me? Why couldn't I stop it?

Our friends shook their heads. Why was I giving up so much to
gain so little? I didn't know. I couldn't explain. I was diving back
into the void that you had helped to pull me out of.

When I moved to an apartment four blocks away, you were so
generous, so kind, that despite the pain that I had caused you, you
continued to stand by me, helping me move, visiting me on nights
when I was so unhappy I thought I might die. Friends asked if
we'd gotten back together. "No," we'd say, as I helped you move
to the apartment upstairs in our old building. We'd cook dinner
for each other, and you'd counsel me when my lover would go off
to the mountains with her boyfriend. You were kind to her despite
her role in our break-up, despite the fact that you were dragging

yourself to work, reeling from the shock, seeing a therapist to help pull yourself together. "You may have to bite the bullet," our therapist told you. You bit the bullet and you swallowed it. I was still firing them.

Meeting Joan

JANE: Your new apartment became my second home. Some days, when I was desperate, I'd let myself in while you were at work: I'd hold Augusta and play "Heart like a Wheel" and try not to feel so scared and alone. You were still my home and my family, and you never seemed to mind my visits.

Three months after I moved out, you were trying to date, had gone on a women's backpacking trip, had spent a weekend at Willow, a women's retreat. One evening—in September, I think it was—a friend invited us to a book-signing party. At that party, we spied a woman, a dark-eyed beauty with white teeth and a movie star's smile. "There's your new lover," I said. "Let's find out who she is." I spoke to her first, then introduced her to you. At least that's how I remember it.

CATHERINE: Here's how *I* remember it: The restaurant was teeming with lesbians. I don't think I saw Joan till you motioned me over to where you two were in conversation, you facing me, she with her back to me. You had an obvious, devilish glint in your eyes when you said, "Catherine, there is someone I want you to meet," and introduced Joan to me. She sparkled like a movie star, and you knew she had me.

JANE: Your relationship took off more quickly than I had imagined. Within weeks, Joan had left her lover and the two of you were together almost every night. Sure, I was happy for you, but I could see the handwriting on the wall. Joan was not going to like me popping in and out of your apartment, getting a hit of my family whenever I liked. And I felt like it a lot, because my lover and I were up and down, on again, off again. It was a blow when you told me that you two were looking for an apartment together, that you were ready to make a lifetime commitment, to create a home, as we had done, or tried to do.

I moved to my lover's house. Six months later, I moved out. Then I moved back, and you helped me pack. Now you and Joan both counseled me, talked to me, listened to my endless stories about the problems of being in love with a woman who could not let go of her man. In 1982, I left my lover for the last time and found my cottage in Sausalito. You bought out my half of Rubber Ducky, our car, and with that, our marriage was formally dissolved.

Sausalito, 1983

JANE: I will always remember the warm summer evening when we hiked out the Tennessee Valley Trail to the ocean, inhaling the sage and salt and the pennyroyal by the creek. Afterwards, I fixed dinner at my cottage in Sausalito overlooking Richardson Bay.

"I have some news."

Your somber tone made my stomach tighten. "What?"

"Joan and I are moving back East."

A tremor jolted my foundation. I stared at you. "Back East?"

"We've saved some money, and we want to buy a house. We can't afford anything in San Francisco, and my mother's been sick and I don't know how much longer she'll . . . "

You stopped. My heart was pounding.

"It's very hard for me to tell you this, Jane. It's harder to tell you than anybody else."

I bowed my head, feeling the tears. "When?"

"In September." That was two months away.

"Is it Joan? Is she making you leave?"

You shook your head. "We want a house. We want to be closer to my family."

"But what about me?" I was being silly. I knew it. You had your life with Joan. I'd made my choices. Still, I was losing my best friend. Who would comfort me when a publisher returned a manuscript? Who could I call when I felt orphaned, scratching on the door to be let in? We were both crying. I am crying now, thinking of that night.

Philadelphia, 1985

JANE: My mother was diagnosed with cancer, and I had come home from California to live temporarily with my parents in Philadelphia, where it was winter—cold and dark. I called you and Joan often, and one weekend you and Joan decided to drive down from Catskill, New York, where you lived now, bringing your new dachshund, Zoe, and the cat. Your energy filled our sad house with love and life. The cat jumped on Mother's bed, giving her quite a start, while the three of us—me, you, and Joan—walked along South Street in the snow.

"You are so lucky," Joan said, as we stopped for Zoe to pee.

"Am I?"

"To have parents who adore you. Who have loved you the way your mother loves you, and you love her." I thought of my mother, upstairs in the bed, struggling for breath. Joan's parents had not spoken to her in seven years.

"You'll always have us, Bun-Bun," you said to me, smiling. "You can't get rid of us."

"I'd better not," I said, wiping my eyes.

My mother died on March 3, 1985. You and Joan drove all the way down from Catskill to the funeral in Baltimore. On the way back, on the Delaware Turnpike, my father and I passed your car. I rolled down the window. "Come spend the night with us in Philadelephia," I called. "Don't drive back tonight."

You followed us to Philly. What a blessing it was to have you in our house, filling up the space where my mother had been. It was not so bad saying goodbye to you, because five days later, my father and I came up to Catskill in the Arctic March air and stayed four nights with you. On the last day of our visit, you and Joan had a huge fight. My father and I heard shouting downstairs. I wondered if the fight had something to do with me, with Joan's resentment of our friendship and our history; there was often tension when I visited. You said it was something else; you said it was her illness, her M.S. getting worse and her feeling helpless and sick and frustrated.

CATHERINE: We've kept this friendship a long time. I've wondered often what the real glue of it is. Not that I don't trust it by its nature alone; I do. We've been loyal dogs, that's for sure. I think it's about interest, respect, difference, family feeling, history, and the friendship created out of this that gives the sense of place in the universe—unloneliness. So we do checks on each other, making sure the other one is doing alright, and we feel secure ourselves.

It's also a particular line of communication we share. Most times we're both able to board the same stream of consciousness and know there's another person in the world who understands what's going on inside where the inexplicable occurs. This is the familiarity between us that people recognize and that makes some people feel excluded. But it's there anyway, and I don't want to know or love you less. And I think this is where the tension has come in from others—new people in our lives feeling left out because we've still got our hotlines intact to each other.

Sailing in Maine, 1989, 1990

JANE: Yes! Joan has said you can go sailing in Maine with me and my father and his girlfriend. He has rented a sloop for ten days, and we'll have time alone together, time to talk and remember and relax. We won't need to worry about hurting Joan's feelings with our memories and jokes, with this old, deep bond that sometimes makes her angry and restless. And so we go on this trip together. Each night, at cocktail time, you and I row the dinghy to this or that little island, talking about our lives. You photograph boats and birds and my father in his hat.

Just before our second sail, in July 1990, I meet Erin. We'd had one date—Chinese dinner, followed by the movie *Longtime*

Companion and a walk under the almost full moon—but I feel the stirring of something important.

Back at home, Erin holds me in her warm, quilted bed. You and Joan listen to my reports of our relationship with cautious optimism. You've heard about so many of my disasters that you're slightly skeptical. In 1992, I rent my house in Mill Valley and move to Erin's. You are both happy for us. You know that I am coming in out of the cold.

California and Catskill, 1992

JANE: I am now used to this long distance relationship. I call you, Joan too, when I'm down and need advice, like in 1986, when I fell in love with my high school crush, and in 1988, when she shocked me with the news that she had another lover and was finished with me. It hurt, maybe even more than our break-up, because I was older and craving a committed relationship and had had enough of drama and pain.

Cancer, March 1993

JANE: Sometime in February, you tell me you have a lump in your stomach. The doctor says it needs to come out, for it's gotten quite big. "It's nothing serious," you say, hearing the worry in my voice. "The doctor is sure it's benign."

"Benign. Yes." I like the sound of "benign."

Joan gets on the phone. "We like this doctor very much. We trust him. I'll call you the minute we know."

When Joan calls, her voice is choked. "It's very, very bad," she says. "It's ovarian cancer, and it's spread all over her abdominal cavity. The doctor took some of it out, but not all. Some of the cancer is still inside her."

I am in my little office, held up by the couch. "Should I come?" I say, my voice catching.

"Everything is too uncertain," Joan says. "We may move her to another hospital. We don't think this doctor knows what he's doing. She may need another operation."

"Another operation?" I am frightened. This operation was bad enough.

"I'm okay, Bun," you whisper. "Can't talk now." Your voice is very weak, too weak for jokes.

Joan gets back on. "We'll call you. If we move her, we'll call you."

I put down the phone. I am screaming, pounding my fists against my sofa. Erin holds me as you have done so many times, calmly, with infinite patience. Her tenderness reminds me of you, and I cry harder. "I don't want to lose her," I cry.

"Of course not. Maybe you won't."

Two days later, an ambulance takes you to another hospital, a better one, for another operation to remove what the bad doctor didn't take. It is unreal, a nightmare. A continent away they are carving you up, and I am here doing nothing. I find construction paper, and Erin and I make you cards with suns and flowers and cut-out dogs. I want to see you, but it would only confuse things. You need all your strength to survive. And my presence, I know, would be a pressure Joan doesn't need.

Joan drives you home to Catskill. Each day you sound a little better, a little stronger. I plan a visit for June. By then you won't be so weak. By then you will have started chemo.

Catskill, New York, June 1993

JANE: You are so tiny and frail and bald from surgery and chemo that I am afraid to look at you. Your eyes are huge, like a Holocaust survivor's, but the blue and the twinkle are still there. You walk slowly, almost shuffle, in your baseball cap, your corduroy pants hanging off your hips. There's a port in your chest where they put the chemo. I am sick too, with some sort of stomach flu that makes me feel weak and sleepy. We make a funny tableau, the three of us, lying around your living room, watching TV like elderly invalids.

"I don't want you to die," I say finally, one day when we are alone. You are lying on the couch where I'm sitting.

"I don't want to die." You pull your baseball cap down over your eyes.

"You're very important to me," I say, my heart pounding.

"And you're important to me, Jane." You only call me Jane when things are very serious.

"Are you scared?" I feel tears.

"Sometimes I'm very scared."

"Do you talk to Joan?"

"Joan helps me so much. And I'm getting hypnotherapy, because it gets bad at night. I worry about Joan and who will take care of her, and I think maybe I will never see my dogs again, and it's . . . " You stop to wipe something from your eye.

"I love you very much," I say. Why is it so hard to talk when we've been friends for twenty years?

"I love you, too, Bun."

"You're my best friend." I wipe my eyes. "I love you to bits."

You take my hand. "It's hard to see me this way, isn't it?"

I nod.

You smile. "I look good now. You should have seen me a couple weeks ago."

"I'm glad I didn't," I laugh.

We sit for a long time, in the quiet.

The next day I fly to Philadelphia to see my father. He takes me to the emergency room, where we learn that my stomach cramps are a ruptured appendix. I am in the hospital for six days. Erin flies East. You and Joan send flowers and call me every day. I'm scared. I've been up all night throwing up and having diarrhea. They want to operate and talk about a problem with my bowels. I remember my mother and her colostomy. Then, suddenly, I'm better. Erin and I fly back to California. They'll operate on me there, after the infection heals.

Catskill, June 1994

CATHERINE: I'm so glad to be alive, to have made it through last year's cancer and chemotherapy. I think of the terror I felt at losing my life, not to be here any longer, not able to understand what that apartness was about. I felt so bad and scared for you last year when you had that awful time in the hospital with the appendicitis. And I could really feel your fear around the medicine, the doctors, the vomiting, the sense of abnormalcy. So we shared a lot of that particular thing at the same time, and came to see the daylight at the other end.

Today, August 1994

CATHERINE: I'm fifty-three now, loving my life with Joan. We both wish we lived closer to you and Erin. I'm happy that our lives are in favor with each other's! I tell you on the phone how many houseguests we've been having, and you say don't let anyone else come here but you; I say OK and really mean it. I love your visits to Catskill, laden with stories of cousins and old loves and crazy California lesbians.

It's a perfect August day—clear air and blue and green all around. I'm on the back porch with my dogs. I'm feeling good that you and Erin have each other, that your lives are blessed with caring. A baby sparrow has been nearby all day while I write this; she's been learning to take care of herself. I'm watching her, and I'm watching you! With much love, I'm watching.

JANE: Writing this, I have thought so much about our lives, about those days in New York, about Hudson Street, when we loved on the edge, and there was so much we didn't know. I think of your blue eyes and your beautiful house and listening to that pop song, "Two Strong Arms," that you used to sing to me, drinking Grand Marnier late at night. I think of Diane and Allison and Janet and Susie and Hillary and Lisa and Claire and Marilyn and Dunham and Lynnsy and Margo and Michael and John Spina and Bobby Hobbs and Paul and Caroline and all the people I know because of you. I think of what is over and wonder what's to come.

You are well now and have hair and energy, and you're working again in your darkroom, and you can drive and take the dogs for walks, and your cancer is in remission. When I think how close we came, that we could, still, will, at some point, come to that place again, I start to cry.

Have we said it all, sweet Catherine? Have we said any of it? I have left out so much, like "the girls" at Village Casuals in New York—the first middle-aged lesbians I'd ever met—who owned the store where you bought tailored blouses and beautiful silk-lined slacks. I remember the sad night we buried Augusta in the Presidio in San Francisco. I remember learning of your mother's death, and then your father's.

I am thinking of Lynne, who introduced us, who is married now, with children, and who never answers my Christmas cards, afraid, I fear, that her lesbian past will somehow tarnish her happy family life. I am thinking of the white iron bed and the living room on Hudson Street and Augusta lying curled on the couch, where you and I listened again and again to Linda Ronstadt. I met Linda Ronstadt recently, in San Francisco, at a fundraiser for abortion rights. I told her about you, about us, about our friendship, about all the years we listened to her album in New York and San Francisco. At my request, she signed the evening's program and wrote a little note to you in scrawling script. I don't know what she thought, but it doesn't matter. What matters is that I'm seeing you now, as I hear her voice belting out a song about a love that never ends, just bends and grows and widens, like a circle, like a wheel.

FIVE

Ruth Benedict and Margaret Mead: Portrait of an Extraordinary Friendship

HILARY LAPSLEY

In her autobiography, *Blackberry Winter* (1972), Margaret Mead, in a simple and telling obituary, memorialized her lifelong friendship with Ruth Benedict: "When she died, I had read everything she had ever written and she had read everything I had ever written. No one else had, and no one else has" (p. 125). Friendships between women have seldom been accorded their true importance in the lives of women who have made a mark on public life, and the extraordinary relationship between Ruth Benedict and Margaret Mead is no exception.[1]

It was while surveying biographies of women in order to find material for a project on women and their mentors that I was first drawn to Benedict and Mead, who provided an example of woman mentor and woman protégée, respectively, a combination not easy to identify in accounts of women's lives. When I came to realize that Mead and Benedict's relationship included a sexual dimension, I was even further interested. As a lesbian scholar, it is endlessly thrilling to find more skeletons in the closet of history, to find more evidence that women have loved each other against the tide, more evidence that heterosexuality is not as secure as its propaganda would have us believe. That excitement is tempered by a sense of sadness at the ways in which lesbian relationships are often suppressed, overlooked or distorted in accounts of women's lives.

As I studied Mead's and Benedict's work,[2] I began to realize how in a very real sense their anthropological preoccupations related to their personal lives and this, too, became a focus of investigation. But what emerged was really the story of an extraordinary relationship, which moved beyond mentor and protégée, becoming a love affair and then an enriching lifelong friendship.[3]

The Restless Woman and the Punk

Ruth Benedict was born Ruth Fulton in New York City in 1887. Her childhood was overshadowed by the death of her father when she was four years old. She later told Margaret Mead that her "primal scene" was her mother weeping over her father's open coffin while she urged Ruth to look at him and never forget him.[4] Growing up with her mother, sister, and extended family on a farm in New York State, she was a quiet, withdrawn child with a rich imaginative life. Partly deaf from measles, she was given to occasional ungovernable tantrums until her mother, despairingly, made the eleven-year-old Ruth invoke the help of Jehovah and solemnly promise never to give way to another fit of rage. This tactic succeeded, but the rages turned into lifelong bouts of "the blue devils," as Ruth called her depressions.

As a young graduate from Vassar, her mother's alma mater, Ruth surveyed her options. The unmarried lifestyles of the generation of career women who taught her seemed dreary and unfulfilling. Yet to live out one's destiny as a woman through marriage and children meant sacrificing the chance to do meaningful work. Ruth made forays into teaching and social work, which she found unsatisfactory, as these professions merely transferred women's traditional skills into the public sphere. She took a predictable way out of her dilemma by falling in love with Stanley Benedict. Like her idolized father, Stanley Benedict too had made a career in medical research. But the marriage quickly became unhappy and no child came of it, initially a deep disappointment for Ruth had hoped that children would give her a reason for living.[5] After toying with becoming a writer (her topic: the lives of restless women), her escape route became the world of anthropology. As an adult student in her early thirties at the New School for Social Research after World War I, Benedict was encouraged to take up graduate studies at Columbia University. Franz Boas, elder statesman of American anthropology, Germanic, austere, and forbidding, generously mentored this awkward, shy woman, who must have looked unlikely to succeed, handicapped as she was by age, gender, marital status, and partial deafness. Boas and his disciples took issue with the biological determinism of the day, believing that the origins of cultural characteristics lay in history, not in racial differences. With so many "primitive" cultures dying out under the influence of colonization, there was a sense of urgency about the tasks of anthropology, which excited his students.

Margaret Mead, born in 1901, came from a Pennsylvania family with a tradition of strong and opinionated women. The oldest child, she was home-schooled by her feminist grandmother while her mother tried to fit sociological research and radical social activism around domestic duties. Her father, a university professor of economics whose imaginative business schemes and inventions put the family finances at risk, nicknamed Margaret "Punk." When her brother was born, she became "the original punk" and he "the boy punk," which was, as she said later, "a reversal of the usual pattern, according to which the girl is only a female version of the true human." [6]

Margaret Mead was clever, extroverted, an organizer of people, and an optimist with boundless energy. If there was cake, she was going to have it *and* eat it *and* share it around with her friends. Undaunted by realism, her childhood ambitions were to marry a minister, have a career, and have lots of children. She selected a prospective husband early on. An early engagement to Luther Cressman, a theology student, enabled Margaret to avoid adolescent agonies about boys. At Barnard College, she and her women friends, the Ash Can Cats, had a motto: "Never break a date with a girl for a man." Nevertheless, Mead was coming of age in an atmosphere of sexual defiance; the "New Woman" of the 1920s was to be (hetero)-sexually adventurous (see Smith-Rosenberg, 1991).

"I Shall Lie Once with Beauty,/Breast to Breast"

Mead first met Benedict when she was twenty and Benedict thirty-five, in a class Boas taught for Barnard students. Mead became fascinated with Boas's shy assistant, who spoke quietly and hesitantly but who had gems of insight that showed, behind the mask, a creative scholar. Benedict always wore the same dress to class, a drab creation that offended the clothes-conscious Barnard students but was apparently Benedict's quiet rebellion against expectations of women (the men always wore the same suits without prompting comment). Mead, along with fellow student Marie Bloomfield, set out to get to know this curious woman. Instead of going directly to the Museum of Natural History for their class, the pair would travel to Columbia and ride down with Benedict on the streetcar, chattering all the way. Benedict soon invited them to attend the regular graduate seminar at Columbia, and gradually they began to know each other better.

The growing closeness between Mead and Benedict was accelerated by Marie's suicide. Benedict sympathized with Mead's mixed feelings about her friend's death, since she understood from her own experience the wish to die. Mead later said that from that time "our relationship became one of colleagues and close friends" (Mead, 1972).

Benedict encouraged Mead, who was majoring in psychology, to consider anthropology for her future career ("I hope she does. I need a companion in harness!" [Mead, 1959, p. 68]). They began to meet outside class and spent hours talking about poetry (both had literary ambitions, Benedict publishing during the '20s under the pseudonym "Anne Singleton"), anthropology, and their own lives. Benedict wrote in her diary, "She rests me like a padded chair and a fireplace. I say it's the zest of youth I believe in when I see her. Or is it that I respond understandably to admiration?" (Mead, 1959, p. 67). She made a practical contribution to Mead's future career when the younger woman failed to receive a scholarship for graduate studies. Benedict gave her, from her own purse, a three-hundred-dollar "First Award No Red Tape Fellowship." Mead said later, "By electing anthropology as a career I was also electing a closer relationship to Ruth, a friendship that lasted until her death in 1948" (Mead, 1972, p. 124).

At first this mentoring relationship may have had a mother-daughter flavor. Margaret saw Ruth as "middle-aged"; she said that she was "the child Ruth never had. I had all the things she'd have wanted in a child; joy of living, positive affirmation of life" (Howard, 1984, p. 57). But it was not long before the two became lovers, though that story is hard to dig out of the published accounts of their lives. This side of their relationship was kept secret, most vigorously by Mead, who in later life feared any publicity which might detract from her role as a popular commentator on American culture. Their sexual relationship was only hinted at by previous biographers until Mary Catherine Bateson, Mead's daughter, in her moving memoir of her parents, revealed that Mead and Benedict were lovers over a long period of time (Bateson, 1984). Only the most recent biographer of Benedict, Margaret Caffrey, deals frankly with their love affair, and even so has few materials to draw on. The most intimate aspects of Mead's and Benedict's lives are hidden in unpublished letters, some of which have only recently been made available to researchers and some of which are still restricted.[7]

Both Mead and Benedict may have known physical love with women before their own relationship became sexual. There is considerable evidence that Mead engaged in passionate relationships with college friends.[8] And at a time when Benedict's relationship to Mead was most likely still that of teacher to student, one of her poems seems to refer to lesbian experience, claiming "I shall lie once with beauty, / Breast to breast" (Mead, 1959, p. 56).

But loving Margaret called Ruth's lesbian self into being, releasing her ability to love a woman completely, with sensual abandonment and with the investment of all her emotions. She wrote about the physical satisfactions of love: "Here only bliss is for our taking," she declared and asked, how could anything "compete with sleep begotten of a woman's kiss?" (Mead, 1959, pp. 480, 67-68). In peace, "I lie so in quiet at your breast. . . . I am so safe with you, so blindly blest."[9] To all lovers, the beloved is beautiful. Ruth remembered her lover's body with striking eroticism in her poetry, sometimes metaphorically disguising, but not hiding, its woman-inspired imagery. She sang "songs of her great loveliness," her "beauty sudden-fluttering," recalling her "slim white hands upon their naked flesh" (Mead, 1959, pp. 482, 488, 483).

But a truly passionate love is not a comfortable experience. Ruth was tormented by "nights of long loneliness" when she could not be with Margaret, when flesh "cries out for flesh" (Mead, 1959, pp. 481, 486), when she longed to go to her lover for comforting, to "escape from walls and safety," to relax into "your lazy flag unfolding to the fling and caress of the wind that so shall be in beauty naked to my sight." [10] She saw her hopes and dreams as foolish. The harsh reality was that "all our fires go out in nothingness" (Mead, 1959, p. 480). Depression was never far behind the celebrations of sensuality and its short-lived satisfactions. Loneliness and acute feelings of loss were their natural heir.

Knowing at heart that she could not find an exclusive place in Mead's life, Benedict continued to shelter within her arid marriage. She was not to separate from Stanley Benedict until 1930, seven years after she met Mead, and it was he who initiated the separation. Meanwhile, Mead married her fiancé, Luther Cressman. However, she discovered early on that relationships that excluded other possibilities were not to her taste. Her independence was foreshadowed when she kept her own name after marrying, a move so unusual that it was commented on in newspapers.

Margaret showed her capacity for complexly woven relationships when, not long after her marriage, she began a love affair with another mentor figure, Edward Sapir, the anthropologist and linguist. Sapir's wife had died after a long illness. He now wished to marry Margaret and urged her to divorce Luther so she could marry him. [11] Margaret's affair with Sapir must have been difficult for Benedict, who was Sapir's closest friend and who had herself loved him, although their relationship had never been sexual. Ruth did not possess Margaret's ability to manage simultaneous intimacies. Given the deepening bond between Mead and Benedict, the affair seems oddly timed, although testing out heterosexuality is not uncommon in the early stages of lesbian explorations.

But whatever the vagaries of their sexual relationship, the women's friendship was solidifying. It was well grounded in similarities of values and interests and complementarities of style and temperament. Ruth had a cautious approach to the world, contrasting with Margaret's leaps and bounds of the imagination. Benedict was depressive, reserved, the self-doubter, tempering Margaret's extroverted enthusiasm. Physically they were very different. Ruth was tall, willowy, and athletic with "the beauty which had been hers as a young girl misted over by uncertainty and awkwardness," whereas Margaret was short, dumpy, and plain and hated exercise (Mead, 1959, p.9; see also Caffrey, 1989, p. 187 for contrasts between the pair).

Loving Margaret did not make Ruth ungenerous or possessive, much as she may have yearned to capture her butterfly. It was she who encouraged Mead to take her first fieldwork expedition in Samoa, a big step for a young woman who had problems with her health, being plagued by muscular pains whose source was not identified. Mead had never been on a ship, had never stayed in a hotel on her own, had never conversed in a foreign language, and had never spent a day on her own in her life. Edward Sapir, no doubt self-interestedly, counseled Boas against allowing Mead to go to Samoa. It was Ruth Benedict who championed her. Benedict surely knew the right course of action for another "restless woman."

In the summer of 1925, after Mead had secured a job at the American Museum of Natural History, which was to prove a lifelong base for her career, Benedict and Mead took their leave of each other. They traveled together to the Grand Canyon, and in this romantic landscape they made a personal commitment. They agreed that they were each more important to the other than Sapir was to either of them (their relationships to their husbands did not appear to absorb such intense attention as did the triangle with Sapir). Ruth said that she would be measuring the year apart by the three week intervals between steamers carrying the mail, "as the Indians do with their prayerstick plantings" (Mead, 1959, p. 292). Yet when they were reunited a year later in Europe, Margaret, to Ruth's intense disappointment, had fallen in love with Reo Fortune, a young scholar from New Zealand whom she had met on shipboard. Reo, melancholy, neurotic, and intense, was on his way to graduate study at Cambridge University, England. The young woman who would "never break a date with a girl for a man" must have demonstrated to Ruth once and for all that she would never make a primary commitment to a woman and that her affection for Ruth would not prevent her from having relationships with men. Mead did not want exclusive relationships, but she did want the conventionality and protection of a companionate marriage which would enable her, as a woman, to undertake fieldwork in risky places.

Benedict's poetry had anticipated her loss, and the crushing of her hopes led her to wrestle again with the idea of suicide. She lamented: "Passion is a turncoat but death will endure always" (Caffrey, 1989, p. 193). She was seared by memories: "Had I the milk-white fairness of her body, / The quiet of her brooding fingertips" (Mead, 1959, p. 482). She lost heart: "Admit no hope, / Warm-lipped upon your breasts, nor folded flower, / From any south-turned slope" (Mead, 1959, p. 481). And despaired: "This hand that may not lie on your hand, / These lips that lacking you find nothing worth" (Mead, 1959, p. 486). Many years later Mead hinted that strong feelings were not on Benedict's side alone when she said that Benedict, whose hair had "turned white prematurely," had her hair cut in Europe and "was once more extraordinarily beautiful" (Mead, 1974, p. 34).

This was a crucial time in the relationship, and the bond between Ruth and Margaret could have ruptured at this point. However, it continued and evolved; they were always friends, and perhaps occasionally they were lovers. Regular correspondence played a central role in enabling them to sustain a lifelong relationship. Mead spend most of the 1930s on extensive field trips, always in partnership with a husband. In New Guinea with Fortune, she met Gregory Bateson, who became her third husband.

After her separation from Stanley Benedict in 1930, Ruth set up house with Natalie Raymond, a physiology student who was, like Mead, much younger than she. Their relationship lasted seven years and was succeeded by another domestic partnership with psychologist Ruth Valentine, which lasted until Benedict's death. During that time Benedict remained based at Columbia. After having struggled for years to obtain an assistant professorship, she was blocked from promotion for many years by Boas's successor, Ralph Linton.

Women Speaking to Each Other? Sex and Deviance in the Anthropology of Benedict and Mead

How did Benedict and Mead's personal relationship shape their work? Did they look to anthropology for solutions to the issues raised by their relationship? Did their anthropology reflect their personal preoccupations? These are scholarly questions which are only beginning to be addressed, since biographical materials on the two have mostly obscured the lesbian aspects of the relationship and, in so doing, have dislodged its centrality to the life and thought of each. The view I take suggests that submerged in the writings of Benedict and Mead in the late 1920s through the 1930s is a muted conversation about lesbian sexuality and relationship (see Lapsley, in preparation; and for a feminist analysis Nardi, 1984). Martha Vicinus illuminates my approach to their work when she says of lesbian historiography, "If we look to the margins, to the ruptures and breaks, we will be able to piece together a history of women speaking to each other" (Abelove, Barale, and Halperin, 1993, p. 434).

Mead's *Coming of Age in Samoa* (1928) and Benedict's *Patterns of Culture* (1934b), first books for each, were produced after the pair had become lovers. In these works their mutual influence is evident, most notably in the concept of deviance, which was Benedict's central interest. *Coming of Age* portrays women's sexuality as culturally shaped, including lesbian sexuality (although "lesbian" is a word that she does not use). In Western cultures repressive practices distort the natural range of sexual expression, causing frigidity or fixations, whereas in Samoa, Mead argued, homosexual activities are common, casual, and unremarkable. Mead distinguishes between homosexual practices, which are within the normal range of behavior for women and men, and "psychic perversion," the incapacity to respond heterosexually. She noticed only one villager, a male, who was exclusively homosexual, and she was apparently unaware that "fa'afine" (loosely, transsexuals, or womanly men) have a distinctive role in Samoan society. She did recognize, though, that same-sex preference can be linked to lifestyle choices rather than evidencing psychic perversion. Young Samoan women who valued Western education sometimes chose same-sex relationships and avoided young men, in a similar manner to some American college women. Both cultures disapproved of women avoiding marriage, even though the Samoans appeared not to be concerned about same-sex sexual behavior. Mead classified these girls as "upward deviants."

If Mead, as she surely did, applied this understanding of sexuality to her relationship with Benedict, she would not have regarded either Benedict or herself as a "psychic pervert," because of their histories of heterosexuality. Unlike her own culture, Samoa is a sensual utopia, a romantic island culture where pleasure and choice are a feature of women's sexuality and where lovemaking is skilled and separated from emotional entanglements. [12] (However, it is not an intellectual, cultural, or even emotional utopia, for individuality and the possibility of deep intimacy and self-exploration, which she valued in her relationship with Benedict, are sacrificed.) Mead must have wondered, too, about professional and social implications had she chosen to be partnered with a woman ("upward deviance"), thus gaining freedom to pursue her career, but at the expense of social disapproval and childlessness. As always, Mead's "have your cake and eat it too" philosophy prevailed. She chose to exercise freedom in her career, enjoy the socially sanctioned partnership of marriage, have a child, and love both men and women, without the bonds of possession.

Ruth Benedict's *Patterns of Culture*, published in 1934, has a quite different focus. Benedict's interest is the misfit, the deviant, the abnormal person whose favored ways of responding to the world, resulting from temperament or early childhood "set," are "not supported by the institutions of their civilisation" (Benedict, 1934b, p. 187; see also Benedict, 1934a). The deviant is created by the accident of being born into an uncongenial culture.

For Benedict, the homosexual faces difficulties in Western civilization, where he (*sic*) is regarded as abnormal and "exposed to all the conflicts to which aberrants are always exposed. His guilt, his sense of inadequacy, his failures, are consequences of the disrepute which social tradition visits upon him, and few people can achieve a satisfactory life unsupported by the standards of their society" (Benedict, 1934b, p. 191). The Western attitude contrasts with that of the ancient Greeks, who regarded homosexuality as honorable, and with that of American Indian cultures, in many of which homosexuals were seen, according to Benedict, as having unusual gifts.

Benedict was very careful to obscure all possible allusions to herself in her discussion of homosexuality. She insisted to her publisher that she should appear on the title page of the book as "Mrs. Ruth Benedict" (1934b, p. 212), despite the fact that by 1934 she had been separated from Stanley for four years and was living with her first lesbian partner, Natalie Raymond.

But one could argue that her portrayal of the Western homosexual as guilty, inadequate, and a failure is not a mirror of her own feelings about lesbianism. Benedict felt guilt, failure, and inadequacy as a young single woman and also as a married woman; as a lesbian she became a "sexual subject," [13] and she flourished, once she had made an adjustment to her disappointment over Mead's lack of commitment. "Loving Nat and taking such delight in her I have the happiest conditions for living that I've ever known," she wrote in the same year as the publication of her *Patterns* (correspondence cited in Caffrey, 1989, p. 203). Even her physical being was transformed from awkwardness into beauty, as Mead (1974) noted. The woman used by Abraham Maslow as an example of his "self-actualising person" (Caffrey, 1989, p. 255) was in no way crippled by negativity, although she valued privacy, felt like an outsider—"a stranger in this land" (Caffrey, 1989)—and was perceived as remote by many who knew her.

"You Belong Especially to Seasons When There Are No Devils"

Mary Catherine Bateson (1984, p. 117) tells us that Benedict and Mead remained lovers throughout Margaret's marriages and Ruth's lesbian partnerships. In some ways it is surprising that Benedict managed to integrate a continuing sexual association with Mead into her life, given Benedict's more reserved nature, her disappointment in Mead's remarriage, her belief in permanence, and the establishment of her live-in lesbian relationships with Natalie Raymond and, later, Ruth Valentine. But their letters during the 1930s do suggest something more than merely the loving affection of friends. In 1932 Ruth wrote to Margaret, who was at that time in New Guinea with Reo:

> Darling, I wish you were here. I'm getting on well, no devils and more drive than I can remember. You'd be quite pleased. . . . But you belong especially to seasons when there are no devils—you belong to both, but I've a special hunger for you when my blood pressure goes up. And I'm terribly impatient for letters. I love you, darling. *And be good to yourself.* Ruth.[14]

In a 1939 series of letters Margaret, planning to come back to New York after a long trip (Ruth: "It will be manna in the desert to have you back"), asks Ruth to arrange a hotel for them to "have dinner and have the evening and night together" and "no one else need to be told I am back till Monday" (April 7 and 13, 1939).

Although Margaret was not encouraged to get to know Ruth's family, husband, or partners well, Ruth formed friendships with all three of Margaret's husbands. She encouraged Luther Cressman to become an anthropologist, despite the risk to his ego from his world-famous ex-wife. Although crushed by the news of Mead's intention to marry Reo Fortune, Benedict corresponded with both Fortune and Mead while they were in New Guinea and, in *Patterns of Culture,* she drew extensively on Fortune's work on Dobu. Her letters show a somewhat noncommittal response to Margaret's excited announcement of her forthcoming marriage to Bateson, but she became friendly with Bateson and enthusiastically welcomed the news in 1939 that Margaret, now in her late thirties, was pregnant.

One exchange of letters suggests that jealousy was not entirely outside Margaret's emotional range. At that time Margaret was in New York in the middle months of her pregnancy and lonely, while her husband, Gregory Bateson, was looking for a role in the war effort in Britain. Ruth, who had recently separated from Nat, was on sabbatical in California, and Margaret was eagerly awaiting her expected return. Unbeknown to Margaret, Ruth was getting to know Ruth Valentine. She decided to delay her return to New York, and Margaret was furiously disappointed:

Ruth darling, well, after a couple of hours of futile tears and a sleepless night, I have got myself into the mood to call it "bad luck" with at least fair grace. They could always just keep the baby in the hospital until you came East, if anything happens to me. (October 2, 1939)

Ruth, in her reply, professes to be surprised at Margaret's reaction and asks her to "write me what bothered you the night you cried" (October 5, 1939). In return, Margaret explains that she was upset because she thought Ruth would return early from California and she cannot see any positive reasons for her staying out there. She thinks that Ruth is avoiding the stresses of New York, which include "Nat's working out an adjustment for herself independently of you." She then goes on to hint that Ruth may be holding something back from her: "[I]f there were someone you terrifically wanted to be with in California, I'd have been sad and disappointed not to have you here, but it wouldn't have felt nearly as miserable" (October 7, 1939). Ruth, who was to move out from her sister's and into Ruth Valentine's house on the very next day, denies this suggestion but laments, "I feel all the time that I'm paying high for it by being away from you; I wish there weren't always prices to pay for everything" (October 10, 1939).

Margaret's tone became a little cooler, and in a later letter she says, "I lead a kind of surface life, not giving my imagination much leeway these days to wish for Gregory or wish for you." By return mail, Benedict tells her how wonderful Ruth Valentine is and says how comfortable the two have felt together "from the moment we saw each other," adding, "I know she [R.V.] thinks God made me out of a rare and special clay, but she doesn't bother me about it" (December 1 and 4, 1939).

In any event, Ruth did not return for the birth, but cheered Margaret on enthusiastically from a distance:

I love you, darling, and I never minded so much being so far away. I love you double, for I wonder if I don't love your baby as much as I love you. . . . Marie says Gregory has applied for a sailing permit, and I can't think of anything that would make you happier. (December, 1939)

No permanent cooling resulted from this minor disloyalty of Benedict's.

One cannot overemphasize how much the relationship was shaped by anxiety about exposure. In 1938 Benedict agreed to testify in a male friend's divorce case, a decision which so angered his wife that she told Mead she would expose Benedict's lesbianism to the world. In the field at the time, Benedict received a "furious" letter from Mead, who thought her stance was foolhardy. The impact of the letter was such that Benedict spent three days in bed recovering from the upset (Howard, 1984).

This anxiety is shown explicitly in letters to and from Margaret Mead after Ruth Benedict's death. Mead corresponded with Ruth's two female partners as she prepared material for her memorial tribute to Benedict, *An Anthropologist at Work* (1959), and they show themselves to have been more concerned at the risk of publicity than even Mead herself. They did not want to be mentioned in the book, even though Mead made it clear that such references were to be quite discreet. Ruth Valentine wrote: "[I]f you include Nat's and my purely personal association with Ruth, I think that you will be doing violence to Ruth's private life—invading it in an inexcusable manner. As I wrote you, I just can't see what Nat and I have to do with Ruth as an anthropologist."[15]

Much later in life, Mead took the risk of writing about bisexuality in her *Redbook* column. There she said that bisexuality was linked with creativity, innovation, and individuality, that sexual preferences may change serially over a lifetime, instead of being fixed, and that "we shall not really succeed in discarding the straitjacket of our cultural beliefs about sexual choice if we fail to come to terms with the well-documented, normal human capacity to love members of both sexes" (Mead, 1975, p. 29). But she was never to publicly acknowledge the true nature of her relationship with Benedict, let alone its impact on her work, for at heart, she believed in maintaining appearances.

The survival of Ruth and Margaret's loving friendship through all its vicissitudes owes much to Margaret Mead's talent for nonexclusive relationships. Mead did not harbor grudges against former husbands, and she had affairs with both men and women. She also built deep, abiding, and not necessarily sexual relationships with other men and women. She collected people around her whom she found stimulating or useful and managed to extract a tremendous amount from them, which they usually gave ungrudgingly, perhaps because the gift was not for Margaret personally but for the causes to which she was devoted.

Though Ruth Benedict also had a talent for friendship (and was a wonderful mentor to many of her students as well), it is hard to believe that she quite shared Margaret's ability to weave such a complex web of relationships. However, her sense of privacy and her remoteness enabled her to rise above the whirl of emotions that tend to surround emotional entanglements. She was able to distance herself, keeping people in separate compartments, but it seems that for her, Mead always had a place in the center.

Their rich relationship came to an end in 1948, when Ruth Benedict died suddenly at the age of sixty-one. Mead was at her deathbed and was treated by many in their world as the chief mourner. Friends acknowledged the closeness between Margaret and Ruth, but sadly, in a fate typical for lesbian couples, Benedict's partner received less attention. Ruth Valentine, after all, had shared a household with Benedict for years and was the chief beneficiary of her will.

Ruth Benedict and Margaret Mead's twenty-five-year relationship illustrates the progress of a truly great friendship between women. It began as a mentorship, survived the snares of romantic entanglement, and resolved into something which encompassed friendship, sexual love, and collegiality, persisting through many changes in each woman's life. It was an enriching relationship for both women, different as they were, reflecting a generosity of spirit on both their parts which allowed them to survive each other's transitions.

NOTES

1. How different the heterosexual friendship of Simone de Beauvoir and Jean-Paul Sartre, which has proved a topic of perennial fascination. Ironically, de Beauvoir's adieux to Sartre is quite similar to that of Mead to Benedict: "This is the first of my books—the only one no doubt—that you will not have read" (1984, p. 1).

2. I was assisted by a study leave from the University of Waikato that I spent in the United States as a Fulbright Scholar, at the Center for Research on Women, Wellesley College. This enabled me to examine unpublished papers at Vassar (Benedict) and in the Library of Congress (Mead). The mentoring project is now on the back burner, and I am writing a full-length book on Mead and Benedict for the University of Massachusetts Press (*Margaret Mead and Ruth Benedict: Love, Friendship, Anthropology*).

3. This article is adapted from a longer paper being published in the proceedings of the Lesbian Studies Conference, Wellington, New Zealand.

4. A key source of information on Ruth Benedict's life is her collected writings, edited by Margaret Mead (1959), containing several biographical chapters by Mead, as well as Benedict's own autobiographical piece and selections from her poetry, letters, and anthropological writings. Mead's *Ruth Benedict* (1974) is a shorter version and the selections are not identical. There are two recent biographies of Benedict, which have been consulted extensively in the preparation of this article. They are Modell (1983) and Caffrey (1989).

5. Two commentators on Benedict (Bernard, 1964; Modell, 1983) have seen Benedict's infertility as central to her adult character, Modell arguing that she wished for a child to prove her womanhood, and Bernard going so far as to call Benedict a "reluctant scholar" (p. 24), who saw her life work as but a poor substitute for children. These stances are predicated on obscuring Benedict's lesbianism and on a sense of childlessness as a lifelong state, rather than on a more psychologically sophisticated understanding of the process of coming to terms with infertility. Even in Benedict's early journals (*Anthropologist at Work*) there is an expressed ambivalence about children as a solution to her unhappiness, and although she clearly regretted not having children, she never apparently thought her work came second.

6. The main sources of biographical detail for Margaret Mead's early life are her own account (Mead, 1972) and Howard (1984).

7. Parts of the Mead-Benedict correspondence lodged in the Library of Congress had just been opened to researchers when I visited there in May 1992. Unfortunately the earlier letters between Mead and Benedict are still not available. It is these letters that Mead (1974) refers to when she says, "Ruth Benedict's own fullest comments on the years between 1925 and 1933 are contained in the letters she wrote me while I was away on field trips in Samoa, in Manus, and in the Sepik area of New Guinea" (p. 25). Recently released material is explored in some detail in my forthcoming book on Mead and Benedict (see note 3).

8. This assertion is explored in more detail in my forthcoming book.

9. "For Faithfulness," Box 43, Ruth Benedict Papers, Vassar College.

10. Box 44, Ruth Benedict Papers, Vassar College.

11. The most detailed account of the affair is in Regna Darnell (1990). This biography also minimizes the lesbian nature of Mead and Benedict's relationship: "Benedict, unwilling to risk further intimacy with a man, turned to a close but unthreatening friendship with Margaret Mead which centered around women's

issues—particularly the breaking up of both women's marriages and the role of professional commitments in their lives" (p. 181).

12. Interestingly, Suzanne Raitt (1993) says that the island figures as "a crucial image for lesbian writing after Sappho" (p. 95) and refers to Vita Sackville-West's statement, "An island! and that had slipped the leash of continents, forsworn solidarity, cut adrift from security and prudence!"

13. The concept of "sexual subject" comes from Carroll Smith-Rosenberg (1991). I argue that because her lesbianism emerged during the 1920s rather than earlier, she would have been able to view herself as sexual subject. The single women ("spinster") teachers whose path Benedict, as a young woman, rejected because she believed they led emotionally unfulfilled lives, may well have had passionate, indeed sexual, attachments to other women. But Smith-Rosenberg argues that in their time "sex in the absence of men was inconceivable" and that "having eschewed men sexually, they had no language in which to conceive of their erotic relationships with other women as sexual; they could not construe themselves as sexual subjects" (p. 273). In the 1920s, the era of the ":New Woman," women's sexuality became more agentic and erotic relationships between women, no longer "innocent," were named as lesbian and stigmatized.

14. Letter to Margaret Mead, April 2, 1932, Margaret Mead collection, Manuscript Division, Library of Congress. Permission to quote from these and subsequent letters to Mead and to Benedict courtesy of the Institute of Intercultural Studies.

15. Ruth Valentine to Margaret Mead, July 23, 1957. Margaret Mead collection, Manuscript Division, Library of Congress.

REFERENCES

Abelove, H., M. A. Barale, and D. M. Halperin, eds. 1993. *The lesbian and gay studies reader.* New York: Routledge.

Bateson, M. C. 1984. *With a daughter's eye: A memoir of Margaret Mead and Gregory Bateson.* New York: William Morrow.

Benedict, R. 1934a. Anthropology and the abnormal. *Journal of General Psychology* 10: 59–82.

———. 1934b. *Patterns of culture.* London: Routledge and Kegan Paul.

Bernard, J. 1964. *Academic Women.* State College: Pennsylvania State University Press.

Caffrey, M. M. 1989. *Ruth Benedict: Stranger in this land.* Austin: University of Texas Press.

Darnell, R. 1990. *Edward Sapir: Linguist, anthropologist, humanist.* Berkeley: University of California Press.

de Beauvoir, S. 1984. *Adieux: A farewell to Sartre.* Vol. 1. London: André Deutsch.

Howard, J. 1984. *Margaret Mead: A life.* New York: Simon and Schuster.

Lapsley, H. In preparation. *Margaret Mead and Ruth Benedict: Love, Friendship, Anthropology.* Amherst: University of Massachusetts Press.

Mead, M. 1928. *Coming of age in Samoa: A psychological study of primitive youth for western civilization.* New York: William Morrow.

———. 1959. *An anthropologist at work: Writings of Ruth Benedict.* Boston: Houghton Mifflin.

———. 1972. *Blackberry winter.* New York: William Morrow.

———. 1974. *Ruth Benedict.* New York: Columbia University Press.

———. 1975. Bisexuality: What's it all about? *Redbook* 144(3): 29.

Modell, J. S. 1983. *Ruth Benedict: Patterns of a life.* Philadelphia: University of Pennsylvania Press.

Nardi, B. A. 1984. The height of her powers: Margaret Mead's Samoa. *Feminist Studies* 10: 323–37.

Raitt, S. 1993. *Vita and Virginia: The work and friendship of V. Sackville-West and Virginia Woolf.* Oxford: Clarendon Press.

Smith-Rosenberg, C. 1991. Discourses of sexuality and subjectivity: The new woman, 1870–1936. In M. B. Duberman, M. Vicinus, and G. Chauncey, Jr., eds., *Hidden from history: Reclaiming the gay and lesbian past.* London: Penguin Books.

SIX

Namasté[1]

LAUREN CRUX

Her skin
a warm brown turns
dark mahogany
in the ardent sun.
Her body compact
strong.

We trekked Nepal together
She held me as I cried
exhausted.
I urged her
across chasms.
We lay each night
not touching
but laughing, irreverent
all the hardships made bearable.

When someone asked
why we were not lovers
she quipped,
"She's too tall, and I
have a poor sense of direction."

She works hard—calls herself a
bureaucrat
earns more than her parents' dream
feels guilty, proud.
Animals speak to her,
and spirits.

She wants a woman who has her
own sleeping bag,
pays her own way.

But she is slow—
to ask, to touch,
"They never held me,"
she explains,
"And I'm still not sure
I'm good enough."

When I lay the purple roses
on her doorstep,
"I have loved you for years,"
she hesitates,
calls me, "Giant."
"Yes," I say, "But I have
an excellent sense of direction."

She invites me in.
Places the flowers
in the vase
one
by
one.

Why not us? was my question. But she was my best friend, and why would I want to mess it up by becoming lovers? The answer was, we had so much in common. We loved to bicycle and backpack and we traveled together at the same pace, even though my legs were much longer. Her speed matched my stride. We both liked to work hard, but could lie back in the high Sierras and watch clouds for hours. There were important differences too. I loved British comedies and she couldn't stand them. Her idea of a great breakfast was a plateful of refried beans, mine was scrambled tofu and vegies. I suffered the torments of being an overly ambitious, middle-class, alienated WASP, and she carried early childhood wounds of being a dark-skinned, Portuguese woman whose mother dressed her in beige so people would not think she was Mexican. We both knew childhood brutality, but it played itself out differently in our adult lives. To our credit, we usually could work out our differences—through the enjoyment of each other's company; the love of poetry, nature, things simple; and a shared delight in physical movement.

To up the ante, both of us had been single for years and were lonely for a lover. We helped each other play the personals by writing witty want ads. We talked dirty, called each other early almost every morning in a tradition begun in Nepal, where the porters would greet us at 6 A.M. with tea and a high-pitched sing-song, "Gooood Moooorning, Didiis." (*Didiis*—loosely translated—means "sisters.") Using nicknames given us by the sherpas, she called me Lamu, which more or less means "big," and I called her Choto, which more or less means "little." We were buddies. What could be better? So we decided to screw it up.

I remember when I came up with the idea. We had been backpacking in the western Sierras. I was recovering from a knee surgery and we had picked an easy trip to break my knee in again. All had been going well until the hoards of men arrived. I do not exaggerate when I say "hoards." It was a Saturday morning, and we had left for a mid-morning hike to a nearby peak. While we lolled on some boulders, inhaling the view, several men hiked past us down to the lake. As we watched, another ten passed by, then eight from another trail. By this time, they were pouring in like ants from the north and the south. Finally, I saw a group begin to walk around our tent, apparently intending to take over our campsite. Emerging from our stunned incredulity, we mobilized.

Hustling back, we discovered two tents, one in front of ours, one to the side. The place oozed testosterone. Four men were even setting up a tent on a boulder slab that sat out on the water right in front of our cooking area. Internally I went berserk; I felt Jodi's fierceness. I started out with my polite Canadian behavior: "Excuse me, but you seem to have set up camp on top of us." The men looked at us, said nothing, and continued to hammer in tent stakes. I quickly abandoned polite: "You are setting up in our campsite. Stop it." This captured their attention. One man stood up, looked us over, and growled, "You girls aren't from around here or you'd know that this is how we do it here. We fishermen always camp like this at this lake." Then he and his friends turned around and started to fish.

Jodi and I had a brief consultation and decided that although we would like to commit mayhem, preserving our equanimity was more important. We quickly packed up and moved on down the trail, leaving what once was a pristine lake now covered with fishermen shoulder to shoulder. Fortunely for us, a mile or two away, off the trail and cross-country a bit, we found a place by a stream that was so private we were able to walk around naked, unseen, unknown, and untroubled. It was a good resolution to what could have been a disastrous trip. Jodi dubbed the lake "Weenie Lake," and we vowed never to return.

That evening, sitting around our cookstove, staring at stars, now able to laugh over the day's events, I realized just how much I loved this woman. I would travel with her anywhere, trusted her absolutely. Why aren't we lovers? I asked myself. I wanted to reach out, put my arm around her, hold her. But she wasn't an easy person with touch, and I didn't want to offend. Later, driving home, I brought up the subject. I said something terribly romantic like, "So, how come we're not lovers?" She said she would think about it.

A few weeks later, vacationing at Tassajara Hot Springs, I noticed that she was making constant sexual innuendoes. I am a little slow picking up when someone is coming on to me, but even I got this one. I asked her if what I thought was happening was, and she answered, "Yes."

It is very difficult to transition from a good and intimate friendship to being lovers in an unselfconscious way. Courtship behavior with an intimate is meaningless. We both felt awkward with each other, even disoriented. I'm a little butch-of-center and like to take charge, but so is she. We couldn't tell who was seducing whom. Here I was doing my best to be stunning and charming, put on my best show, be flirtatious, with a woman I had known for years, with whom I had shared some of the nastier details of my psyche. She knew my aches and pains, the knots in my personality, the stuff that good friends know and tolerate in each other as part of the gift of friendship. We were already intimate, but being clever and creative women, we invented new rules: ours was an "informed courtship"; love and lucidity would coexist.

Both ambivalent, struggling with the shift, we did the dance of intimacy, to coin a phrase. At times I would be the one in close, while she backed away. Then she would move forward, and I would back away. I was relieved when she came over one night and said, "It feels unnatural, and I miss you as my best friend. Like, you're not going to tell me about your sexual exploits anymore, are you?" (Although we had become lovers, we were not in a committed relationship.)

"No."

"That makes me mad; that was a part of our friendship I really liked."

We decided it was too awkward, too difficult, to change established feelings and patterns; we were happiest as buddies. We had only slept together three or four times so we thought we could cut our losses and make the transition back to friends. We went to a movie, as "best friends" once again, then came home and had great passionate sex. "Is this us being best friends?" I asked. "No," she said, "it's our fond farewell."

We made another mistake. We had plans to go to Hawaii and bodysurf our hearts out; we didn't change those plans. The bodysurfing was fabulous, but our hearts were hurting. There was all the unspoken between us. I was feeling guilty, because I initiated the whole thing. My friend did not open her heart easily and at my beckoning had opened it for me. But it wasn't working for me, nor, I think, for her. I tore my shoulder up on the last wave of the last hour of the last day. That's what I did with my pain. I don't know what she did with hers.

There is no happy ending to this story. There may never be. The friendship never made its way back to what it had been. I used to be able to lay my spirit up against hers and rest in the warmth of our friendship. But no more. As they say in Nepal accompanied by a shrug of the shoulders, Ke Garné, "Oh Well."

But I am a romantic, so I will create an ending, one that I think honors what passed between us. I imagine one day in a faraway place, after a day of strenuous hiking up the mountain, finally reaching the pass. There, trudging up the last few feet on the other side, will be my friend. Time and trouble will have healed our wounds and like the two Nepalese women we saw in Katmandu while trekking in Nepal, we will greet each other not calmly, with palms together in front of our chests, bowing slightly, but rather with arms outstretched, pumping wildly, as we run into each other's embrace shouting, "Namasté! Namasté!"

NOTE

1. *Namasté* is a reverential Nepalese greeting that means "The divine in me salutes the divine in you." It is traditionally accompanied by a gesture of pressing the two palms of the hands together in a "prayer" position in front of one's chest and bowing.

B. Erotics in Friendship

SEVEN

On the Other Side of Silence

CAREY KAPLAN AND ELLEN CRONAN ROSE

Two years ago we published "Strange Bedfellows: Feminist Collaboration" (Kaplan and Rose, 1993), an essay about a profoundly satisfying professional relationship that has evolved over eight years and produced one article, two edited volumes, and a book. As we knew—and remarked, in that piece—our work is inextricably bound up in a friendship that began at an academic conference in 1979 and that flourished in the context of our working together. We revealed much about our relationship (and ourselves, as individuals) in "Bedfellows," but collaboration, not friendship, was its focus.

"Bedfellows" emphasizes the professional aspect of our relationship, although it acknowledges the intertwining of friendship with work that we have experienced since we first met and discovered our very compatible intellectual interests. As we continued to encounter one another at subsequent conferences, to have a drink or dinner together to talk about work, we also talked about our personal selves, our families and friends, our emotional and affectional needs and involvements, our likes and dislikes. We learned that we could laugh together and share jokes. We found that we could cry together and console each other. In short, we realized that we liked and understood one another on a variety of levels: emotional, as well as intellectual and ideological. As a result, we wrote a grant proposal together and, in the process, found that we also liked to write together.

Our published work was one result of our relationship. Since we have always lived in different places, a decade of letter writing was a second. We write one another a weekly diary letter, sharing not only intellectual insights and suggestions, but also our dailiness: cooking, gardening, friends, films, books, music, lovers, fights, reconciliations, children, menopause, sickness, and health. Our intimacy is sustained and intensely verbal. And yet, as we progressively deconstruct our connection in various essays, we learn that even in the midst of such candor and so many words, there are reticences, silences.

We intend here to engage one of the unspoken subtexts of our essay, "Strange Bedfellows," and of our relationship: the dynamics of friendship between a lesbian and a heterosexual woman. Briefly to position ourselves, we are white, middle-class, middle-aged tenured professors, of English and history respectively. Both of us have been married and divorced. Carey has been a lesbian for the past twenty years and lives with her partner, while Ellen now describes herself as a heterosexual celibate and lives alone. Carey has defined herself variously as heterosexual, bisexual, lesbian; Ellen as heterosexual, political lesbian, asexual, celibate, but ineradicably straight. Ellen has three children, two birthed, one adopted, with whom, over the years, her relationship has ripened. Carey acquired children (and grandchildren) in middle age, through her partner's family's generous adoption of her. We have never felt sexually attracted to one another. We know we love each other, we are physically affectionate, and we are comfortable acknowledging and discussing the powerful energy that informs our connection. We feel great attraction but not sexual longing.

Nevertheless, and despite the continuing controversy over what is requisite to claiming lesbian identity, we describe our collaboration as an "erotic," "lesbian" relationship—erotic, because of the energy that surges between us when we are working on a project; lesbian, because of the nonhierarchical reciprocal intimacy that characterizes our exchange. We used this description in "Strange Bedfellows"; in fact, the original subtitle of that essay was "The Erotics of Feminist Collaboration," and one paragraph in it employed sexual metaphors to describe our writing process.

"Bedfellows" took a long time getting published. The straight editors of the anthology for which it was originally solicited asked us to "theorize." So we rewrote the essay, but we did not resubmit it to the anthology. Instead, we sent it to a feminist journal, whose external reviewers were uncomfortable with the sexual metaphors that still informed our now-theorized piece. We discussed our problem with a lesbian friend, who recommended that we submit "Bedfellows" to *Signs: Journal of Women in Culture and Society.* Although our essay was eventually accepted for publication in *Signs,* the most explicitly sexual passage in the essay was taken out at the editors' suggestion, even though they asked us to be specific about our individual sexual orientations. By the time "Strange Bedfellows" was published, we had so theorized and abstracted lesbian Eros that it had no physical, genital resonance. It was, therefore, presumably no longer threatening.

Why were so many reviewers and editors uncomfortable with the sexual language in our essay? "Strange Bedfellows" was repeatedly censored, and by the very people who should have been most responsive to its refiguration of Eros: feminists, some of them lesbians. The frustration at having been silenced has lingered, especially because our friendship and collaboration continue to discomfit some people—friends, children, and lovers, as well as editors. We have concluded that this must have to do with the aura of mystery and exclusiveness that surrounds our relationship. When we work together, we devote ourselves to each other, selectively tolerating but not welcoming phone calls, invitations, visitors. This degree of absorption in one another, which extends beyond the working hours to shopping, walking, eating, watching movies, connotes for most people a love affair. Everyone who knows us knows that we are not lovers. Yet we appear to them to behave like lovers. Hence the mystery—which is kin to the mystery attendant on lesbian sex: "What *do* they do?"

To alleviate our friends' and intimates' unease, we half-consciously set about protecting ourselves and others by such evasions as, "We're just good friends," "Creative work demands isolation," and "Of course you're just as important." When, in "Bedfellows," we dropped subterfuge and used sexual language to assert the singularity of our connection, we were censored at every turn.

What we would like to do now is resurrect that censored paragraph and compare it with the desexualized version that finally passed muster and made it into print, in order to try again to make the paradoxical but absolutely essential point about our relationship: though we are not "lovers" in a genital sense, our collaboration is drenched in sexuality, pulsating with erotic as well as intellectual tension, striving for and frequently achieving a kind of orgasmic fulfillment. The sanitized version of the original paragraph reads as follows:

> Because we are mature women and because we have been working together for years now, we know a great deal about ourselves in relation to one another. . . . Our relationship is increasingly resonant and profound. Our repertory of communication is complex, varied, and always in flux. And, because we remain sensitive to and excited about one another, we keep learning new modes of expression. . . . We learned to prepare for our time together by stimulating each other with ideas and hints in letters. . . . We learned to read the same books at the same time and to exchange our different but complementary responses. We learned the pleasures of delaying our time together until we were both ready to explode or implode with new words, new ideas. We learned each other's best hours for work, for relaxation, for solitude. We learned an accretive interplay in which one of us roughs out a chapter, then sends it to the other for expansion and clarification, and then we go back and forth until we are both satisfied. (Kaplan and Rose, 1993, pp. 555-56)

Unfortunately, we can only dimly reconstruct the original language, because once the piece was accepted for publication by *Signs*—having gone through the regime of editorial discipline we described earlier in this essay—we threw out all earlier drafts and even erased them from disk. We have tried repeatedly to recover our lost language, by rifling our computer and desk files and by sitting together and recalling phrases and parts of sentences. We know that its content was roughly that of the paragraph we quote above, but the language was subtly eroticized, playfully using half-explicit tropes of foreplay and orgasm to figure our writing process. The original, however, is irretrievably gone, erased from our computers, our papers, and even our minds. When we try to rewrite it, we find ourselves with an unsubtle and uninteresting paragraph. It would seem that we have colluded in our own silencing. Why would we have done so? As we settled into the project of conceptualizing and writing this essay, we discovered some possible answers to that question in an unexpected and hitherto safe space, our friendship. We discovered to our chagrin that self-censorship sometimes characterizes our unusually open, intimate, and above all verbal relationship.

An anecdote comes to mind: A few years ago Ellen told Carey the story of a mutual friend, Andrew, who had lost Sarah—according to Ellen the love of his life—at the tragically young age of twenty-one. For some years thereafter, he had brief affairs with women, but no committed relationship. The next serious love was Kevin, and since then Andrew has defined himself as gay and has had several long-term, monogamous relationships. Ellen explained Andrew's sexual orientation to Carey by saying, "I think the reason Andrew is gay is because after Sarah, there could be no other woman." (This is the interpretation of Andrew's history that Ellen's two straight daughters, who knew him and Sarah, also espouse.) When Ellen concluded the story in this way, Carey's inner reaction was a kind of horror: "How could Ellen be so heterosexist?" She did not at the time take Ellen to task, but for years she carried the incident in her mind as demonstrating a deep division between her interpretation of the world and Ellen's.

Only when we sat down to discuss writing this article did Carey reveal her memory and reaction. Inwardly Ellen said, "Shit! Did I really say something heterosexist? Me? When so many of my friends are gay?" Aloud, she asked, "Why didn't you tell me at the time? Were you afraid I'd be offended?" The answer was not simple or immediate, and it involved discussing more than Andrew and his sexuality. Ellen remarked that she never censored herself in conversations with Carey, because she trusted their long friendship and knew that Carey loved her unconditionally. Carey suddenly realized that she did, sometimes, censor herself with Ellen (and with other straight friends), usually about issues of gay and lesbian sexuality. When Ellen told her Andrew's story, shaping it according to the conventions of romantic love, Carey first thought that it might hurt Ellen to know how heterosexist she was being; then she thought, "Besides, I am angry, and I don't want to unleash that anger on my dear friend Ellen."

Among the questions that emerged from our exchange were: Is there parity in friendship between lesbians and straight women? Are there silences and/or evasions imposed by one on the other, or self-imposed? To what extent do even two highly educated, feminist, caring friends accede, however unwittingly, to such dominant ideologies as heterosexism? And where does power come into all this?

Our discussion led to this formulation: Friendship between a lesbian and a straight woman replays, in microcosm, the dynamics of imperialism. The subordinate and marginalized person does not speak; the master cannot hear. The colonized subject knows the master's language, while the master remains ignorant of the vernacular. But, although the colonized subject knows more than the master, her superior knowledge can only, at best, mitigate the master's power over her. A subordinate may laugh at the colonizer's stupidity, but she can never wield power over the master.

To particularize, using Andrew's story: Carey did not tell Ellen how offended she had been by Ellen's interpretation of Andrew's history, in part because Ellen might not have understood that her "obvious" and "natural" reading of Andrew's assumption of a gay identity was ideological. Since in any society, the beliefs and practices of the powerful are not perceived by them to be remarkable or even noteworthy, Ellen might not have been able to "hear" Carey's alternative reading of the story ("Andrew once had a deeply meaningful sexual relationship with a woman, but there is no necessary connection between her death and his subsequent coming out as a gay man."). Moreover, as a member of the dominant sexual group, Ellen enjoyed the privilege of not *having* to hear Carey; in that sense, she had the power to silence Carey (whether or not she wanted to deny her the right to speak is another point, not the one at issue here). Her question ("Were you afraid I'd be offended if you told me you found my remark heterosexist?") reveals the extent of her privilege and her lack of awareness of it. Ellen's question assumed that "of course" no one would find her heterosexual interpretation of

Andrew's story bothersome. The reality was that Carey actually was offended.

While Ellen's "privilege" (of not having to hear Carey) conferred on her the power to silence Carey, Carey's knowledge (that there was another reading of Andrew's story besides the one that seemed "self-evident" to Ellen) gave her a kind of power, too, although not equivalent to that enjoyed by a member of the dominant sexual group. Carey could see the limits of Ellen's knowledge and could choose whether or not to inform her of alternative meanings. As we analyzed the five years of silence between Ellen's casual remark about Andrew and Carey's admission that it had offended her, we realized that, although on the one hand the silence felt empowering to Carey, on the other it served to confirm Ellen's hegemonic power: Carey did not want to risk hearing Ellen say that her, Ellen's, reality was more real than Carey's. Despite our long and deep friendship and mutual respect, Ellen's unexamined adherence to dominant values conferred enough power to be at least temporarily hurtful. In the event, since Carey chose silence, our mutual candor was, however minutely, diminished. Carey chose to exercise the qualified power of the subaltern, to laugh up her sleeve at the master's ignorance.

Indeed, had we not decided to write this essay, this "telling" silence between us might never have been explored; difference, distance, and a small power manipulation might well have remained in our relationship. Carey told her story to Ellen because she could see no way to begin to write without taking the risk of crossing a new threshold of honesty, and without giving up her hidden and guarded power. Sitting in the bright sun of a June morning in Carey's kitchen as we began to unravel the implications of the anecdote, Ellen asked, "How could there be such a silence between us when our relationship is so verbal? You and I talk the same language. We've written together for eight years, and nobody—including ourselves—can tell which of us wrote which sentence. We have always written and talked nonhomophobic feminism." But, Carey explained, we have written the master's language, the language of (straight) academia. Even feminist theory, considered by most an oppositional discourse, is frequently marked by unexamined and unacknowledged heterosexist bias (see Adrienne Rich, 1980, for a critique of such germinal texts of feminist theory as Nancy Chodorow's *The Reproduction of Mothering* and Dorothy Dinnerstein's *The Mermaid and the Minotaur*).

Our experience in getting "Strange Bedfellows" published illustrates the unacknowledged, untheorized, but nevertheless ineluctable heterosexism of most academic discourse (for a review of this issue, see Teresa de Lauretis, 1994). What we have learned in the process of writing this second essay suggests how profoundly the codes, conventions, and discursive possibilities of the master's language have shaped even our personal and intimate conversations. Moreover, exploring the dynamics of our friendship has given us some insight into how the master's power is maintained and reinforced. As a member of the dominant heterosexual group, Ellen exercised, however unwittingly, the master's power to silence Carey, who— partly to preserve a friendship she valued, partly because her silence gave her at least the illusion that she had greater power (because greater knowledge) than Ellen—colluded for some years in reproducing Ellen's (heterosexist) "knowledge" about why Andrew was gay. It no longer baffles, though it continues to sadden, us that we threw away the early, sexualized version of "Strange Bedfellows." As scholars, we value our "friendship" with the academic publishing establishment enough to have learned to speak decorously.

We have chosen to focus on some of the difficulties accompanying our unconventional relationship—most having to do with silences and censorship—but we would like to end by celebrating the ways in which our different sexual identities contribute to and enhance communication and knowledge. For instance, there have been areas of experience that were closed to each of us; children for Carey, lovers for Ellen will do as illustrations. Despite the lack of relevant experience, each of us strove to empathize with the other in our letters, phone calls, and work sessions. The unanticipated benefit of our mutual generosity was that, having vicariously experienced an array of alien emotions, each of us was predisposed to enter new territory.

For years, for example, Ellen eschewed any sensual/affectional relationship. Work and family were her loves. During that time, she willingly, but with some difficulty, made an effort to understand Carey's fraught, rich, and complex sexual life, and the importance to Carey of a monogamous commitment. Recently, however, Ellen fell in love, and what was foreign now makes sense. When Carey suggested that we arrange a working weekend before the brief time in the summer during which she can vacation with her partner, Ellen readily agreed, because she now understands the selfishness of desire.

Similarly, for years Carey sympathized with, but only dimly comprehended, Ellen's passionate involvement in the lives of her children. Over the last three years, however, she has become progressively more engaged with her partner's four grown children, four grandchildren, and two AID (Artificial Insemination by Donor) children birthed by a former partner. Carey now understands Ellen's feelings for her children. Further, partly because of the years of taking Ellen's feelings about her children's triumphs and griefs seriously, she is able wholeheartedly to support, enter into, indeed feel as her own, her partner's profound commitment to family.

Lesbians often shut themselves off from the straight world, and straight women, by the same token, are frequently ignorant of and uncomfortable with the lesbian world, as our experience with editors and reviewers demonstrates. Not the least of the many benefits of our long and increasingly rewarding friendship are bilingualism and biculturalism. Because our friendship is built on trust, we can ask each other things we might not feel comfortable asking other women of different sexualities. We can take risks with potentially touchy questions—"Isn't that a kneejerk gay/straight reaction?" "Did you really think *that* about the sexual politics of that movie/book?" "Don't you think you're being overly accommodating to that man/ woman?" "How can you let him/her walk all over you?"—because of our almost completely uncensored freedom of communication. We can also exchange information: "Do you feel the same way about the person you love as I do about my partner?" "How do you talk to your children about sex?" "Would you mind if your child were gay?"

"What's aging like for you?" "How do you feel about menopause?" "How do you use your sexuality professionally?" "How do you deal with students who have crushes on you?"

In fact, so thoroughly have we become bilingual and bicultural that it is difficult for us to determine how, specifically, our different sexualities enhance our friendship. Our differences, yes—Carey's ebullience checks Ellen's reserve and austerity; Ellen's elegance and dignity smooth Carey's irreverence—but how are these differences associated with our sexualities? Surely there are staid lesbians and jolly straight women.

As we survey our decade and a half together, we see ways in which our interactions are influenced by our sexualities. But at the same time we have been, however incompletely and imperfectly, "there" for each other simply as friends—in times of crisis, or growth, or joy. Indeed, we have found that our different sexualities sometimes complicate and enrich our professional collaboration and friendship—and sometimes seem utterly irrelevant.

REFERENCES

Chodorow, N. 1978. *The reproduction of mothering: Psychoanalysis and the sociology of gender.* Berkeley: University of California Press.

de Lauretis, T. 1994. *The practice of love: Lesbian sexuality and perverse desire.* Bloomington: Indiana University Press.

Dinnerstein, D. 1976. *The mermaid and the minotaur: Sexual arrangements and human malaise.* New York: Harper and Row.

Kaplan, C., and E. C. Rose. 1993. Strange bedfellows: Feminist collaboration. *Signs: Journal of Women in Culture and Society* 18: 547–61.

Rich, A. 1980. Compulsory heterosexuality and lesbian existence. *Signs: Journal of Women in Culture and Society* 5: 631–60.

EIGHT

Guided Journey: The Road to Myself

KATHLEEN M. JONES

Dear Sharon,

Recently I've been reorganizing my room and while doing so I came across many of the letters you have written me. Reading those letters was like a trip down Memory Lane. It was interesting to see how much we had gone through over the last six years and how our relationship has changed.

In the beginning, we were teacher and student. Our relationship was tenuous at best. I was shutting down and had no desire for new people in my life. Yet from the first time I saw you I knew you would have an impact on my life. I was frightened and overwhelmed by what I felt. It would take another two years for me to realize what I was feeling and, as we both know, I'm still trying to deal with it.

On those occasions when I stop to think about what makes our relationship work, I get stumped. The standard answer of course is hard work. It took us a long time to learn to understand each other. I was a guarded young woman and you were yet another maternal figure thrown in my path, but you were different. It was hard for me to grasp that a white woman could understand me, a young black woman. It meant that I had to reexamine all that I had been taught both formally and informally. Our commitment to each other seemed to happen almost immediately.

The nature and quality of our relationship changed when my life came apart and I fell into despair. It was the beginning of my awakening. I was hurled into a sea of confusion. My mind couldn't understand how I could have sexual/erotic feelings for women. I just wanted to be "normal" and, if I couldn't be, then I didn't want to live. In one of our usual Friday conversations you told me I had to make peace with who I am. I wanted to know how, and instead of telling me, you showed me. You taught me how to love and nourish myself. You showed me where to find resources and encouraged me to reclaim my friends. When I had finally gotten my act together and was about to take it on the road, you started to get tentative about me doing so. My head began to spin as to why you wouldn't want me to be proud and tell everyone. Then you wrote to me, "Gay is *OK*. But it carries a lot of baggage in our culture and sometimes one pays a price for wearing it as a badge." Those words proved to be very valuable and very true. Your tolerance and unconditional regard for me has always been an inspiration for me.

> Gentle woman who knows and
> loves me
> makes me a star that burns brightly
> against
> the dark of life.
> Strong woman who pushes me
> to be a stream that carves a
> path in the sea of humanity.
> Silent woman who gives me
> a voice to state my purpose
> so that
> I may change the course of events.

I think the critical point in our relationship was when I fell in love with you. I felt as if I would die, it was so intense. How could I tell you that I was in love with you? I felt like a foolish child and I was frightened that you would push me away. Finally, when I could take it no more, I told you. Your response was so nonchalant that I couldn't believe it. You weren't offended or repulsed; instead it seemed as if this were a normal course of events. You had me read Fromm to learn his theory of love. The reality of love, however, was revealed to me through our talks. It was the way you smiled at me and said, "Kath, you're going to be all right" or "I know it's tough but it's going to be all right." Your letters at that time were laced with supporting messages like this one: "That's important to me . . . your being more comfortable with life and with yourself." This was such a simple expression and yet it is the cornerstone of our relationship. Eventually I would move away from the desperate love that I felt for you. It would take months of separation, marked by an occasional visit to transform my love. As I wrote one late fall night, "I can love you and still live with myself. I've found out what loving you means and my days are better for it." This, however, was not the last time that I would struggle with my love for you. The first time I felt an attraction for someone other than you I was unhappy. It was hard for me to share my feelings and thoughts with anyone but you. You were my world. I went through a mourning period when I felt that you were giving your attention to other people (i.e., my roommate).

The other side to all of this, of course, is my need to have you approve of my love interests. I want you to release me, but you can't do that, because we're only friends. Our relationship seems flat on paper. I don't think I can adequately capture the way I moved from being in love with you to loving you nor explain the real difference in those two states. If I never love anyone again the way I love you, I can die happy. My quest for a partner is tempered by the fact that I am looking for a tall, sensual, highly intelligent, and compassionate woman. I haven't decided if I want her to be old enough to be my mother; maybe she could be in the older-sister range.

In our talks about relationships we discuss the qualities that make a good partner. I notice that you also give me sage advice about the nature of relationships. You once wrote to me, "Loving, intimate relationships are probably the most difficult thing to understand and make peace with. We want too much and we want him/her to fix everything from the trivial to the impossible. So, do the best you can and try to make your expectations of yourself and your lover realistic."

After reading your letters I always feel invincible and that I've mastered a small part of living. The only bad part about that is that reality comes crashing in without warning. It reminds me of my relationship with D. and how I struggled to make some sense out it.

My impatience was at its maximum and I wanted to be in a relationship *now.* This matter was complicated by our sometimes present mother-daughter relationship. I was in what could be termed my adolescent period and was not talking to you as much. I wanted to explore my sexuality by myself. I thought, "I am a lesbian, and this is so different from being a heterosexual that you could no longer understand me." This was a limiting point of view. You, of all people, the woman who is the most understanding and knowledgeable person in my world. Sharon, the scholar who studies women and their worlds. You, who give me resources to help me establish a network that will help me feel less lonely and isolated. What was I thinking? I thought that I had to be different from you and reject all that had been before. You called these feelings growing pains. I was searching for yet another identity. I spent many days in turmoil: writing, painting, and crying. I spent time not talking to you and reading *The Little Prince,* learning to let go. It was the act of leaving that let me return to the caring fictional lover, mother, and friend who holds me until the tears stop and then puts me back on track. What would I do without you? A topic I tend to dance around. You always say I'll be fine without you and that the ultimate test is our separation.

I was thinking that I am getting closer to being thirty and how scary it is to get older. We have a date to have the biggest party of my life on my thirtieth birthday. But sometimes, in the middle of the night, I am frightened that you won't be here. You and I have often talked about growing older and about death. We both agreed that we could do without death, but you said that becoming physically and mentally mature was comfortable for you. What a relief! I often wonder if your words of wisdom will comfort me when you are no longer with me. You said to me, "Death is sad. It means saying good-bye. It represents loss of someone you care about. The positive part is that you've allowed yourself to get close to someone, to touch their life and let them touch you. I think that's what it's all about."

I know that's what it's all about. Your many life lessons "say" that to me. You insist that I finish my education, get a well-paying job, and become productive. You are flexible and yet also unyielding. I'm only now beginning to understand why a well-paying job is important. You would think, considering where I came from, that money would have been more important to me. But it wasn't until you explained about choices and how money gives you freedom that I began to understand. Who would have guessed that I could learn the value of money from an upper-class woman? You know, I started to write "white woman" but I stopped myself. I have moved past my limitation of seeing you as just a white woman. You are more than that, just as I am more than a black woman. We are a collective of experiences. When necessary I represent the black view and you represent the white view, but you have taught me that I am more than a sum of my parts. I am a complex piece of work that's still in progress. It's like you always say, "I've just begun to live."

I almost feel as if our story is a fairy tale. It's a unique story of two women, but is it really that unique? And was it really that smooth? Hell, no. It was a long and difficult journey, marked by self-doubt and self-exploration. I had to learn to communicate with you. It felt as if I had to learn to speak all over again. The walls of self-protection that I had erected early in life came down slowly but steadily. I had practiced and perfected being close-mouthed and a minimalist. The idea that I was a person with legitimate feelings and wants overwhelmed me. I was like a small child that had just learned to walk. I would toddle away from you for a while and then run back when it became too much. And you were always there waiting for me. If it is possible to have a second childhood, then I've had mine. You were the best mamma a girl could ask for. I never had to wear pink dresses or lace socks for you. I have, however, learned a few tricks of dressing to look sophisticated. Further, you have taught me that clothes are only wrapping and that the true gift comes in the interaction. My relationship with my own mother has also become less of a hassle. It is far from perfect but it's getting better. It was your challenge to me to see my mother as a person that put everything in motion. I have never forgotten how sad you were when you lost your mother or the gentle message you wrote about waiting for the good part with mine. She and I are like dancing partners who have not found their rhythm.

I guess when we can dance in time the good times will be upon us. I can be so demanding sometimes. But I don't have to tell you, because you know firsthand. You are a saint, a portrait in patience.

I guess the one area left to talk about in this crazy relationship is the world of work. Somewhat like a child, I want to be like you when I grow up. But as we know, I have to be like me, because I have to make different decisions. I must always remember that what people "see" about me is often where their search stops. I must also continue to be careful about where I go and what I do, because I could get killed, fired, or abused for being a lesbian. At one time I was despairing about all of these things but you helped me put it into perspective. Your repeated adage, "One thing at a time keeps me calm," and your advice to "whistle a happy tune" give me courage when I ride the rough terrain. When I'm faced with doing something that I don't want to do, your voice comes to me and reminds me, "You don't have to like it, you just have to do it." Sometimes I want to scream bloody murder because I feel like you're always telling me what to do. Then you remind me that I'm an adult and that the choice is mine. I have to laugh, because I know that I've given you the power that I want you to have. I think that's a thing called trust.

I have tried several ways to capture my feelings for you. I used our friendship as the basis for a short story. I've written several poems for you. My favorite is entitled "Because She Loved Purple."

Oh, woman of joy
so gentle, so tough
sensing, knowing, touching
the depths of emotions.
A vast sea of talent
that inspires
love of self and others.
Oh, woman of knowledge
so smart, so inquisitive
seeing, looking, understanding
filling the caverns of emptiness with fullness.
A range of support that enables
growth, change, renewal.

I think it captures how I feel for you and it serves as a goal for me. I need to become a strong woman like you. As I've come to learn from you, being born female is not a guarantee that I will become a real woman. I must always remember who I am, what my needs are, and I must never compromise myself for anyone. Further, I need to remain mindful that my love of women is not enough to make my relationships successful. I will have to work hard to keep my relationships honest, supportive, and fun. I am ready for the challenge, because I know that in the world there is one person who loves me unconditionally.

Affectionately,

Kathleen

Marcia Munson (left) and Martha McPheeters (right) took the formal attire they wore at the twenty-one-year anniversary celebration of their relationship in 1994 to their 1995 celebration event. Pictured here on Medicine Bow Peak in Wyoming (September 1995), Marcia and Martha remain good friends after now twenty-two years of "open love, uncommitted sex, firm friendship, and wild adventures." They wish to note that they usually dress more appropriately for their wilderness adventures.

NINE

Celebrating Wild Erotic Friendship:
Marcia and Martha

MARCIA MUNSON

"Martha McPheeters and Marcia Munson request the pleasure of your company at their 21st Anniversary Party. . . . We are celebrating 21 years of open love, uncommitted sex, firm friendship and wild adventures."

As we read over the invitation, we knew our friends would focus on the phrase "uncommitted sex." Because we both like to have sex with friends, and because we have both been in open relationships, we've each been seen as "loose women" by various lesbian communities over the years. But sex, though fun, has never been central to our relationship. First of all, we have been friends. The words that inspired us most were "wild adventures." Both of us have done plenty of wilderness travel over the last two decades, but very little of it has been together. As we embarked on the adventure of planning our anniversary party two months away, we dreamed of seeing more wild landscapes together in the future.

The idea for this anniversary party had been brewing for nearly a year, but when we saw each other in October 1993 after several months apart, it took hours to come up with the simple wording for the invitations. On the back, after the directions to the University Club, we would add, "We hope all our women friends and lovers from the past 21 years will join us."

The next eight weeks were filled with late night talks. We compared invitation lists, brainstormed about party favors, discussed

125

other lovers, and wondered what to wear. From the start, we knew
we wanted to each wear evening gowns for part of the night and
tuxedos for the rest of the party. Political discussions of butch/femme,
butch/butch, femme power, and gender-bender got pushed aside once
we realized comfort was the real issue. Marcia would start out in a
tux, Martha in a dress. To get everyone's attention we would switch,
right before our noncommitment ceremony.

To help us celebrate open love, we each planned to bring a date to
our anniversary party. We wanted to emphasize the point that we
were not, nor had we ever been, a couple. When we started plans for
the event, Martha and I were enjoying one of the rare sexual phases
of our friendship. Her primary partner, Nancy, was two thousand
miles away in graduate school. Martha hoped to bring Nancy to Fort
Collins, Colorado for our party, and in the beginning Nancy thought
the idea was great. Eight weeks before the event, I invited my long-
term friend and occasional lover Betty to be my date. In the weeks
that followed, Nancy became less comfortable with the sexual side of
the Martha/Marcia friendship. Martha and I quit sleeping together,
and Martha found another date. I became involved with Barbara,
who was very helpful and supportive in creating the anniversary
event. Energetic and imaginative herself, Barbara was the perfect
date. When I asked Betty at the last minute if she would mind being
the photographer instead of my date, she happily agreed.

The last and hardest detail of party planning was writing the vows
that we would read at the event. Our first versions seemed too
personal to make public, so we started over. The second version,
though less revealing, did not meet with approval from our current
partners. The next version was simply too long and boring to keep
the attention of a late-night crowd of one hundred women. We left
out all but the most significant and juicy stories. As we read aloud
our words to each other on the night of our twenty-first anniversary
party, it was hard to tell whether our friends and lovers packed into
the ballroom at Colorado State University were laughing or crying. It
was an emotional night.

Our dates, Gail and Barbara, escorted Martha and me to the
podium to begin the ceremony. The dance music stopped, and we

proposed a toast to open love, uncommitted sex, firm friendship, and wild adventures. We faced each other, held hands, and read our vows.

MARCIA: Martha, when I met you twenty-one years ago, I had no idea we would still be friends today. You were the first lesbian I had ever met, or at least that's what I thought. I remember coming to Yosemite to visit my friend Dara and meeting you. My third day there, you announced that your lesbian lover was coming for a visit soon. I had to knock on your door that night to ask you just exactly what a lesbian was. You explained so clearly, and then said you thought I was one, too.

You were the first person who had ever talked to me about loving women. On that night twenty-one years ago, and over the years, you have been the first woman I remember who would talk openly about butch and femme, s & m, dressing for success, open relationships, financial stability, and other hard topics dykes often avoid.

MARTHA: Marcia, when I met you in December of 1972, I was a wobbly, new lesbian. The relationship that spurred you to ask me, "What is a lesbian?" was my first intimate affair with a woman. My lover was coming to visit for Christmas and I was excited. Not so excited, though, that I didn't see your striking red hair or your willingness to scramble up a rock face without a rope or the obvious pleasure you took in hiking on a cold, rainy day in December. It was our shared love of the outdoors that kept me interested in your life in the 1970s.

MARCIA: Over the last twenty-one years, we have usually lived hundreds of miles apart. When we have found ourselves in the same part of the country we have arranged to meet. We have backpacked, skied, bicycled, danced, and made love together on many visits. Sometimes you have rejected me when I wanted you, sometimes you have propositioned me when I was involved elsewhere, and sometimes we have been open to intimacy with each other at the same time. I love you for all those times. In the years I have known you, I have been in three different long-term committed relationships with women I have lived with and loved for years.

Today, I know where all three of those women are, and I have warm memories of them, but I'm not as close to any of them, and I don't expect to share real affection with any of them again. With you, Martha, I don't have plans beyond this month—but I expect to share more years of open love, uncommitted sex, firm friendship, and wild adventure. After twenty-one years, I realize you are one of the long-term loves of my life. Martha, ours is one of the relationships I most value.

MARTHA: I, too, have had three important long-term relationships during the last twenty-one years. The first was monogamous, the second was defined as an open primary relationship, and the third was a seasonal partnership. You have had a significant effect on this evolution. During our visits in each phase, your input would provide an extremely useful mirror of my couple behavior and the trigger I needed to change the relationship to better reflect my needs and desires.

Ten years ago, we lived geographically close enough to have one date per week for an entire year. You were a stabilizing influence during this very turbulent period of my life. I discovered you were an excellent confidante. I would and did tell you my hopes and fears, joys and rejections, worries and wonders. Your curious mind, open ears, and warm embraces were instrumental in extricating me from not one but two significant relationships, a job that was destroying me, and a geographic area I found distressingly distasteful. I came to trust you with my emotions, with my mind, and with my body.

It was during this period that we defined our love, deciding we could love each other without "falling in love" and that a committed relationship was not for us. We could and would remain uncommitted, sharing love, sex, adventure, and friendship in the moments we found ourselves together.

Upon occasion I've arranged to visit you, only to find you preoccupied with a job, a woman, or your life. After my initial disappointment, I remember that when we choose to live in the moment, not every moment is wonderful and joyous. It becomes my turn to let go—let go of expectations, let go of those plans for a romantic evening, let go of all the walls and barriers I put on my path. My path will cycle and circle, rise and fall, in a rhythm that is not mine but rather belongs to life itself. It is you, Marcia, who, more than anyone else, teaches me these things.

Besides philosophy, you have taught me some very practical life skills. You provided my initial education about safer sex and have remained a careful practitioner to this very day. As I witness the consequences of careless sexual practices in my friends and community, I am even more grateful to you for making safer sex accessible and fun. Incidentally, I seldom fasten my seatbelt without thinking of you, for it is you who have consistently and rightly asserted that we are far more likely to get hurt in a car crash than to contract any sexually transmitted disease.

MARCIA: Martha, I have never been committed to continuing our relationship. Sometimes I have tried to cling to you, to wrestle from you some kind of commitment. I remember last year asking if you would be willing to commit to one phone call a year for the next three years. You said no. I sighed in frustration, and knew our relationship would continue on as usual.

I think our lack of commitment to each other is what has helped us keep on loving each other. Loving you has never kept me from doing anything else I wanted to do or from loving anyone else. In fact, usually there has been some woman or some project in my life that has kept me from devoting more attention to you. For twenty-one years now, you have been always a friend, often a confidante, occasionally a lover, and sometimes an adventure buddy who has reappeared again and again in my life, in different roles. I thank you for your open-hearted, passionate, wild-spirited lack of commitment to me, and total commitment to your own dreams. I expect that our paths will continue to intersect many times in the years to come.

MARTHA [*holding up her necklace of freedom rings*]: Rings are often used to symbolize commitment. However, in keeping with my contrary nature, I wish to use rings to celebrate my connection without commitment to you. These particular rings are called freedom rings. They represent the freedom that oppressed people seek. In the case of bisexuals and lesbians, this freedom is the freedom to love whom we choose in the way we see fit.

[*Martha kneels.*] Marcia, will you help me distribute these rings to our guests? It would please me greatly if each woman received a ring this evening symbolizing her freedom to love whom she wants, when she wants, and how she wants. Perhaps the ring will further remind these women of the loving community that exists in this very room and the abundant opportunities for friendship, affection, intimacy, and adventure which exist in all our lives. Marcia, will you help?

MARCIA [*reaching for the rings*]: Yes, Martha, I will help you distribute these rings.

The ceremony ended with freedom rings being given to all, anniversary cake being cut and shared, and women dancing for another hour.

Our friendship has continued. We ski fabulous backcountry trails high in the Rocky Mountains. We snuggle, with my curves softening the angles of Martha's muscled frame. I long for Martha when our lives place us thousands of miles apart.

The anniversary party had ripple effects on both our lives. My love affair with Barbara ended soon after the Marcia-Martha anniversary party, partly because of the strain of sharing that event. Martha's relationship with Nancy seems strengthened by their experiences of negotiating and discussing the anniversary party. The publicity surrounding the party led me to a new lover who reminds me of Martha, and whose unconventional approach to love and life matches my own. She supports whatever kind of friendship Martha and I choose in the future: erotic, adventuresome, or wild.

Because Martha has reappeared in my life so many times, I don't fear the goodbyes, though they can be torture. I remember that quick, hot sex ten years ago in a half-packed-up room in Denver. Afterwards, she loaded up a U-Haul, and I didn't see Martha again for over two years. It didn't seem so hard at the time, but my heart cringes at the memory. Martha and I had spent the previous year seeing each other regularly, but intentionally not falling in love, because I was committed elsewhere and her move to the East Coast was imminent. We had fulfilled our promise not to be swept away, but walking that line had not been easy.

When we compare notes, we find that the powerful memories of our friendship are often not of the same episodes. I'll never forget that night in 1972 when I knocked sheepishly on Martha's bedroom door after all her roommates' lights were out and asked her just exactly what a lesbian was. Martha was patient. She told me she thought I was one, too. She speculated that I was in love with both my friends Sandy and Dara and advised that I'd better figure out what to do. I knew a good idea when I heard one: Sandy became my first lesbian lover. Dara became a lifelong friend.

Seventeen years ago, driving to Salt Lake City, I anticipated a visit with Martha, one of only half a dozen lesbians I thought existed in the world. I had hopes that her single roommate would like me. Instead, I found that I was overwhelmingly attracted to both Martha and her current lover. The experience opened my mind to fantasies of open relationships.

It was Martha who took me to my first lesbian bar. I knew from that experience that the lure of city life was an unknown I longed to explore as thoroughly as the mountains I called home.

Several years ago, when I was unexpectedly fired from a park ranger job I loved, it was Martha who happened to be available to comfort me physically and emotionally. (My committed partner was away on vacation.) Martha told me the story of the time she had been fired for being gay and offered observations of the subtle ways homophobia and sexism can poison a seemingly positive workplace. She convinced me that my years of choosing nontraditional jobs had been a courageous political act. She taught me that your lover cannot always be the one "there for you" in time of need. That revelation contradicted my previous notion of "commitment."

Several years ago, when last-minute scheduling changes allowed Martha and me to rendezvous at the Michigan Women's Music Festival, I was thrilled to see her. She helped me colead a workshop I had been struggling with for weeks, and it was a big success. The fact that she had planned to meet another woman at the festival was no problem. The three of us spent the night together. It seemed like the friendly thing to do.

This last Fourth of July, after moping through the early afternoon because my girlfriend was spending the day with her other lover, I cheered up instantly when I started writing to Martha. I remembered fondly the Christmas a year and a half before when we first started to cook up plans for our anniversary celebration. Thoughts of her took the sting out of a potentially lonely holiday. While Martha can't always be here for me, she is always "there for me."

I see Martha as a permanent friend. Each time she has accidentally or intentionally appeared, I have rediscovered that I truly enjoy her. I count on ours as a long-term relationship far more than I could if we were committed new lovers or life partners. It is our history, not any promise to each other, that tells me we will continue to love each other over the years. It is her reappearances, rather than her assurances, that make me believe I'll see her and love her again.

One of the things I like best about knowing Martha for so many years is getting to see the changes in her as she grows older. Because months, or sometimes even years, can pass between our visits, I notice the differences: new wrinkles, a color-coordinated mountaineering outfit, easiness with her feelings.

When I first met Martha she impressed me only as a brilliant, curious scientist, and as the only lesbian I had ever encountered. Today I know her as a passionate, bold, warm, adventuresome friend who can challenge me tenderly or love me wildly.

As I anticipate our next visit, I look forward to catching up on her life over the last six months. We have planned a short backpacking trip in the Medicine Bow Range of Wyoming. I know that she'll be physically stronger and more energetic than I am, and that she will hardly care about the difference. She will have many stories to tell me, and lots of questions to ask. She'll be as curious about my months in San Francisco as I am about her summer with Outward Bound. As I think of our weekend ahead, I find myself smiling at the comfortable memory of an old friend. But also, my heart is jumping as though I were going on a first date with a new woman. Whatever this time with Martha brings, it's sure to be exciting.

From left to right, Shelagh Robinson, Alison McGowan, Karen Dushinski, and Shawna Bradley are "The Gourmet Goddesses" after placing third in a grape-stomping competition. The theme for their team is not hard to guess: the goddesses of wine. Shedonists to the core, says Shelagh.

Going against the Fold

SHELAGH ROBINSON

To Karen, my first love and finest friend. It will.

I kiss her wet hair in the hot tub, while Shawna massages her feet. Karen is unaware of the pressure of my lips, or of my delight at stroking the back of her neck, her shoulders. One day I will let her know the wonder of that secret gesture, of breathing in her closeness as bubbled water falls from the plaster volcano into the terracotta bath. But not now.

Karen, Shawna, and I have impulsively rented the Polynesian Suite at West Edmonton Mall's Fantasyland Hotel. Northern Alberta autumns offer few sun-swept beaches or opportunities to frolic uninhibited, so we manufacture our fantasy, complete with tropical drinks and plastic palms and a wild air of hedonism. Or *she*donism, as it is amended, for we three are surely displaced Dionysians, who live solely for pleasure after the chores are done and who long to play. We discard our bathing suits after the first round, daring one another to pose for pictures straddling the polyethylene mountain, and, temporarily shielded by drifts of bath foam, drink to Karen's toast, which becomes our trio's creed:

> To continents left untraveled,
> To friends unmet,
> To things yet experienced, but most of all
> To now, for it is what we share.

Later, Karen, Shawna, and I retire to the catamaran bed with the mirrored ceiling, where we circumnavigate the topics of past lovers and intimate encounters. We covertly watch each other's bodies and relate our cleanest heterosexual secrets, but not the real ones. Because we're only friends—and that's all we can be, for we are three women alone, not a man among us—we're not supposed to feel more than friendly. And nothing to be done with the desire that we all feel.

Fall is the time that the dreams begin coming to me. Dreams of Karen, slipping through wet tunnels, down dark slides. Archetypal symbology. The female.

One night I meet her twenty years in the future and she tells me of her marriage—to a woman—confessing that she'd desired me when we were younger but had feared the implications, and so we'd never had the chance to acknowledge our love. We'd missed. At forty-five years old we hold one another, crying at what has not become, and I awake in the morning feeling cold fingers of regret, an insistence that I not allow my fears to hold me tight. When I tell Karen at work the next day that I have met her future spouse, I am embarrassed that it is a "lesbian" dream and so omit that fact. I can't tell her; we are constrained by the "shoulds" and "musts" and "have tos" of our prairie upbringing. And she is my supervisor at the catering company where I recently began to work.

Edmonton begins its long slide into winter's depths. Days are cheerless grey, and our November hibernation starts in earnest. Work at the catering company loses its new-job glow, but I realize that I am not sinking into the usual depression brought on by the sunless season. Why? I know that merely seeing Karen's car in the parking lot sends an adrenaline rush through my chest. But that's a feeling reserved for men, is it not? How is this possible, and when did it begin?

One day I catch her in a similar sentiment: "I thought it was your day off today, but then I saw your car and I was so glad . . ." Her smile reaches into me.

Karen likes me. She thinks like me; we are so much the same. Too much serendipity in our lives for it to rest unacknowledged. Synchronicity, everything for a reason, nothing is a coincidence, we tell each other over pâté platters. Karen and I were meant to meet; we only have to figure out why. We both have a secret awareness of the reason, but do not tell even ourselves. We reveal other things, however. She and I discover that our families know one another, though we did not meet prior to working together. We have the same friends; we share the same hobbies, special stars, significant song. We discuss life philosophies, the importance of spontaneity; read from each other's diaries and relate significant dreams. I write to myself that she is creating a yellow joy glow in me and inscribe her Christmas card:

> Two in limbo. Two waiting. So why did we meet? I have my theories; we'll see . . .

signed with my love. Teasing myself, and her.

The bonds holding Karen, Shawna, and me are knit more tightly as winter presses us close for warmth. We "create" in the kitchen all day, confiding in our triad, buoying one another up, drawing strength from the peace we feel kneading one another's tired shoulders. But eight hours a day becomes too short, and the three of us discover an oasis in Shawna's apartment: "Shawna's Sauna," which quickly becomes our "Wooden Womb." We decorate the cedar walls with splashed water and beer and infuse it with stories of our pasts, stories which, when the lights are lowered, become sexual and daring. Small confessions by the other two let me know that what I feel is not so uncommon. But our truest narratives remain too hard to share; unfulfilled desires on the edge of mutual awareness.

Unspoken words addict us three. So tantalizing to hear only the edge of a fantasy. Each of us presses the others for more detail, learning that it is easier to answer questions than volunteer the truth. An almost-ménage à trois, an encounter while camping, an athletic coach, a best friend. We all have our timid tales of brushes with women, but none can tell the others just how deep the dreams are.

The rumor at work is that we share "one brain," are complete unto ourselves, which is true. I no longer telephone my "real" friends; neither does Karen. And Shawna now only infrequently sees her husband; with him she shares a different life. I see less of my parents, making excuses for missed dinners, forfeiting friends' parties. Our work days become marathons of hors d'oeuvres plates and fruit bonanzas as the holidays approach, and we assert that we deserve the time to decompress at night, alone with each other.

Post-sauna, we begin to move onto the bed that Shawna shares with her husband, who is away at work. Wrestling matches are inevitable, rough, and Karen straddles my chest, holding my arms, her long hair hanging in my eyes, lips very, very close. I close my eyes to imagine a more appropriate male weight, but smell her skin on mine.

When we have to behave correctly in mixed company, we use every excuse to be near one another, attached in some way, and touching. Karen and I are allowed to be closer to each other than Shawna can be with either of us because Shawna was sealed into holy wedlock two years earlier. Karen and I, two mere single females lacking the life-giving force of a male in our spheres, are free to remain solo, together. Thus we are indulged in our silliness, free to go to parties with the other as date, to snuggle in big round chairs, bodies close. We sit on one another's laps when no other space is free and hold each other like children, innocent, arms around shoulders; we are pals, buddies. It is not possible, of course, for there to be illicit activity between two women, and so no one, least of all any of us, suspects that when we advertently tip cranberry martinis onto one other, it is an excuse to touch the other's hands, feel a body beneath fingers.

One day after Christmas Karen boosts my car in a snow-filled alley. We remain outside, both our bodies chilled and pink, but unwilling to let the other go. She smiles at me, knowing the risk, and tells me she loves me. My heart jumps with excitement, but my returned grin is hesitant; I can't form the acknowledging reply. What can her words mean? As a woman, I may love other women with friendship and compassion and simple happy attachment; anything deeper, I have been taught, must be reserved for the male. I give nothing back to Karen for her courage that day but the smile. Later, alone, I mentally translate her sentiment into platonic emotion, thus not requiring the examination of my own feelings, which are heated and fearful.

On evenings alone, I spend hours in my bathtub, making love to Karen with my mind. There, and only in that warm space, my imagination may move freely. I smooth the inside of her elbow, kiss her neck, feel her mouth. I am curious to know her warm hands on the curve of my breast, the press of her thigh on mine. After, however, I rub away the images and the wet with my towel, and meet my boyfriend, rarely seen, for an evening of what I think is passion. He and I have little in common compared to the connection I share with Karen, yet I ignore the implications of hearing her voice whisper in my ear rather than his as I drive home alone in the dark.

I want and fear a relationship with Karen that is more than friendship. I am scared to contradict the decision-by-default that my culture has prescribed for me, but when I see my life story being written by others unconcerned with my happiness, I long to seize the pen and recreate the script for myself. Karen makes my story that much brighter; should I, then, not live by my shedonistic sensibilities? But I recall my younger days and memories of girls who were taunted as tomboys, and think, "If I desire a woman, then I must be one of *them,* and they are everything I do not want to be: different."

Daily, however, this fear diminishes, though slowly.

Unsurfaced desires begin to ascend when I invite Karen to house-sit with me under the pretext of fear of sinister intruders. She will spend the night, but at the critical moment of allocating sleeping space, I freeze and direct her away from my generous king size mattress to a cramped guest room with a single bed. Later, when she comes to steal a blanket and take playful refuge on my pillow, I slide to the wall so her body will not press against mine, as she seems to intend. I do not know what to do; I am filled with desire, but also with revulsion that I should long to reach over to her, that I would presume to go against the fold, the ways of propriety, in such a manner. So I turn my back on her, and possibility, and awake in the morning as friend, not lover, again safe from myself.

New snow and a day off. Never a thought that Karen, Shawna,

and I wouldn't spend the magic of the day together. Toboggans are wonderful things which require tight claspings of the woman in front and breath down the neck. When we spill, we toss together, legs and arms entangled in calculated chaos. Then there is freedom to lie, for a moment, faces together, inhaling one another's frosty breath, laughing, until a devious hand covered in freezing white comes up to brush another's face. We lie in the forest and listen to the chickadees and the flakes hitting dead leaves. We make Rubenesque snow angels in our down parkas, and sit, melting the ground beneath us, eating snow, tasting childhood, watching tongues.

Work is chaotic: New Year's platters of smoked salmon and mousse sprinkled with slivered almonds command our time. The three of us spend long hours preparing for the enjoyment of others and fantasize about running away to Belizian beaches for snorkeling, toplessness, and our own pleasure. More strongly I feel that I do not know the real Karen and will not be able to unless we are allowed to indulge in some Anything-You-Want-to-Do-Land time. We must be away, we say, to arrange our futures, to be silent for a while. To be alone with her, I think.

In the evening, exhausted from work and the heat of the sauna, and emboldened by wine, I lie with Shawna on her bed, waiting for Karen to arrive. I confess that if Karen and I do manage our escape to the beaches of Belize, we'll probably have an affair.

Amazing thought; I feel suddenly fearful as my covert up-until-now-unconscious plans become words, physical and real. I still cannot place Karen's relationship with me into a context apart from that of coworker/friend, except in the bath when I am alone with my thoughts. Does "affair" mean sexual intimacy, and if so, how can I think, much less speak, such things? Now I must face my own deviance and am anxious that I will be looked upon with disgust by friends most close to me.

Shawna is tantalized. Clearly amused and aroused by my confession, she lies quietly, hoping that I will elaborate. Later, after the wine has taken effect on us all, Karen teasingly bites Shawna's earlobe while I sleep, and Shawna shares my secret with her. And is rewarded by a small smile, revealing that it is not only I who have been thinking about possibilities.

Nothing more is said that night, but all three of us understand what has happened. In the subsequent week, work is punishing as I face Karen and Shawna every day, not knowing their thoughts about my revelation. The jokes between us cease, and I try to work alone as much as possible or with other coworkers besides my two friends. I confuse Karen and Shawna by my silence, and hurt myself with the separation. We are all aware of the implications of my words, that they are too big to put back in the box, to take back. The three of us understand that to return to one another, there must now be a confrontation; I am repelled, scared that I have made a mistake by speaking the unspeakable.

A night when my parents are out, a large bowl of sangria, and a staff party appear to be the solution to our silence. We make plans to "get it all out." Karen and Shawna arrive, and my stomach twists, knowing that we three have come to a place that will shift us, and our relationships, onto an entirely different path. It is time to move, to be self-determining, and to state what is most important, so before I have time to curb my words, I ask them, "What has been going on? It's been such a crazy week."

Karen and Shawna stare at me, knowing that someone had to start us off, and I understand that they are as shy as I am. But Karen takes the initiative, and watching my eyes, she speaks words that echo through me with shock that she can actually verbalize such sentiments:

"I'm attracted to you, Shelagh; the least you can do is look at me when I tell you this."

But it's terribly difficult to do—too close, too real. I am very near tears, with the emotions of the entire winter suddenly confronted. But I owe her something in return for her courage, and, finally able to look across to her, say, "I'm attracted to you too, but I'm not sure what to do about it."

Still, we know enough to touch hands, and acknowledge with our fingers that what we feel in the other's grasp is a very new kind of contact.

Time speeds when Shawna leaves us to be alone and Karen moves to sit beside me. I feel her hip against mine; now she is too close to look at directly.

"But it's good, huh, Yosh?" comes the old Karen, saying my nickname with a Slavic accent, and now it's easier to look upon the familiar face and remember why I love being with her so much, why we're friends. We sit, moving hands, happy with our new proximity, enjoying the warmth of the other's skin in unfamiliar caresses—until I hear a sound from the kitchen: Shawna is crying.

I move, step behind her. "What's happening, sweetie?"

She won't turn around, so I hug her from behind, feeling her sadness, knowing that she has somehow been separated from Karen and me by what has just passed. Shawna says she doesn't think she can watch this happen between Karen and me, this joy, the new circumstances. She feels excluded; she wishes she too could find a woman to be her lover but feels constrained by her marriage. I am not certain what to say to comfort Shawna; I am filled with such happiness and relief at what has emerged between Karen and me. So I tell her, gently, that none of us knows where this is going, that we've still got a lot to figure out; it's still the three of us. Which isn't really true. Karen comes over, reaches for us both, and the three of us merge into a close, arm-bound embrace.

"You're important to us, Shawna," Karen says. But then Shawna's husband arrives to chauffeur us to the party, and there is no time to put temporary closure on what has just occurred.

Crouched in the dim backseat of the car with Karen, it's easier for me, still cautious, to feel but not see her. She moves her arm to draw me close, and pressed against her in the dark, I feel smooth, warm fingers slip into the cuff of my glove, stroke my wrist. It's perfect and comfortable, and I am able to breathe more freely, enjoying the sensation of a woman who touches me, in the most simple manner, the way I want to be touched. I settle back against her more closely, and, for the first time, allow myself the thought that this is good and appropriate and allowed. Because we have willed it to be so, and that is all that is required.

The party becomes a frolic—our catering group has had to postpone its Christmas revelry until the law firms and accounting companies and advertising executives have finished with their holiday celebrations. But now our turn has come, our time to indulge. And so we dance with abandon in a dark basement. As we do, colleagues become sentimental shoulders, move with soppy tenderness ("I love working with you . . . ") But the words are genuinely tender when I say them to Karen, and I find myself reaching out to her, more comfortably, when I think no one notices; the evolution of intimacy.

The three of us spend the night on Shawna's living room floor on a makeshift bed of couch cushions and quilts. Shawna lies with us, her husband sleeping in the bedroom. The three of us wait for silence from him, listening to one another's breathing in the dark, knowing that too much has occurred for us to move quietly into sleep. Hands begin to wander, but I am suddenly still with apprehension, unmoving, until Karen, recognizing that she must be the decisive one, turns towards me, face close, and kisses me on the mouth. I bronze that kiss in my memory to later resurrect and gaze upon with awe. No small thing, the first romantic touch of a woman's lips to mine; I hope I kissed her back.

Shawna has deliberately placed herself with us, desiring inclusion, longing for our triad to remain intact in this new dimension. But while Karen worries about Shawna's husband only a wall away, I feel an ecstatic awareness of wonderful new feelings and have no reservations about sharing them with Shawna. True, it is Karen for whom I feel the greatest desire, but I wish to confer my joy, and so touch Shawna in return when her hand moves towards me.

It is an evening of communality and tenderness between the three of us, but we are tired, the space is not comfortable, and we feel limited by the presence of Shawna's husband. Fingers on bodies and freed lips move, but eyes shut with fatigue, and we leave off our explorations; sometime in the night, Shawna returns to her bedroom. When morning comes upon Karen and me, there is little of the usual discomfort that I have felt so keenly with men. All three of us have waited too enticingly long a time for that to occur, become too close; we will not mar it by being stilted with one another, or embarrassed.

Although there is some shyness, the result of our new connection, it disperses quickly when Karen, with a sudden awareness of where she lies, rolls towards and kisses me, this time in full light. Karen with her mouth on mine; I become aware that this is exactly where I want to be and return her soft stroke, my lips to hers, with wonder.

Comes the spring! Life so changed; work becomes a game of who can trap whom in the walk-in cooler for a kiss. I become fearful of moving into the back rooms, afraid that I'll be maneuvered into Karen's embrace and we'll be spotted by a coworker. One afternoon in the large refrigerator when I am defenseless, arms full of lemons, Karen ambushes me and I, wanting, kiss her with exaggerated passion. When we are caught by a cook who double-takes at our posture, eyes wide, we make vigorous, silly excuses in our retreat. Mischief makes light work.

Shawna gradually realizes, with foreseen sorrow, that she cannot join Karen and me as we progress into this different relationship, but work remains a study in flirtation between all three of us. Making sandwiches, I startle to feel a hand move up my thigh, and our fantasies, now given full liberty, compel Shawna and me to blush and stare lewdly at one another. Cold water and ice shards become instruments of a wonderful torture among the three of us, and our changing friendship becomes even closer.

Time in the Wooden Womb becomes progressively more intimate, and the lights remain on only long enough for the three of us to settle onto heated benches. Although bathing suits are still the costume de rigueur, hands now lower shoulder straps and stroke warm breasts. Foot massages become calf massages and progress upwards. Eventually I must release myself from Karen's fluid fingers to douse my overhot skin with cold water from the shower, plan my next advance; I return to find Shawna gone, and am finally free to press my length against Karen. Since our first evening, we haven't had the opportunity to be fully together, and I appreciate the freedom to kiss her salt lips and stroke a body undressed.

"I love you," I hear whispered, and am taken back to the alley, cold, where I'd been so regretfully silent. It has taken much inner strength to come to this point, more than I'd known I possessed, and on this day, finally, I am able to reply to her words, tell her what I have held in my heart for many months.

"I love you."

Karen hears me, and is aware of the stretch of the journey that I have taken to come to such a place, to be able to say this important thing. At last she can know her significance to me, and an important obstacle between us disappears.

Boyfriend exits scene. Time alone becomes the main priority for Karen and me, and we take grateful refuge in "house-sitting" regularly for a friend who has been admitted to our confidence. Together Karen and I are free to explore and learn about one another in new and intimate ways. Without pretension, we have little anxiety about what is, and is not, possible between us, and I am stunned by the sensitivity of Karen's touch, her awareness of my pleasure, the equal of which I have never experienced with a man. I am her first lover, of either gender, and with me she finds freedom to be completely with another person, giving herself up to gain herself. As do I. We feel no modesty as we sit, breasts touching, legs scissored by candlelight, the softness of the female at hand, and she responds easily to my, "So what do you like?"

She shows me.

It's play time, pure "us" time, and though we think no one at work but Shawna is aware of our transformation, it's hard to keep the joy from our faces; we are so in love. We secretly caress each other in darkened movie theatres, others oblivious, and park on quiet side streets in the spring evenings, seats reclined, gear shift awkward, her neck so damn soft. Driving becomes dangerous as I unclasp my seat belt to whisper in her ear and slip a hand inside her shirt. She grins at me when, as we walk a forest footpath, holding hands, a passerby catches us, our lips touching with a smile. We decide not to care.

Karen and I have no other lesbian friends; we don't know where to find them and we do not need them. We aren't aware that there are books to be read relating situations such as ours, or magazines which describe this way of loving. There are movies whose images reflect our desires for a woman, and singers as well, but beyond k.d., a local girl and our acknowledged idol, Karen and I have no clue that there are women who sing of being intimate with women. We don't even think to go to the one gay bar in town to investigate. We are isolated and without role models.

Summer emerges late in June, dawn of Alberta warmth, and Karen, Shawna, and I come to the proverbial career crossroads. It is time to set a new course. Shawna wavers between earning her journey papers as a chef and entering the army. Karen ponders opening a restaurant with her brother but is attracted to a women's studies degree, to add to her B.A. in anthropology. And after traveling, playing, and undergoing the rigors of the real world at work, I long to return to the haven of academia, where I am accountable only to myself and continue to learn.

All three of us desire change, and perhaps having earned it by demonstrating the courage to be self-determining in our love, the Goddess presents us all with opportunities and great challenges. Shawna is given a lucrative and promising new job, away from us and requiring independence. Karen learns that she is eligible as a special student and begins to plan her upcoming calendar around "Fundamentals of Feminism" and "The History of Women." And I receive a telephone call at work that I have been admitted into an M.A. program in psychology. In Ontario. I cry with relief that my professional life, which has felt so chaotic and fruitless, is resuming, but through the tears and congratulations, I see Karen move to the back room, to be hugged by a friend who understands the meaning of the news and consoles her.

Later, alone, Karen and I hold one another. Recognizing that our time together is now limited, we begin to make plans for only us in the remaining days. How much money do we need to escape, and where will we go? How soon can we quit our jobs? What will we tell our parents?

Our remaining summer time is at a premium. Karen and I make plans to go camping and spend glorious days at bed-and-breakfasts throughout British Columbia. We camp in the rain and spit cherry pits at each other as we drive through the Rockies. We hold hands and read Susan Griffin and Jean Shinoda Bolen to one another, listening to the songs that have been the soundtrack of our time together. We do not attend Gay Pride; we are hardly aware that it is happening.

Later, at Folk Fest, Karen and I stare with wonderment and big smiles when two women pass us holding hands. Although we are not yet free enough to do this, we store the images of the two and notice that they, like us, attend all the side stages where the female singers are scheduled. People like us; Karen and I feel the connection and, for the first time, desire to talk of common experience.

Impending autumn—Karen and I do not speak of my leaving, for it endows my departure with a solidity and reality that we choose not to acknowledge. Shawna telephones with a revelation: she has met someone at work, a woman. ("She might be a . . . like us.") Inevitable. And so before I am to take my plane east, Shawna hosts a potluck and invites her new woman friend to meet us, the rest of our friends, and Shawna's husband. I am excited for Shawna: typical shedonists, we do not look at the potential outcome of such a situation, are mischievous. Karen is less enthusiastic than I, but we are both excited by the prospect of potentially meeting another woman who is like us.

When we are introduced, unable or unwilling to contain myself, I tease this new woman, asking if k.d. isn't her favorite singer and why she wears the woman symbol as an earring. I query her about boyfriends with a smile on my face and examine her short fingernails, laughing. She smiles back, understanding.

Our evening closes in Anything-You-Want-to-Do-Land, as promised: the sauna, goblets full of red wine resting on the cedar slats, disclosures of Karen's relationship with me, and interrogations of this new woman's life story. Of course she's like us, a . . . lesbian, something easier to acknowledge now, to say.

And so as Shawna finds a friend on the eve of my leaving, the three of us become aware that an idyllic and significant chapter in our story is finishing. The Goddess closes one door, opens another. We speak of this shared tale, now many pages long, noting that its author persists in incorporating different characters and novel settings into our lifescapes. And through these new elements, we are aware, our individual stories will progress, sometimes with joy, sometimes in pain, sometimes with others, but inevitably entwined. Too soon to lose one another; too much still to be accomplished together.

Karen. I write to her, post-parting, telling her that our relationship is a work in progress and so only has a temporary ending. Separated by a thousand miles, and new, independent experiences, our hearts remain united though our intimacy becomes distant. The love that she and I have for one another, which has progressed from friend to lover, circles back to friendship. Its conclusion? All we can know is that this relationship will evolve, and that as we progress, we inevitably learn who, and what, is important to keep in our lives, knowing that if something should be, it will, regardless of the circumstances of the intimate. It will.

PART III

Friendships across Difference

Kris Morgan (left) and Rebecca Nerison (right) on May 1, 1989, Rebecca's thirty-fifth birthday. The photo was taken in the kitchen of Kris's funny house (note the orange extension cord, the sole supply of electricity to the second story), just days before the friends left together for Alaska.

ELEVEN

Lesbian-Meets-Christian-Heterosexual-Woman-in-the-Midwest-and-They-Become-Lifelong-Friends

KRIS S. MORGAN AND REBECCA M. NERISON

Prelude

REBECCA: In the summer of 1987, I moved from the cool comforts of the West Coast to Iowa City, Iowa. Friends questioned my sanity and joked that I would have to pick corn out of my belongings, as corn was about all that was happening in Iowa. But I was elated. At the age of thirty-three I was starting my life. I was going to graduate school to earn a doctoral degree in counseling psychology. I was filled with doubt and confidence at once, unsure as to whether I had what it took to succeed but determined to follow this dream to its awakening.

I left behind me many people, places, and endings. In 1983 I had abandoned my teaching career but was unable to pursue other studies as I had hoped. My marriage of twelve years had dissolved in 1985, when I left my home in Ketchikan, Alaska.

My first year at school was a joy. I discovered that I was as smart as everyone else. I made good friends and learned to drink beer. The wounds of the past slowly began to heal. And suddenly, I was a second-year student in the program—a veteran. As a veteran, I was assigned as Big Sister to a new student. I learned from her advisor that my protégée's name was Kris and that she was coming to Iowa from Seattle, where I had once lived, with her partner and a small menagerie.

KRIS: My decision to enter a doctoral program in counseling psychology was an outgrowth of my own recovery. I truly believed that my therapist had saved my life, and I wanted to put good into the world in the same way that she had done. I think I had been clean and sober about a year and a half before the fog cleared enough for me to realize that I was probably going to have a future, and that I could make some choices about it. I returned to school to finish the undergraduate degree I had abandoned.

My partner and I had been very isolated, and that began to change, too. The process was very slow, but eventually we began to discontinue old, unhealthy friendships and to experiment with new ones. I found a couple of women at school with whom I could share real things about my life. It was hard, exhilarating work, but I wanted healthy friendships.

Beginnings

KRIS: Once I was accepted to graduate school I got a letter from Becky, saying that she was to be my Big Sister, which meant that she would help me get acclimated to school. (Note: Rebecca was known as Becky back then. Although she now thinks of herself and introduces herself as Rebecca, she has encouraged me to keep calling her by the nickname.) She talked about her love for the Pacific Northwest, which indicated to me that she was a sensible person. She apologized for having written the letter on a word processor, explaining that school had left her handwriting undecipherable. This led me to feel that she was a thoughtful person. Her letter, in addition to being friendly and warm, was also well written. These metacommunications caught my attention, and I felt respect and liking for this woman.

I first met Becky in July of 1988, when I went to Iowa City to find housing. The professor who was to be my advisor had graciously invited me to stay at her home and use her car while I looked for a house, and she introduced me to Becky while showing me around at school. I inferred from Becky's initial reaction to me that she was taken aback by my appearance: I am a very large woman. Although she was courteous, I thought I read dismay and disapproval in her face. But reactions like that are part of my everyday reality, and here was the woman who had promised to help me out, so I couldn't afford to let her write me off so easily.

REBECCA: Yes, I was taken aback by Kris's size at our first meeting. I wish I could object at this point and say that I did not feel dismay and disapproval, but I probably did feel—and communicate—these things. Like most people in our culture, I equated the presence of fat with the absence of health and style. As a result of meeting and befriending Kris, however, these assumptions were challenged, and I had to struggle with my feelings and attitudes about fat. It wasn't okay anymore to cling to my prejudices, because Kris was somebody I cared about. But there was something else that struck me at our first meeting: Kris was wearing shorts and a sleeveless shirt. I remember thinking, What a gutsy thing for a large woman to do! It was as if she had nothing to hide and nothing to be ashamed of: Here I am, world, like it or lump it! I liked that quality about her, partly because it was something I didn't share at the time and secretly envied.

KRIS: It was in these first hours together that I began to understand how unhappy Becky was. I didn't know why, but she seemed sad, dissatisfied, lonely, and hopeless, as if her life didn't feel right, like she had no hope that it would ever feel right. We spent some more hours together before I left Iowa, and I truly began to like this woman. When I took her to see the large, dumpy house I had rented about twenty miles out of town, she was both tactful and humorous. (REBECCA: My first response to the house was alarm. The floors of most of the rooms sloped in various directions, and each room was clothed in new carpet remnants of different colors and patterns. It soon became clear, however, that this was the best house that Kris had found and that it would probably suit her family's needs. As she felt anxious about making the decision alone, I resolved to be supportive and encouraging, saying only that I thought the house would be a fine rental but that I probably would not buy it. I prayed that the house would hold together.) I think it was when her humor began to show that I realized she was not going to be just a charity case, and that this Big Sister/ Little Sister relationship might really be fun. I left Iowa feeling secure that I had the beginnings of a friendship, though Becky and I had very little in common.

Differences

REBECCA: Apart from our West Coast origins and the graduate program, my perception was that Kris and I had very little in common in terms of fundamental lifestyle issues. Kris was an "out" lesbian feminist who was not in the least shy about sharing this fact with her classmates. My exposure to out lesbian feminists was limited, and so I was quite struck by Kris's openness about so private and culturally unpopular a matter. I thought of myself as a heterosexual divorcée who was in no hurry to find another man. And I, like Karen Thompson,[1] had voted for Reagan, twice. In the years prior to our meeting, I identified as an "evangelical" Christian, by which I mean that I approached the Christian scriptures in a literal sense. Although this identification was waning by the time we met, I continued to hold my religious beliefs relatively near and dear. Another major difference between us was our attitude toward animals. Kris and her partner, Sarah, came to Iowa with three cats, one aging cocker spaniel, and a gray rabbit named Rodeo. They adhered to a strict vegetarian diet out of respect for animal spirit. I, on the other hand, consumed meats without a qualm, except for consideration of cost and nutrition. I had no pets, although I enjoyed animals that belonged to others. Also, Kris possessed a body of substantial size, and she carried herself with pride and confidence. My culturally correct slender body enabled me to tiptoe through the world without causing much of a stir. Finally, Kris was quite serious about being clean and sober, while my newfound enjoyment of beer added an important dimension to my social life. It seemed unlikely to me that we should become friends based on shared interests and commonalities alone.

KRIS: I don't know when I first saw that she had a Bible in her desk, but it was pretty early on. I was shocked and horrified but tried to laugh it off. To me at that time, identifying as religious was an unforgivable admission of stupid and sheeplike thinking. But Becky wouldn't let me laugh it off. She let me know that being Christian was part of her fundamental being and that she took it very seriously. This really threw me, but, by this time, I liked her a lot. And didn't this revelation really fit into the hypothesis that I had formed about Becky's unhappiness? She was a victim not only of our sexist society, but also of the sexist Judeo-Christian tradition. Probably she just hadn't been exposed to the right feminist influences yet. No wonder she wasn't happy—who could be under those patriarchal influences? All the more reason for me to bide my time and show her that there might be other ways to live and be happy.

So I began talking to Becky about her faith, and I started going to church. Not surprisingly, Becky was more than willing to talk to me about her beliefs, and we also visited at one another's churches. I think the first time she came to my home for a meal was Sunday brunch after church—broccoli quiche. In this way, talking about Christianity and about the effects of religion on psychological functioning became part of our relationship. This difference between us that I thought might be insurmountable began to nourish our growing closeness.

Alaska

REBECCA: The summer of 1989 I arranged to work at a mental health facility in Ketchikan, Alaska. I had lived in Ketchikan between 1980 and 1985, and I looked forward to returning for the summer. Since I was staying for three months, I decided to drive my bright yellow 1979 Ford Fiesta, a tiny but trustworthy box of

a car. I asked Kris to accompany me on this trek, flying back to
Iowa via Seattle and returning to Ketchikan in August to help me
drive home. Kris and I joked that the trip would be a real test of
our friendship, as it involved three days together in tight quarters
each way.

KRIS: I know it was a very important period of time for our friendship, but I don't remember many details. I remember talking and
talking. We read a lesbian novel aloud, one with lots of sex in it
(my favorite kind), and talked a lot about our own sexual experiences and preferences. We talked about our bodies and about fat.
We had conflict about one another's driving. We had a blazing
argument about religious education and cramming religion down
the throats of innocent, unsuspecting children. We discussed our
families and our loves. We talked about politics—and, as a radical
lesbian feminist, to me almost everything was politics. We talked
about feminism and identity development of all kinds. We talked
about our spiritual beliefs and found that once we put the seman-
tics aside we agreed far more than we differed. I think it was on
that drive to Alaska that I fell in love with Becky.

See, you have to remember my friendship history. I had none.
Okay, I had very little. I had begun to make a couple of friends
before I left for graduate school, but those friends were clearly
temporary, because we all knew I was moving. Becky was the first
person, other than a lover, that I had been this emotionally open
with and close to. So I think it was only natural for me to associate
the closeness we had with being in love. I didn't tell anybody how
I felt, and I had no interest in or plans to have a sexual relationship
with Becky. After all, I was in a committed, monogamous relationship. Besides, she was (probably-maybe?) a straight woman. Plus,
she was repelled by my body. And she had just told me, during the
sex talks, that she believed that she could never have sex with
anyone without being married to them. But I fell hard for her, and
enjoyed the crush thoroughly (most of the time). I missed her
dreadfully that summer that she was in Alaska. I wrote letters and

I called her often. I mailed her my copy of Loulan's *Lesbian Sex*[2] because she had been so full of questions. That feeling of being in love with Becky probably lasted off and on for a couple of years.

Middle

REBECCA: I spent over two years struggling with feelings, theological issues, and practical questions concerning my sexual identity. This process began about eight months before I met Kris. Kris was not my first lesbian friend, but she was the most proximate during my coming out period. She took a supportive role in my process and talked at length with me about the many concerns I had with identifying to myself and to the world as a lesbian. She never proselytized or pressured. She spoke freely of her own struggles concerning being a lesbian and the joys and difficulties of her longtime partnership with Sarah. In this, Kris and Sarah were role models par excellence. I spent a lot of time with them and their animals out at their house in the country. I saw for myself their love for one another, their commitment to their relationship, and the everyday irritations and conflicts common to couples of all affectional persuasions. In short, my observations of Kris and Sarah served to normalize a type of relationship that I heretofore believed was alien to humankind. Their relationship was not in the least alien; it was simply a variation found in nature. And so my own coming out became firmly rooted in a calm, secure sense of rightness and normalcy. Despite the formidable theological difficulties I experienced, I felt confident that I was discovering and following my true nature. I attribute much of the calm in the midst of this major transition to Kris's presence and influence in my life.

KRIS: After the drive to Alaska, our friendship was firmly established. I no longer thought of myself as the ray of sunshine I thought Becky needed, nor did I think of her as a "project." Rather, I had come to rely on her for the many wonders that daily contact with a close friend provides. During the next couple of years, while Becky was coming out and experimenting with lesbian life in all its glorious complexity, her daily presence in my life spurred my own personal growth in a number of ways. As I've already touched on, she was my first adult friend, and I was learning a lot about how friendships work and what the limits are and what it was like to count on someone in addition to my partner. Also, I continued to learn about religion, its effects, and my reactions to it all. Another struggle with which Becky helped a lot was graduate school.

Transitions

KRIS: During this time, the initial differences between us really began to disappear. Yes, Becky is still six years older than I am, and I am still large and she is not. But she came to identify as lesbian, and she calls herself a feminist now. She seems to have made some kind of peace with my body size. (She recently asked me to pose nude so she could paint a portrait of me.) I gave up being vegetarian. She came to a crisis in her faith and is transforming her belief system. In the meantime, I have become much more tolerant of religious persons and of the role of faith in people's lives, and much more understanding of how my own spiritual beliefs are analogous to a number of Judeo-Christian traditions.

Becky and I were not initially drawn together because of our similarities, but we deliberately chose to befriend one another. And becoming more similar over time has not insulated us from ups and downs in the friendship. I lost my crush on Becky somewhere in there and at times believed that the friendship would not survive the various physical and emotional distances between us. Sometimes I didn't even care that I might lose her, because I was now getting pretty good at having friendships, and, frankly, this one seemed to need a lot of work.

Once the shine of the crush was gone, I began to pay attention to some things that I had dismissed before. I realized that Becky often didn't follow through with plans she made, and that made her seem unreliable and distant sometimes. I began to be frustrated with her unhappiness, and, like her, I felt doubtful that she could ever make her life joyful and satisfying. I think now that I was angry about this unreliability and unhappiness because I had expected to have more impact on her and had counted on her caring for me in the same blindly loyal way that I cared for her. During that time I began to think of her as selfish, as I recalled all the things my partner and I had done for her, all the times we had opened our home to her, fed her, given her shelter and comfort. Never mind that she had never asked me to provide these things for her.

The turning point for me came when Becky and a guest came to our home in Kansas for a weekend. (My partner and I had moved there for my clinical internship.) One morning, fairly early, I crawled back into bed to read, after having seen that my partner and Becky's friend were happily drinking coffee and talking downstairs. Becky got up soon and, to my surprise, came and got in bed with me. She asked about the changes in my attitude and behavior toward her, and she told me about the work she was doing in therapy to understand and change how she related to people. We talked for a long time. Afterward, I felt that the closeness we had lost had been restored. Once I understood what was going on with her and knew that it wasn't just about our friendship but about all her relationships, I felt compassion for her again.

While I still try to protect myself from being disappointed by Becky by remembering to give her room to change her mind, I am now able to do so in a more loving and empathic way. I also have accepted that the difficulties we had were also partly my responsibility and sprang from my own lack of knowledge about what is normal in friendship. I think I am a better friend for having learned more about reasonable boundaries and expectations.

Colleagues

REBECCA: Kris and I have evolved from graduate student buddies into lifelong friends. In the process, we have shared a great many anxieties, trepidations, vulnerabilities. Sometimes the questions seemed endless: Will I ever be finished? Will I get a job? What if I don't know what I'm doing? We have thus supported one another through some difficult, and prolonged, academic processes, during which we have developed an intimacy born of trials by fire and celebrations shared.

In addition to the professional tribulations, however, our friendship has survived the vicissitudes of personal growth and circumstantial change. Over the years, I have continued to work hard in therapy and to change the way I do relationships. There were times that I found Kris distant and detached, and it was a major breakthrough for me to find the courage to talk to her about what I was perceiving. The physical distance between us has been challenging, as well, since I now live on Cape Cod and Kris lives in Seattle. Keeping in touch thus requires greater creativity. I look forward to growing older and wiser, knowing that Kris is in my corner.

The Effect of This Writing Project on Our Friendship

REBECCA: The process of writing this chapter was much more challenging to me and to our friendship than I had imagined. This is what happened. Kris and I divided the work into sections and wrote our respective parts. We then exchanged drafts and reviewed what the other had written. My first reaction to Kris's writing was surprise. She had revealed much more personal detail than I had. I wasn't sure how I felt about that. In addition, she talked a lot about me in terms of her perceptions that I was chronically unhappy and unreliable. The part that stung the most was the section on how she pretty much gave up on me because of this. I felt as if I had failed her and found myself thinking ruefully about the kind of friend I had been to her. However, I did not allow myself to *feel* my reaction, which was hurt and anger. I rationalized my feelings away, reminding myself that Kris is a straightforward and, at times, blunt woman. So I told her that I had no objections to the piece, that it was fine as it was.

As time passed, however, I grew less comfortable with what she had written. This discomfort manifested itself in a dampened enthusiasm for the project, which led to avoidance of it altogether. I finally recognized that I felt angry. It seemed that Kris had portrayed me as a depressed victim who couldn't get it together, who needed rescue. And when I didn't respond favorably to her rescue attempts, she became angry with me. This made me mad. And there seemed to be something missing from her piece, namely, an explication of her expectations of me and how she dealt with her disappointment when I did not meet them.

And so it was that I communicated these feelings to Kris shortly before the deadline for the first draft. Kris was understandably angry that I had waited so long to bring up these issues, as I had said at first that her piece was okay and we now had little time to make changes. Her anger was what I had feared all along, I think. When it comes to close relationships, the kid inside me is afraid that people will go away if they get angry at me. So here was this golden opportunity to face my fear and work through a conflict. Kris and I agreed to persevere with the writing and to work through the anger that we felt toward one another. We have had several conversations toward this end, mostly at professional conferences, where we have the opportunity to talk in person and to hug each other. This friendship is giving me a chance to practice conflict resolution in a safe context and to heal that which has been hurt. That's just one of the reasons why I cherish my friendship with Kris.

KRIS: Yes, I was angry that Becky had taken so long to voice her concerns. But I was also glad she told me, because I want her to tell me the truth. I listened to her concerns, responded honestly, and told her what I wished she would change about her portion of the piece. The result was that we both made changes. I think our chapter is better and more honest for the work we did on it, and I believe our friendship is better and more honest for the work we did on that, too.

NOTES

1. Karen Thompson wrote a book after her partner, Sharon, was critically injured in an automobile accident and Karen was involved in a lawsuit to obtain guardianship of her (*Why Can't Sharon Kowalski Come Home?* [San Francisco: Spinsters/Aunt Lute, 1988]). Prior to this event, which forced Karen to come out, she admits to having voted Republican.

2. JoAnn Loulan, *Lesbian Sex* (San Francisco: Spinster's Ink, 1985).

Ruth Hall (left and Suzanna Rose (right) renewing their friendship at the 1993 March on Washington for Lesbian, Gay, and Bi Equal Rights and Liberation.

TWELVE

Friendships between African-American and White Lesbians

RUTH HALL AND
SUZANNA ROSE

The racial divide between African-American and White women has not been healed by the balm of sisterhood as feminists once hoped would happen. Awareness of a shared gender oppression did not result in the desired cross-race friendships and political ties, even among lesbian feminists who highly value both sisterhood and women's friendship. Instead, the alliance between African-American and White women has been tense (hooks, 1990). The tension has extended to the lesbian community. Lesbians of color have issued challenges to White lesbians to confront their own racism; others have withdrawn from multicultural work (e.g., Lorde, 1981; Smith and Karp, 1988). White lesbians, in turn, often have responded to women of color with confusion, guilt, anger, or dismissal (Frankenberg, 1993). This social context has had a direct impact on friendships between African-American and White lesbians. For example, African-American lesbians who seek friends in the predominantly White lesbian community report facing three negative consequences (Mays, Cochran and Rhue, 1993). They may be rejected because of their race, they may be accepted but exposed to racism within the community, or they may be expected to minimize their own African-American culture.

But racial segregation within lesbian communities also has influenced some White lesbians to begin a process of self-examination that eventually will help them build friendships and alliances with African-American lesbians (Pratt, 1991; Segrest, 1994). Although cross-race lesbian friendships have not materialized on the large scale predicted by feminism, a productive dialogue about racism has occurred in some circles that has encouraged cross-race friendships. One example is the friendship we, the authors, share. Our friendship developed through our involvement in the Association for Women in Psychology. Suzanna was already a member of the Implementation Collective when Ruth joined it as the first coordinator of the Women of Color Caucus. A series of antiracism workshops in which Ruth and Suzanna participated as members of the collective facilitated the friendship. We took the business of undoing racism seriously, became political allies, and learned to laugh together, too. Our friendship is now eight years old and we consider each other to be family. Reflecting on our friendship caused us to wonder how representative our experience was of other cross-race friendships among feminists. We decided to explore this question by examining friendships between African-American and White lesbian feminists.

In this chapter, our intent is to illustrate some of the considerations, problems, and rewards of friendships between African-American and White lesbians by drawing on twelve in-depth interviews conducted in St. Louis by Suzanna.[1] Six of the participants were African-American lesbians whose ages ranged from twenty-one to sixty-one; six were White, aged twenty-one to forty-seven. Three of the African-American and two of the White women described themselves as working-class; the remainder were middle-class. Our participants represented a very select group. Individuals chosen were at a high level of racial awareness; many had participated in or led antiracism workshops or confronted racism in the lesbian community. They also had been successful at establishing intimate ties across race lines; for example, all had at least one close cross-race friendship.

The interview questions were aimed at exploring the defining characteristics of cross-race friendships. It was assumed that cross-race friendships would share the features of close friendship, including a sense of belonging, emotional stability, opportunities for communication, assistance, reassurance of one's worth and value, and personality support (Duck, 1991); thus, these general processes were not investigated. What interested us was how the politics of race and racism would affect the formation and development of friendships between African-American and White lesbians. The ten questions selected for the interview focused on: (1) friendship initiation, including the criteria participants had for cross-race friends; (2) common problems in cross-race friendships, particularly in terms of building trust concerning the issue of race; and (3) the political and personal rewards associated with cross-race friendships.

Friendship Initiation

The process of initiating any friendship is a complex one (see, e.g., Derlega and Winstead, 1986). Previous research has shown that demographic factors such as age, race, sex, social class, sexual orientation, and geographic location to a large extent dictate with whom individuals come into contact and, therefore, with whom they can become friends. As an acquaintanceship develops, personal factors, such as attitude similarity, physical attractiveness, personality style, and interests, become increasingly important. Four behaviors also appear to be related to successful friendship development: companionship, consideration, communication and self-disclosure, and affection (Hays, 1984). In addition, friendships are governed by certain informal "rules"; failing to follow them can impair the friendship (Argyle and Henderson, 1984). For example, it is expected that a friend will stand up for you, share good news with you, give emotional support, trust and confide in you, offer you aid when needed, and try to make you happy when the two of you are together.

Cross-race friendship initiation as described by our participants largely fit the pattern described above. However, the usual demographic factors limiting contact between people differing in age, race, and social class appeared to have less effect on participants than is normally the case. Instead, sexual orientation (a demographic factor) and political activism (a personal one) were the two similarities most often reported as promoting initial contact. These two factors "located" the participants in situations that allowed them to interact with lesbians of different races, backgrounds, and neighborhoods. However, other criteria for cross-race friendship were likely to come into play once initial contact occurred. Thus, we asked participants what criteria they had for determining if someone of another race was "friendship material."

Responses to questions about friendship initiation revealed that racial awareness was the most important criterion for potential cross-race friends. Racial awareness was described by participants as having two components. First, a racially aware person was described as someone who recognized and appreciated differences in culture, values, aesthetic standards, and so on among races and did not regard these differences as signs of superiority or inferiority. Second, a racially aware individual was able to identify and challenge the ways White people actively or passively participate in and benefit from racism. This concept of racial awareness corresponds to the most recent view of race to develop historically, according to Frankenberg (1993), one that includes a recognition of how race oppression is institutionalized within our society, as well as a positive valuation of cultural differences. As such, it represents a definite rejection of the two dominant views of race prevailing in the United States until recently. According to the first or essentialist view, people of color are regarded as biologically inferior to White people. In the second, the color-blind view, all people are held to be the same under the skin. Those holding this view tend to deny that race affects how they treat people or how they are treated (Frankenberg, 1993).

That participants defined racial awareness in a way that has only recently emerged suggests that they themselves were at the most advanced stage of racial identity development (Cross, 1991; Helms, 1990) and were looking for friends who were at a similar stage. For African-Americans, the fifth and highest stage of identity development is *integration*. Integration is said to occur when a strong pride in one's African-American background exists alongside a willingness to establish meaningful relationships with Whites who are respectful of one's self-definition (Cross, 1991). For Whites, the fifth and highest stage of racial identity is *autonomy*. At this stage, a positive White identity is internalized along with an appreciation for racial differences and similarities; cross-cultural interactions are sought out as opportunities for growth (Helms, 1990).

Participants regarded individuals as potential candidates for friendship if they appeared to share a highly developed racial awareness or identity, as described above. Those holding the essentialist or color-blind views were not seriously considered as likely candidates for friendship, particularly by African-American lesbians. Generally, African-American lesbians assumed that White lesbians were, at least to some degree, lacking or less developed in terms of racial awareness. This assumption set up a dynamic that required the White women to pursue the friendship, if one was to occur. Most of the African-American lesbians felt positively toward White women who made an extra effort to establish a friendship. For example, Renee Upshaw[2] (aged thirty-one) remarked, "The first thing that they see is that I'm Black. I would think, is she just trying to be diverse in her friends? It doesn't stop me if that is her motive. If I'm the first [Black friend], I can pave the way for more." Friendship initiation was a sign to African-American lesbians that the White woman had done some work on understanding her racism. Tonya Hutchinson (aged twenty-two) noted, "I guess I would wonder, 'Why would they want to hang out with me as opposed to someone White?' . . . Or, I would think that they were curious about Black people . . . or that, 'Man, that person must be really cool or dealing with race shit." Similarly, Lynn (aged sixty-one) asserted, "When a White woman becomes friends with a woman of color, it's a kind of migration as opposed to a need. . . . [T]hey have an education [about race] or they wouldn't be approaching a Black woman as a friend. . . . She's not coming with overt racism or prejudice."

However, several of the African-American lesbians also expressed caution about forming friendships with White women. Some of the more serious concerns were explained by Alicia, a forty-year-old African-American lesbian:

I would assume that she didn't know much about race relations . . . that she wants to learn about Black people . . . that she wants to know me so she can tell her friends she has a Black friend . . . that her world is White and that she has no or few people of color as friends, which means she's had little experience with cross-cultural relations except maybe in work situations where she was most likely the boss or supervisor or serving clients of color . . . that she thinks she's smarter than I am or that she has more to offer in the friendship . . . that she has access to more resources than I . . . that [she believes] her Eurocentric values are superior to mine and will assume when any conflicts come up that I should change . . . that she will be pretty uncomfortable in my world, at least at first . . . [and] that she will have misconceptions about Black women, for example, that Black women are stronger than her, as in "You Black women are so strong you can do anything."

In general, White lesbians saw their race, as well as any unidentified racism in themselves, as being a drawback in terms of initiating friendships with racially aware African-American lesbians. Monitoring oneself constantly for signs of one's own prejudice put a psychological strain on White women that made the friendships more stressful to initiate. However, the self-examination process also made the White women aware of the reasons why African-American lesbians tended to be reserved about cross-race friendships. Janey Archey, a thirty-nine-year-old White lesbian, indicated:

I always have to screen what I say, because I'm afraid what I say will be racist . . . because I've had so little experience with African-Americans. I can't say, "I know how you feel" related to race. It almost comes out of my mouth and part of the screening is that I can't say that. . . . It takes a lot of effort. It's very tiring and then I feel guilty about it—I'm the White person—Black women are tired all the time [from dealing with racism], so I shouldn't be tired. I feel irritated that we're not more alike. I was always raised to think "different" was bad. Now I'm looking at it as something good, but sometimes I still think, "Why can't we be the same?" . . . So, I think African-American lesbians are guarded about having friendships with White women. . . . I learn a lot from them. . . . I'm not sure they get as much [from the friendship as I do].

Marlene Schuman (aged forty-seven), a White lesbian, expressed similar anxiety: "I'm concerned that I will let them down, that I won't be there for them in the way they expect me to be. Even when there is a close bond, there is still a space between us when it comes to the pain [of racism], a space I can't cross because the White person—myself—hasn't really walked in the other person's shoes."

White lesbians described friendship initiation to be largely their responsibility in cross-race friendships, due to African-American lesbians' perceived and actual cautiousness. Marlene, just introduced above, predicted, "I would expect a certain level of resistance [from African-American lesbians] to becoming friends. Sometimes that means I don't push as hard. I try to give it time. Their experience would suggest they would be wary of my motives.... [W]hat is different about me? ... [W]hy should they get into something [with someone White when] they've probably been hurt by [one] before?" Similarly, Connie, a forty-four-year-old White lesbian, described friendship initiation with an African-American lesbian as follows:

> I would expect her to be cautious, possibly suspicious about my trustworthiness, particularly around race issues.... She probably wouldn't trust White people.... She might be sensitive, guarded, waiting to see how I respond to a Black perspective.... She may have various "tests" for me that might involve finding out what my views are about different issues, especially regarding my possible response to acts of discrimination against Black people.... She might want to know if I am an advocate for people of color.... She might see me as having little to offer her on a personal level.

Likewise, Dana Long (White, aged twenty-one) reported, "I've never had a Black lesbian initiate a friendship.... I usually approach them in a political context to develop a friendship, as I did with Tamara. I had to prove to her that I was interested in fighting racism and have the friendship develop out of that.... Most Black lesbians will stand back and see where you are. Of course, that's self-defense. As a lesbian, I do the same thing with gay men."

As a friendship develops, similarities of attitudes and values become more important. The similarities facilitate communication, influence how much emotional support friends will be able to give each other on issues they care about, and affect whether the companionship provided will be fulfilling. Being at a similar level of racial awareness was seen as providing the basis for communication, emotional support, and companionship. African-American lesbians were more stringent about applying the racial awareness test than White women, although both groups mentioned its significance. For instance, Tonya (African-American, aged twenty-two) explained:

> I have more stringent guidelines for White people as friends. I'm not as naive and uneducated as I used to be. I still feel race should not prohibit friendships, but many White people *and* Black people would never think of callin' up a person of another race. I don't trust White people as quickly as I have in the past. I am constantly questioning. I would be more apt to let an African-American woman come to me with a clean slate. The White person's slate would be blotted. I would have to know she liked me for me—no ulterior motive. Because of the world we live in, I have to use stricter guidelines. But once they are my friend, I trust them implicitly.

Lynn (aged sixty-one), another African-American lesbian, echoed the above sentiments: "What political views she holds are important. Is she educated as to the cultural difference [between Blacks and Whites]? Does she realize racism is alive and well? Is she a civil rights activist? I don't want to hear statements like, 'Is it true all Black people [whatever]?' How the fuck do I know? I'm not all Black people." Similarly, Alicia would want to know, "Does she know anything about race? I won't want to know her if she's totally ignorant. Can she think? Has she fooled herself into thinking she's more in tune with her racism than she really is? Has she ever had any Black friends before and what were they like?"

It also was quite important to African-American lesbians that the White woman respond empathically to people of color's experiences with racism. Deborah Clayton [aged forty-plus], an African-American, indicated that a White lesbian who wanted to be friends "has to be able to realize that we are in two entirely different worlds. People will respond to me differently [than to] her." A similar point was made by Renee (African-American, aged thirty-one): "Is she able to go to an Anita Baker concert and be a minority? Is she able to see what it's like for me in her world?" Current events sometimes set the stage for revealing White women's attitudes. For Renee, "Rodney King was a litmus test. . . . A lot of Whites don't understand Black America's viewpoint. It's been a loss for me to realize they weren't as cool as I thought. [Some White lesbians said], 'He's a criminal. He shouldn't have run. Don't you think he deserved it? White people get beat up, too.' But not by Black cops. To have to explain [to them] why he might have run! . . . I've lost friends since [the King case]."

White lesbians also looked for racial awareness in cross-race friends, but identifying as a feminist activist was seen as being equally important. Other research also has reported that White lesbians place strong emphasis on the "feminist" criterion in choosing friends, even to the extent that many actively avoid friendships with nonfeminist women (see, e.g., Rose and Roades, 1987). For example, Laura Ann Moore (aged forty-seven) stated, "Their politics are most important to me. I would want them to be able to articulate their oppression as women of color, as a lesbian in the world at large, as a woman, and to be aware of class issues, too." Andy (aged forty-one) said, "I look at their ethics, politics, and sense of humor. It's important that we have shared politics—a respect for a sense of justice, a craving for a different kind of world." According to Connie, a potential African-American friend would have to "be proud of her race," as well as be a feminist activist. However, Connie indicated that the standards of feminism she applied to African-American lesbians might differ from those applied to White lesbians, in recognition of the cultural differences in how feminism is defined by the two groups.

> Black women are less likely to be tolerant of White lesbian separatist views, for instance. They cannot afford to be isolated from the Black community as a whole. Also, Black women may not identify with White feminist priorities. School desegregation or employment discrimination are more likely to be major concerns for them. White lesbians are often uninterested in those problems or unsympathetic to them—in fact, White lesbians sometimes contribute to those forms of oppression! What I look for in a Black woman, then, is whether she supports issues that bridge the race gap, like reproductive freedom and equal educational opportunities.

In summary, initiating cross-race friendships appeared to add another level of complexity to the usual process of friendship development. The assumption that White women were unlikely to be racially aware inhibited African-American lesbians' interest in establishing friendships with them. White lesbians' standards for feminist commitment, along with their lack of knowledge about African-American women's experiences, made them more tentative about pursuing cross-race relations. As a result, the process of friendship formation was much more gradual than it would be for same-race friendships.

Establishing Trust

Questions about how to establish trust in cross-race friendships formed a second major theme of the interviews. Trust is necessary for close relationships to develop. According to Holmes and Rempel (1989), "Issues of trust have their origins in the dialectic between people's hopes and fears as close relationships develop" (p. 187). As people become more intimate, they become more vulnerable to one another. Trust requires reciprocity and equity (Hendrick and Hendrick, 1992). Reciprocity is present when both people are equally involved in the relationship; equity exists when both are equally benefited by it. Holmes and Rempel (1989) proposed that trust also is based on the belief that your partner will be responsive and even, at times, sacrifice her own self-interest in order to help you. The process of building trust in friendship is fostered by self-disclosure and intimate communications, as well as the buildup of consistent behaviors (Hendrick and Hendrick, 1992). Over time, friends become increasingly secure with each other and reassured about the partner's intentions.

The lesbians we interviewed indicated that the most effective way to build trust in cross-race friendships was to become *allies* against racism. Such an alliance signaled that the two women viewed each other as equal partners in the relationship and that each would keep the lines of communication open about race issues. Little extra effort was required from African-American lesbians to signal their commitment to antiracism, because their involvement in that work typically was obvious. White lesbians, however, had to work to establish their status as allies. They could begin by taking responsibility for their own education about race. To be an ally also required White lesbians to take both public and private stands against racist attitudes and acts, even at the expense of alienating other White people. These actions provided the reassurance African-American lesbians were looking for in cross-race friendships.

The ability of White women to listen nondefensively to African-American lesbians' views of race was considered a hallmark of an ally. For example, Tonya indicated that she knew a White lesbian was a potential friend when she (Tonya) had made a comment about all the Black men on TV being in handcuffs and the woman replied, "That's really fucked up." The woman's lack of defensiveness about hearing racism mentioned was interpreted as a positive sign that the friendship could go forward. Similarly, Lynn, an African-American lesbian, said, "I want respect first, trust later. White lesbians have to learn to hear what Black people are saying. When a woman of color says, 'This is a racist statement,' don't go all defensive. Find out why she said that." Alicia, also an African-American lesbian, echoed that sentiment: "White people aren't used to having to listen and learn from a Black person—they resent being in the 'inferior' position of student. It's important that [potential friends] don't act like they know it all. They need to do a lot of listening."

White lesbians indicated that they were able to establish trust with African-American lesbian friends by developing their listening skills and by not abandoning the relationship as soon as the conversation became uncomfortable. Dana, a White lesbian, explained:

> The first thing in building trust is that there has to be a level of openness and honesty . . . some understanding that who you are—who I am—is based on race and class and that it affects every dynamic between you and another person. There has to be a willingness to talk about those things. . . . Concretely, this means, in my friendship with Tamara [an African-American lesbian], that we have many discussions about fighting racism. . . . We disagree a lot, but I am not willing to retreat from argument because of guilt or fear. This is part of the foundation of trust between us.

Another White lesbian, Janey, also pointed out the importance of responsivity:

> It's important that I be open and honest about myself and my ideas. . . . I might not necessarily agree with a Black friend about them. I know not to shut them [Black lesbians] off. I've learned from African-Americans that I'm not always right. It's important to enjoy each other's company and not have to screen for race. Just to have a free flow. If race comes up, to be able to say it. . . . What I've been hearing lately from Black friends is to be myself. I now don't always have the need to take a particular stand. I own up to who I am and be White.

Responsiveness was seen by White lesbians as extending to the political arena. Most felt strongly that the lack of participation by African-American lesbians in lesbian, gay, and feminist political activities was due to the failure of the (mostly White) organizations who sponsor them to address the concerns of people of color. Marlene, a White lesbian, explained:

> It's actually been hard to involve some friends of color in [lesbian and gay] political work. . . . There's a certain lack of trust from Black women friends. . . . Their issues aren't being addressed. We [the gay community] are leaving people out. I've learned that from my Black friends. I've heard them say, "The Amendment Coalition [to repeal gay/lesbian civil rights] isn't gonna affect me one way or the other. I'm more interested in how much I'm gonna make per hour than worrying about rights I already don't have. Getting involved isn't gonna take care of them." They feel pretty betrayed. That's taught me that we White people really don't get it—we don't get it that it isn't possible to build coalitions without making social change.

A willingness to confront White privilege in oneself or in other White people also was a major indicator that a White lesbian could be trusted. White privilege refers to the advantages that unfairly accrue to White people as a result of racism (McIntosh, 1989). These advantages can range from being served more quickly in a restaurant to getting a job, mortgage, or housing more easily. For Deborah, an African-American lesbian, "The bottom line is for a White lesbian to admit that she has an advantage over me in this society and that it's not fair. . . . In our daily struggle as lesbians, the only thing a White lesbian has to do is put her arm through that of a White man and she has all the benefits and status White society has to offer."

White lesbians were well aware of the requirement that they address their White privilege if they hoped to make cross-race friends. According to Connie, "The White woman must take the lead in building trust. For instance, try not to act White all the time. That is, if something goes wrong, don't take charge because you're used to taking charge as a White person." For Laura, a White lesbian, only a strong personal commitment allows trust to be established:

> Trust comes about by being there when people express that they need support, by challenging racism wherever you see it. If you are a poor

person or a person of color, you don't know if the other [White] person is really on your team. Will she walk away when the comfort zone gets too hot? That's why, when I'm committed, I stay with the program. I've made a long-term commitment to social change. For eight years, I've been involved in housing and health care issues for the poor. You build trust by showing that you're steadfast. You have to show you have a personal stake in it.

In general, White lesbians felt that trust was enhanced when the White person took the initiator role in establishing the friendship; being the initiator also was viewed as well worth the effort. As Dana explained:

There has to be a more conscious attempt to build friendships with African-American lesbians. "I have to work a lot harder to be your friend," I tell my African-American friends. . . . I think that continues to be true [in the relationship]. Even when intimacy is there, it is still a fight to maintain the friendship, because there are so many ways society tries to divide us. You constantly have to bridge the gap. . . . The friendship is constantly being tested. . . . In personal terms, the payoff is worth it—you have the feeling you can really trust someone. . . . My relationships with other White lesbians have been more comfortable, but not as deep.

Another White lesbian, Janey, concurred with Dana. "It's a different kind of trust. Once they're formed, there's a good amount of trust in both White and Black friendships, but there is less screening with White people. Race adds another dimension. I have to work harder at the trust and for a longer time than with White lesbians, especially at the beginning. . . . But I'm looking at that more—easy doesn't mean better."

Race was not always the singular focus for developing trust. Participants recognized the need to establish other common interests. Several African-American lesbians questioned the relevance of race. For instance, Jeanette (aged fifty-six), an African-American lesbian, claimed:

I can't assume anything on the basis of race. You have to remember that I'm fifty-six [years old]. I look for different things in people than when I was twenty, thirty, or forty. . . . I listen to my innards—whether I feel this is a good or bad space or person. I'm extremely trusting of a person who makes me feel good . . . a comfort level. . . . I will pursue that person's friendship. There has to be mutual respect . . . enjoying the same types of things or, if the things we enjoy are different, at least we can respect each other's territory. I prefer friendships where race is not the basis for it. Race is insignificant to me. I don't want to be described as a Black friend—I'd rather be described just as a friend.

Two other African-American lesbians, Deborah and Tonya, also pointed out the need to judge people on an individual basis. Deborah asserted, "There are some White women I would trust before Black women. My brother was killed by a Black cop. Witnesses wouldn't come forward. . . . I learned you can't trust anybody just because they're Black. You can't hate anybody just because they're White. . . . You have to have openness and honesty in any friendship." Tonya also wished not to be judged or judge others based on race, while recognizing that it was not easy to surmount the color barrier:

> I would really like [to see] the day when we don't see color. I don't think race should be a criterion for friendship. It's very possible to have cross-race friendships. I know it's possible, because I have one, Sandra. I've known her for five years. She is the dearest friend. We've been through lots of shit together. It's not easy. It's easier for me to be friends with other African-American lesbians who grew up poor. It's definitely harder to be friends with someone of another race. If you can be friends across race lines, you are really doin' something big.

The path to establishing trust was not always smooth, however. Three inequities or conflicts were identified as common in cross-race friendships, including expectations for African-American lesbians to fill a "nurturer" role, cultural misunderstandings, and racial segregation of social activities. First, a racial dynamic originating in the era of slavery—the expectation that African-American women would fulfill a supportive, nurturing "nanny" role in relation to White women—continued to permeate and cause conflict in African-American and White women's relationships. Renee, an African-American lesbian, explained:

> African-American women have always been the mother figure, the peacekeeper. They have always bounced from one race or class to another. . . . Black women have always been educators, caretakers. We have been able to make Whites feel comfortable. . . . I get angry when I have to soothe them [Whites] to make them comfortable. Why don't I get to be comfortable? . . . We've always been entrusted with White people's children. Even my employer wants me to babysit his kids. History is full of Black women taking care of someone else's business. African-American

lesbian to the rescue! . . . I am a walking, talking example. I'm not a threat to have as a friend. If you had a Black friend, she would be like Renee. . . . I can work it if I have to.

The nurturing role also was imposed on African-American lesbians when it was assumed they would be responsible for teaching White women about race. The inequity of the teacher-student relationship made the African-American lesbians feel "used" and underbenefited in the relationship. As Lynn explained, "The woman of color does most of the education or work [on race issues]. I don't want to do that education." Alicia made a similar point:

> I would have to be ready to commit a certain amount of energy to teaching about race relations in order to be comfortable. . . . I don't expect White people to know a lot about race, but if I have to teach them everything, it's boring. If I was going to get a lot from the relationship, I would be willing to do it—if, for example, they were really trustworthy, a *really* good listener, or owned a ranch with horses. . . . In general, I don't think White women care about having any friends of color. . . . I don't even think they think about it. . . . White women don't want Black women around. It makes things difficult. It makes them uncomfortable. They only want us around if they have certain politics. . . . Then, it's a show of power to have Black friends. It shows they're an expansive person.

White lesbians responded to this issue in their cross-race friendships by assuming responsibility for their own education about race. According to Connie, this could be done by "educating yourself about Black culture—not assuming she sees things the way you do—and getting that across to her." However, this sometimes proved to be difficult, as Janey indicated: "One of my Black friends says [for White people] not to come empty [to the relationship]. I still feel like when I'm myself, I'm coming empty, because that's what it means to be White."

A second source of problems in trust-building pertained to incidents in which White lesbians did something that was interpreted as racist by African-American lesbians. Usually, the incident itself was identified as less important than the resistance the White woman typically had to hearing the African-American lesbian's point of view. Cultural differences in attitudes concerning women's roles, in the use of slang, or in food and clothing preferences all were potential sources of misunderstanding. For example, Lynn, an African-American lesbian, remarked: "One of the major problems I have to deal with [in cross-race friendships] is that I was raised as a free female. I can express my thoughts. A lot of White women can't express their feelings, especially anger, and they don't want me to either. . . . What I think about them is 'You've already got problems with who you are. Why do you want me to be like you?' " Tonya elaborated on the cultural gap:

> I'm frustrated when I have to explain everything because there's a language difference. Black folks have a totally different vocabulary. I mean a word I use to be good, but White people may think it's bad or else they don't understand it *at all!* Or, here I've been saying the same phrase the same way for fifteen years and they correct me because they want me to use 'proper' English. . . . When White people do recognize a cultural difference, it is usually stereotypic. They automatically assume that because I'm Black, I like fried foods, or that I can sing, or that I really must love Anita Baker, or that I know every Black author.

Another African-American lesbian, Jeanette, pointed out problems that sometimes arise when the White friend makes assumptions about how African-Americans have been treated:

> It's irritating when a person assumes I'm going to react a certain way to a situation . . . when they don't take me for my human value. One friend has assumed I wouldn't be offended by a racial slur. Her son called me a racial slur and she corrected him, saying to me, "I know you're used to being called that, but I don't like hearing it." I said, "No, I'm not [used to it]. This is the first time I've ever been called that to my face."

Problems like the ones mentioned above were only resolvable if addressed directly. Several participants mentioned that bringing such incidents to the attention of the friend had led to some very interesting discussions about race sterotypes and cultural racism, as well as to greater intimacy.

A third area of conflict had to do with bridging the social gap between African-Americans and Whites. African-American lesbians perceived White lesbians who failed to extend the friendship from the political to the social arena as being insincere about the friendship. For example, one African-American lesbian, Renee, said:

I have a problem with them [White lesbians] if they don't introduce me to their family . . . if I hear them talking about certain [White] friends, but I never get to meet them . . . if they have a party, but I'm not invited. Don't just invite me to a meeting or workshop, but into your house. . . . What really ticks me off is when White lesbian activists say Black lesbians aren't doing enough politically. It's only been the past two years that they've wanted to include us. You would think that because we're all lesbians we would have a common bond . . . but if you're White, you may get a job before I do. I tell some White women they should check their racism. White lesbians are very defensive. They say, "I could never be racist. I'm a lesbian!" I say, "Sorry, that is not a 'Get out of jail free' card." If you only come to us [Black lesbians] to fulfill your fantasy of diversity, but keep us out of your inner circle, you are a racist lesbian.

However, Renee admitted that it was not always easy to cross the race barrier socially: "I walk the wire with White lesbian friends. I feel more safe with Black lesbian friends. I have had parties where I've invited both worlds. I have to be a little bumblebee between the two. I'm always on this big educational trip, telling each that the other won't bite."

White lesbians sometimes had to make intentional efforts to bridge the social divide. "Many public events are same-race," stated Andy, a White lesbian. "If I go to one of the lesbian dances, it'll be mostly White women. They [the dances] don't attract Black women as much. It's not easy to maintain the social contact. We have to be conscious about partying and playing together. There has to be a deliberate effort to socialize." Socializing together served to solidify cross-race ties. Two White participants specifically mentioned how attending a funeral had positively affected friendships. "A Black friend's father passed away recently," remarked Andy. "Having lost both my parents, it was important for me to go to the funeral. That required moving into her community . . . being one of the few White people there." Likewise, Janey remarked, "My friend Gloria just died. I was the only White person at the gathering after her funeral. I was very accepted. I felt our friendship made that happen. We never skirted race." Another White lesbian, Laura, stressed the importance of mutual efforts to build social ties:

By struggling together about the differences you have, you come to understand, if not accept, those differences. Working and playing together—

getting to know each other as human beings. Knowing they will be there for you, too—that you don't live on a one-way street.

On occasion, cross-race mingling placed the friends in situations where others were hostile or discriminating toward one of the pair. This usually served as a consciousness-raising experience for the White lesbian. Andy, a White lesbian, addressed this issue:

> A main problem with socializing together is the general racism . . . how people may respond to you when you go somewhere [with an African-American friend]. At a restaurant, the [White] waiter may talk to me, not the African-American friend I'm with . . . . It also exposes me to the general level of trauma, stress, and crises that are part and parcel of the lives of several African-American friends . . . of the destruction caused by race and class oppression. Also, within the lesbian community, people feel they have to tell you they're not racist. So it changes the entire dynamic of the friendship. It shuts down the African-American lesbian and some White lesbians, too.

Another White lesbian, Dana, reported similar experiences:

> For most people, seeing an integrated group of people is a rare occurrence, so being with an African-American friend means I have to feel on a practical level the racism any African-American experiences all the time. We can go into a place and be ignored for fifteen minutes by service staff. I never before experienced that at all. It was a shocking experience the first time. You can't take it for granted that you can go to the same places you would with White friends.

The inequities or conflicts described above could be difficult to negotiate because participants often were unsure of the degree to which race, as opposed to individual personality, was a factor. Marlene, a White lesbian, mentioned, "I have to work at deciphering whether a friend's specific response to something is a personal quirk or if it's a cultural difference. If the person is White, I might just assume it's a personality thing. But if the friend is a different race, I might pause." According to Connie, the less familiar territory of cross-race friendships "might look calm, but land mines could be lurking underneath" that could result in both friends being hurt. However, friendships that survived the conflicts were greatly improved. "When the friendship is built across race, it's stronger," Marlene explained. "You're conscious of it. In same-race friendships, there's a lot of unexamined assumptions that may fall apart. There's not the same thoughtful attention to building [a friendship] that will enable you to get through a crisis."

In summary, the foremost way to build trust between African-American and White lesbians was for a White lesbian to demonstrate that she was a racially aware ally of women of color. Both African-American and White lesbians viewed it as necessary for the White woman to initiate the trust-building process in order to balance the inequities created by historic racism. White lesbians also had to be willing to remain loyal to African-American friends, even if it meant confronting other White people. Although other factors besides race were recognized as playing a role in friendship, most participants believed that race and racism would have to be addressed at some point in any cross-race friendship. The consensus was that a cross-race friendship was indeed subject to unique problems but that, if weathered, they often served to strengthen the friendship.

Rewards of Cross-Race Friendships

Friendship research indicates that "somebody to talk to and confide in" and "to be there when you need them" are the primary and interrelated rewards of adult friendship (Rawlins, 1992). It is apparent from the preceding section on building trust that our participants endorsed similar views with a novel twist. The expectations for cross-race friendship required that friends display special sensitivity and loyalty around race matters; these qualities also were perceived to be among the major rewards. However, because of their commitment to antiracist and feminist work, the participants we interviewed went further in assessing their friendships than most people typically do: they also evaluated them from multicultural and political standpoints. Using these broader perspectives, two additional rewards of cross-race friendships were identified: their contribution to (1) developing a greater appreciation for cultural diversity and (2) more effective political organizing. The first reward is one often associated with being at the most advanced level of racial identity development, when cross-cultural interactions are sought out as opportunities for personal growth (Helms, 1990). The second reward was in keeping with the racially inclusive, feminist philosophy espoused by participants.

The first reward, appreciation of cultural diversity, was described as being highly personal in nature. Participants spoke of the impact cross-race friends had on them in tender, serious, and sometimes humorous tones. The exposure to unfamiliar aspects of White culture was especially noted as a reward by African-American lesbians; being able to benefit occasionally from White privilege by being associated with a White person was mentioned as well. For example, in response to the question, "What are the rewards, if any, of cross-race friendships," Renee, an African-American lesbian, replied:

> Hockey tickets. I never went to a hockey game with Black lesbians. They don't do hockey. I get to share more with White lesbians without being downtrodden. I've been told [by White friends] that I have this or that quality and that I should pursue it—not to let skin color hold me back. It's uplifting. They help me recover from being mistreated for being Black. Also, White people talk about things Black people don't. I wouldn't be playing softball, or have joined the —— organizing committee, gone to New York for Stonewall or to the March on Washington. I wouldn't be involved in the political scene. To boil it down, I've gotten a sense of acceptance from White lesbian friends. . . . I feel that I'm bilingual. I can communicate in both communities.

Three other African-American lesbians, Lynn, Tonya, and Jeanette, expanded on the value of being exposed to another culture and sometimes being able to tap White resources through affiliation. According to Lynn, "One advantage of friendships with White lesbians is that you get to have contact with another culture, to know how the other half exists. There might be other advantages, depending on your needs. White financial resources can help. If you want to get into a job, you have to go that way, use your contacts." Similarly, Tonya noted four advantages:

> The first advantage is learning about another culture. It's so weird how differently you [Blacks and Whites] do things. Neither is better. It's good to know how others live and think. Second, having a different perspective is like having a second mind. It's really neat to have two different opinions. Third, it's important for me to have diversity in my life—to not be sheltered. Fourth, to have access to the power White people have: the

White person has the power position and you're their friend. It's like having the inside scoop. They have things I don't have. It's an inside door. It's good.

Jeanette's remarks continued in the same vein:

[One reward is that] sometimes you get the better tables in restaurants. Also, any of the social things. . . . Sometimes if you are shopping, for example, salespeople will treat you differently than if you are alone or with a Black friend. Also, the White friend will know a different set of people, who will introduce you to even more people. There is more sharing in some areas. I enjoy good literature, symphonic music, good musicals. Most African-American women I know don't like that. . . . But, a main advantage is getting a good table at a restaurant and better service from waiters and waitresses.

For White lesbians, appreciation of cultural diversity facilitated a "paradigm shift" in their way of thinking about themselves and the world. "The advantage is in not compartmentalizing yourself— shutting yourself off," insisted Marlene, a White lesbian. "I cannot imagine life in that kind of all-White vacuum anymore." Another White lesbian, Connie, agreed:

My friendships with African-American lesbians have only increased my admiration for African-Americans' cultural and economic contribution to our society. The [African-American] friends I have are so vibrant, wise, and loving that it has made me aware—and sometimes deeply ashamed— of how much being White has cut me off from what is truly significant in life—from seeing our common humanity, as well as from learning to negotiate our differences and, if possible, to love and value them.

Other White lesbians provided specific examples of how exposure to African-American culture had affected them. For Andy:

One advantage is that it expands my community and my understanding of the world we live in and how we got to where we are. I get to rub my fingers through some really cool hair. I find that African-American lesbians are more physically affectionate [than White lesbians]. It's not sexual. That has been one of the wonderful advantages. I have created with these women a different sense of space—physicality—and I love it and them. I appreciate being challenged. I love spending time with them. That's not specific to race.

Laura also identified cultural awareness as being among the most important advantages of cross-race friendships:

They [cross-race friendships] have given me a lot of opportunities to learn and grow. I would never have had the experience of going into a Baptist church and hearing the preacher and the singing and seeing the type of support it [church] provides if I didn't have African-American friends—or of knowing the meaning of Kwaanza as a celebration—or of going into African-American bars and understanding butch-femme roles when I came out. They're definitely different from White bars. . . . There also is a certain amount of strength to know it's okay to get loud and express yourself with a certain amount of passion. It gives you a clearer under-standing of what's at stake and gives you reinforcement to get in the face of who is opposing you.

The enjoyment associated with learning about others was apparent in Janey's description of advantages as well:

The biggest advantage has been learning from other people's culture. It's enriched my friendships. I've had the same kinds of friendships with [White] people like me for years. . . . I really have enjoyed learning the differences in family—celebration, rules, structure, what people talk about at family gatherings, how they play. The most recent incident was when I went to Valerie's family's—her cousin's—house. I was worried about what I was going to eat (I'm a vegetarian) and not offend her family. So Valerie calls her cousin and says for my benefit, "Well, what kind of food are you going to have?" "Well," responded her cousin, "Black folks' food. What do you think?" Basically, it was nothing I could eat. Then Valerie said, "Oh, I was asking for Janey, 'cuz she's a vegetarian." Then her cousin mentioned a couple of things she'd be having that I could eat. She didn't try to change anything to please me. I thought about White gatherings and how I would've expected my family to fix individual things. I enjoyed her response—she didn't tiptoe around. She just said, "Black folks' food." They were very welcoming. They just did whatever they intended to do. I enjoyed being let into their community.

The second major reward related specifically to cross-race friend-ships had to do with their positive effect on participants' political work. African-American lesbians reported that such ties made a sig-nificant difference in terms of how connected they felt to mixed-race organizations. As Tonya stated, "It's always good to have a White person sitting beside you, thinking the same way, trying to convince White and Black folks of the importance of antiracist work." Like-wise, as Lynn, also an African-American lesbian, pointed out, "If there is a friendship at all, it must've happened during the political process, when you saw eye to eye. But if there is a power struggle, there could be problems. The people in the two antiracism groups I've been in have been loving, caring. They wanted to effect change. They weren't involved in a power struggle."

Alternatively, working together promoted opportunities for friendship. "Political work has made the friendships more secure," explained Jeanette, an African-American lesbian. "Our topic is antiracism. We can talk about things that really hurt—what we feel. That makes us feel good. The antiracism group helps to seal friendships. Some people who came in the beginning were standoffish, especially White women. They've really changed—they see we're not so different after all." Deborah, also African-American, described similar advantages of friendships with White lesbians. "There are obvious political advantages," she explained, "but friendships are so valuable, regardless of where you get them. . . . It helps the organization if there is a friendship. You just need a common goal. My political work has helped form friendships. I don't want to use the line, 'One of my best friends is a White woman,' but one of my best friends is Pam [a White woman]. I know if I call her, she'll be there." Appreciation for White women's political contribution also was a consequence of shared political work for one African-American lesbian, Renee, who asserted, "These White ladies have been doing this political work for a long time. They have tools and knowledge. I can show up with my two cents and I don't have to start from scratch. Don't throw out what they have done. They need our validity, our new blood. I want to add to that."

White lesbians reported tremendous enthusiasm concerning how cross-race friendships had affected their political involvement, too, or at the very least, added to their understanding of why racial integration was difficult to achieve in the political arena. Janey, a White lesbian, elaborated:

> In the past, my political work has suffered from not having real, honest, and long-term relationships with people from different races. That's why I stepped back for a few years; it's part of the reason I wanted to join an antiracism group. I operated as the Great White Hope. I read, I knew, I could change things. One-light-bulb-changes-the-world type of thing. I would read a lot about African-American history and culture and would assume what I was doing politically was right. But the piece I was missing

was real friendships and real collaborative work with African-American lesbians. How the friendships affect my political work. . . . That's probably the biggest area that was missing. The friendships I have now give me the information, impetus, motivation to do better political work—more honest political work. And to be able to have friendships beyond political work! . . . I'm finding that I value that more. Friendship enables it all to come together.

Andy reported a similar effect on her activism: "My cross-race friendships and my political work are totally interconnected. That's true of all my friendships. . . . Working in a multiracial organization has only improved the political work that I'm involved in. It has certainly challenged this White girl to look at things that I had no idea about. It's scary *and* exciting. It's moving me toward the world I want to see." However, another White lesbian, Laura, was more tempered in her assessment of the connection between friendship and politics:

I would like to say that it has strengthened some of the work I do, but I often don't believe that's true. I now am more understanding about why African-American lesbians fail to be politically committed in the way I think they should. I understand their hesitation to jump in the middle of a bunch of White people and be tokenized. I wish more people of color would come forward and kick the asses of White lesbians and gay men and take their rightful place, but I understand that they don't.

Overall, the lesbians interviewed perceived that cross-race friendships had contributed to both their personal and political growth. Personal growth was reflected primarily in terms of enhancing awareness of cultural diversity, including being exposed to the other race's tastes, interests, social patterns, and (in the case of Whites) privileges. Political growth accompanied the friendships in terms of increased commitment to individuals and organizations promoting antiracist, multicultural social agendas.

Conclusions

The way cross-race friendships operated for our participants appears to be an excellent example of the feminist slogan, "The personal is political," in action. The lesbians we interviewed took seriously the idea that racism affected both African-American and White people.

The effects of racism on African-Americans included prejudice and discrimination on an economic, social, and cultural level. For Whites, racism resulted in being miseducated about the contributions of African-Americans, being denied the opportunity to appreciate other cultures without a false sense of superiority (e.g., "White is right"), and seeing oneself as having an individual identity, but not a racial identity (see, e.g., Katz, 1978). At their best, cross-race friendships were seen as healing some of the pain of racism for African-American lesbians, or at least providing a temporary reprieve from it, as well as playing an important role in developing White lesbians' awareness of their racial identity and the privileges and cultural limitations associated with it.

According to Pat O'Connor (1992, p. 21), friendship research has described the ways in which friendships not only meet individual needs but also create "a moral discourse between friends." Applied to the cross-race friendships examined here, the moral discourse of racial equality contributed to creating a universe where participants could enact their vision on both a personal and political level. Thus, our research provides evidence that the feminist notion of sisterhood, if realized, could challenge traditional status hierarchies concerning race. However, it is also apparent from our interviews that the path to such relationships is arduous. One could not simply decide to seek out a cross-race friendship in order to achieve the rewards described here. Cross-race friendships have additional responsibilities associated with them that are not present in same-race friendships. For the African-American lesbians in our sample, they required a willingness to assume, if not a nurturer-teacher role, at least a more patient commitment to the friendship. The White lesbians we interviewed who wanted cross-race friends had to assume the initiator role in the friendship and a significant amount of responsibility for educating themselves about their own racism and racial identity.

Our results suggest that women's cross-race friendships potentially have the power, as Janice Raymond (1986, p. 339) has suggested, "to help tie women's lives together, to make connections that have not been made, and to provide a unifying and directing influence in all other areas of female existence in this world." They also illustrate that "both politics and friendship are restored to a deeper meaning when they are brought together," that is, "when political activity proceeds from a shared affection, vision, and spirit, and when friendship has a more expansive political effect" (p. 339). Clearly, "sisterhood"—if obtained—is powerful. Whether we obtain it, on either an individual or larger political scale, however, is up to us.

NOTES

1. Gratitude is extended to the members of the St. Louis Anti-Racism Group and other community participants and to the Association for Women in Psychology, for creating a space to confront and challenge racism.
2. If a participant is initially identified by her full name, the name is authentic. If initial identification is by first name only, it is a pseudonym.

REFERENCES

Argyle, M., and M. Henderson. 1984. The rules of friendship. *Journal of Social and Personal Relationships* 1: 211–37.

Cross, W. E., Jr. 1991. *Shades of black: Diversity in African-American identity.* Philadelphia: Temple University Press.

Derlega, V. J., and B. A. Winstead, eds. 1986. *Friendship and social interaction.* New York: Springer-Verlag.

Duck, S. 1991. *Understanding relationships.* New York: Guilford Press.

Frankenberg, R. 1993. *White women, race matters: The social construction of whiteness.* Minneapolis: University of Minnesota Press.

Hays, R. B. 1984. The development and maintenance of friendship. *Journal of Social and Personal Relationships* 6: 21–37.

Helms, J. E., ed. 1990. *Black and white racial identity: Theory, research, and practice.* Westport, CT: Greenwood.

Hendrick, S., and C. Hendrick. 1992. *Liking, loving, and relating.* 2d ed. Pacific Grove, CA: Brooks, Cole.

Holmes, J. G., and J. K. Rempel. 1989. Trust in close relationships. In C. Hendrick, ed., *Close relationships,* pp. 187–220. Newbury Park, CA: Sage.

hooks, b. 1990. *Yearning: Race, gender, and cultural politics.* Boston: South End Press.

Katz, J. H. 1978. *White awareness: Handbook for anti-racism training.* Norman: University of Oklahoma Press.

Lorde, A. 1981. The uses of anger. Keynote address to the National Women's Studies Association Conference, June, Hartford, CT.

Mays, V. M., S. D. Cochran, and S. Rhue. 1993. The impact of perceived discrimination on the intimate relationships of black lesbians. *Journal of Homosexuality* 25: 1–14.

McIntosh, P. 1989. White privilege: Unpacking the invisible knapsack. *Peace and Freedom,* July/August, pp. 10–12.

O'Connor, P. 1992. *Friendships between women: A critical review.* Newbury Park, CA: Sage.

Pratt, M. B. 1991. *Rebellion: Essays 1980–1991.* Ithaca, NY: Firebrand Books.

Rawlins, W. K. 1992. *Friendship matters: Communication, dialectics, and the life course.* New York: Aldine De Gruyter.

Raymond, J. 1986. *A passion for friends: Toward a philosophy of female affection.* Boston: Beacon Press.

Rose, S., and L. Roades. 1987. Feminism and women's friendships. *Psychology of Women Quarterly* 11: 243–54.

Segrest, M. 1994. *Memoir of a race traitor.* Boston: South End Press.

Smith, B., and M. Karp. 1988. Addressing racism in lesbian/gay organizations. Workshop presented at the National Gay and Lesbian Task Force "Creating Change" Conference, November, Washington, D.C.

THIRTEEN

Well Worn Conversations

DIANE M. FELICIO

Eileen called me last night. We had not spoken in over a week, because I was out of town, on vacation with my new girlfriend. It is rare for such a long period of time to elapse between our conversations. Without fail, Eileen and I talk at least once a week, rarely for less than one hour and often longer, usually on Saturday or Sunday mornings. During our current conversation, Eileen spoke of the disappointment she has felt in her attempts to build new friendships. She expressed how thankful she was for the quality of our friendship and how grounded and sane it has been throughout the years. She explained that although she did not want to replace me, she felt a sense of sadness about not having more quality friendships in her life.

Eileen is a White, middle-class, Irish Catholic speech and language pathologist living in New York City and I am a White, middle-class, Italian Catholic college professor living in Vermont. Eileen and I have been friends since high school and are both now in our early thirties. I think it is safe to say we are best friends. I never thought that my friendship with Eileen, a lesbian/heterosexual friendship, would be considered a *phenomenon* or something other people would actually be interested in or curious about.

Eileen and I met through some mutual high school friends around 1978 or 1979. We attended a Catholic high school for girls in Rockaway Beach, New York. Eileen was one year ahead of me. I remember smoking cigarettes together—Parliaments, I think. We would talk and smoke on the bus during our thirty-minute ride home from school. Imagine, well over one hundred girls in plaid skirts, white shirts, and polyester vests packed on a city bus, shoulder to shoulder, smoking, talking, singing, crying, and laughing.

We were not allowed to wear jeans to or from school, and wearing argyle socks was cause for being brought to the sock closet by Sister Consuela, a very tall nun with a diagonal posture who roamed the halls in full habit, searching for uniform don'ts. In the infamous sock closet, argyles were replaced by their appropriate solid-color alternatives: brown, grey, maroon, or navy, depending on your year in school. I remember our beloved principal imploring us over the public address system not to listen to the Billy Joel song "Only the Good Die Young," with lyrics proclaiming that Catholic girls "start much too late." Of course, we all knew that we started having sex along with the rest of our teenage peers, well before marriage. Yet somehow we knew that our places in heaven were secure, since we had already spent time in Purgatory, running from Sister Consuela in our plaid skirts, wool socks, and polyester vests.

It was within this context that my friendship with Eileen began. Our conversations on the bus were often followed by phone calls as soon as we arrived home. We would talk for hours at a time. I remember my mother screaming from the other room, "You just saw Eileen! What could you possibly have to talk about? Get off that phone!" There was always more to say. We would talk about politics and world events. We would analyze a topic until we were sure we had covered all the bases. We would analyze sentences, even words, until we reached a mutual understanding of the subject in question. As the years progressed, we found ourselves discussing more personal issues, like family dynamics, work, school, and our relationships with other friends.

These conversations rarely felt like gossip. Rather, through these conversations about others, and our reactions to the lives of others, we got to know ourselves. Although I often had similar conversations with other friends, it was only with Eileen that I discussed the political implications of an event. We shared an interest in the world beyond ourselves (quite a leap for two teenagers), and we were certain that if we had control, the world would be a very different place.

As you might imagine, being a lesbian in a Catholic high school for girls posed many heart-wrenching and complicated dilemmas. In the early days of my coming out, I did not know that loving one woman meant that I was a lesbian. A lesbian was someone who was gay all of the time; she had many girlfriends, just as the other girls had many boyfriends. At that time, there was only one girl in my life, and I believed it would always be that way. It sounds cliché, but something in Karla's eyes brought my heart to life. Before I saw her milling about outside the student cafeteria, my dreams about love and sex were limited to the guys at the park and that once-in-a-lifetime chance of meeting Al Pacino in an elevator.

I have always felt that my lesbian identity development did not match the experiences I have heard other lesbians describe. I did not feel "different" growing up, I loved playing with Barbie dolls, I did not have a crush on my gym teacher, and I never wanted to be a boy. My lesbian awakening seemed much more abrupt and lacking in the early signs often written about in lesbian poetry and discussed at lesbian potlucks. I saw Karla and something shifted. I remember the moment well.

I guess you could say that Karla and I were in a "relationship." We never called it that, but we would hug and kiss and we spent one night in bed together at a friend's sleep-over. It was during that night that I realized I had a lot to learn about being sexually involved with a woman. Karla seemed to know everything already. I remember feeling at once joyous and awkward. Unfortunately, our relationship was fraught with many unanticipated struggles. Karla was confused about her sexuality, and like so many young lesbians and gay men she dealt with this confusion by continually hurting herself. I was her caretaker. When she would ignore her school work, I wrote her papers. When she would cry, I would hold her. When she would disappear, I would find her. I was convinced she was going to kill herself. Then, although she wanted me to take care of her, she began sleeping with other girls willing to take the risk. I was devastated.

For reasons I still cannot explain, I never thought of myself as sick or weird for feeling attracted to and loving Karla. At the same time Karla was struggling with being a lesbian, I was struggling to protect our secret. In fact, I thought my friends, teachers, and family members were overreacting to a very normal situation: I was a teenager in love. I knew my parents suspected something, particularly my mother, who prides herself on her intuitive powers. Although I never admitted to being in a relationship with Karla, my parents did whatever they could to limit my time with her. My phone calls were monitored, they would not drive me to her home (so I walked quite a distance), and they were blatantly rude when she would visit.

To my surprise, one night at a family gathering I will never forget, I was confronted. Everyone, including my parents, brothers, and sisters-in-law sat in a circle around the living room. They said therapy was the answer. I agreed to go, not because I thought I had a "problem," but because I was confused and in pain. I knew I was losing Karla. Luckily, my first experience with therapy was very positive. To my parents' chagrin, my therapist was supportive of my relationship with Karla, and although I do not remember many details, I do know that she had no intention of changing me.

Amidst this backdrop of parental distrust and undue scrutiny, my friendship with Eileen was beginning to develop. In a recent phone conversation, Eileen recalled that she did not consider me a lesbian during our high school years. She explained that because of her own relaxed attitude about sexuality, she viewed my connection with Karla as a "normal" adolescent experience. She had also known of other young women dealing with the same issues. I believe it was my perception of this open-mindedness that drew me to Eileen. As a young woman taking steps toward the forbidden zone (i.e., lesbianism), I knew Eileen would not pass any judgments or make any assumptions about my goodness. She was safe. In reality, we never discussed the specifics of my relationship with Karla until several years later, when I finally discovered the hidden language of lesbian culture. Eileen seemed to have the language already. In those days, I always felt that I had a lot of catching up to do.

Now comes the part where I am supposed to say that one night, after too much to drink, Eileen and I fell into each other's arms proclaiming our passionate attraction and undying love for each other. According to lesbian lore that should have been the next step. To make matters worse, Eileen was a gym leader, and every Meg Christian fan knows what that means! Well, such a love scene never took place. Eileen and I have never been romantically involved. In fact, she has always identified herself as heterosexual and she has never explored sexual relationships with women. Of course I recognize that Eileen's heterosexuality need not prevent me from feeling attracted to her, but suffice it to say that the richness of our relationship has grown from a definitively nonsexual intimate involvement.

Although I had my first lesbian experience when we were in high school together, I never thought about Eileen in *those* terms. Rather, I recognized early on that she was an ally, and informed enough to understand the nature of what I was going through. Today, fifteen years beyond our early conversations, Eileen remains one of my strongest allies. Although I have many loving and supportive lesbian friends, I continue to turn to Eileen for advice about my romantic entanglements, and she continues to seek council from me in her endless struggle to find a "good" man. We continue to analyze conversations and sentences, we still process the decisions our other friends have made, and we still look at the world through the lenses of a cynic. In many ways, our friendship has not changed at all. Yet change, particularly change that results from growth and maturity, is inevitable in any long-term relationship.

The changes that have occurred in my relationship with Eileen have been silent ones; changes that are not obvious at first glance, but nonetheless continue to affect our perspectives, attitudes, opinions, and beliefs. Having matured in a culture that wrestles with questions like "Why do lesbians hate men?" and "How can you be a feminist and sleep with men?" I am sure that we have brought and continue to bring some powerful biases and assumptions into our relationship. For instance, for quite some time I have wondered if Eileen is a lesbian. For years I have listened to her lament her experiences with men, and I have speculated that her dissatisfaction stems from a genuine lack of interest in men. Despite some good friendships with men, she has always found it difficult to trust them. Furthermore, the few intimate (i.e., sexual) relationships she has had have lacked the depth and mutual love I know she wants in her life.

This is not a case of a partnered friend finding it difficult to understand how her single friend could possibly be happy without candy, flowers, and monogrammed "hers & ?" towels. I am aware that many single heterosexual women and lesbians live happy and full lives. I am also aware that "single" is not synonymous with "lonely" (see Hochman, 1994, for alternative views on partnership and single life). However, Eileen has made it clear that she desires a strong and healthy partnership with another person. Unfortunately, despite her own personal growth and development, she has been repeatedly disappointed by the men she has met and dated.

In contrast, I have watched Eileen develop some very intimate friendships with women. I have felt the love she has experienced for these women, and I have witnessed the pain she has felt when abandoned by women she has cared for and trusted. She has spent time with my lesbian lovers and other lesbian friends and I have felt the fit. When she talks about being in love, I hear a description of lesbian love (depth, companionship, passion, mutuality); when she talks about creating community, I hear her describe what I know of lesbian community.

I often wonder if Eileen will ever see the connections I see. Will she ever discover her own hidden secret? Can she be open to the discovery, given the family dynamics she would inevitably confront? Eileen was raised in a strict Irish Catholic household that espoused clear rules about marrying one's own kind (e.g., no Jews or Blacks). She learned early that family secrets were not to be openly discussed, and shameful acts were to be avoided entirely. Being a lesbian counts as a shameful act.

Still, is it fair for me to assume that because Eileen's desires appear to resonate with *my* image of lesbian existence, she is a lesbian? I have assumed that Eileen's dissatisfaction with men could mean that she is a lesbian, as if being a lesbian is about being dissatisfied with men. I have assumed that Eileen's lesbianism is something I could know about before she has recognized it for herself, as if I know her better than she knows herself. I have assumed that Eileen's lesbianism

is a secret that lies hidden away passively awaiting discovery, as if
there is anything passive about being a lesbian. In essence, I believe I
am doing Eileen and myself an injustice by assuming that being a
lesbian is as simple as making some profound discovery about oneself. A lesbian existence involves more than self-discovery; it is a
matter of constructing a life (Phelan, 1993).

I understand that many lesbians and gay men ascribe to the belief
that their sexuality was predetermined, either genetically or hormon-
ally, upon conception. Although there has been much evidence both
to support and to refute this and other hypotheses about the origins
of sexuality (see Money, 1993), coming to a lesbian life (as opposed
to coming out) does not happen automatically. Like Blasius (1992), I
believe that while one's sexuality may be a basic element of one's
being, how one reacts to and lives with this basic element is a matter
of choice. More specifically, as a lesbian, a woman accepts or rejects
a community and in turn is accepted or rejected by that community.
As Ferguson (1990) suggests, along with an objective definition of
culture, which involves the sharing of common social attributes,
there is also a subjective definition of culture, an "identity sense,"
that requires that one be acknowledged by oneself and others as
being a part of that culture.

Coming out as lesbian also involves facing important questions
about sexual behavior. While it is possible for a woman to identify as
lesbian without being sexually active (Rothblum and Brehony, 1993),
sex is often an important part of lesbian relationships (see Morris,
1994, for a discussion of sexual behavior and the coming out process). There are many opinions about what lesbian sex is and what it
could (should?) be. For instance, Hall (1993) and Frye (1990) suggest
that we (i.e., lesbians) should broaden our definition of what
"counts" as sex by thinking beyond the centrality of genital stimulation. But, as offspring of a heterocentric culture, women have been
exposed to a *limited* set of scripts instructing us on our role as sexual
beings, and many of these scripts depict women as victims of male
hatred and violence. Therefore, along with a significant cultural shift,
living a lesbian life demands a comprehensive rethinking of sexual
intimacy and sexual desire.

Given the complexity of constructing a lesbian life, how can I alone determine if Eileen is a lesbian? How can I know if she has any interest in joining a lesbian community? What if she has no interest in being sexual with other women? Most importantly, what does it mean that I do not trust Eileen's own definition of herself? In her discussion of postmodern lesbian politics, Phelan (1993) notes the danger in coming to universalized conclusions about the nature of lesbian existence to the exclusion of more contextualized understandings. She maintains that "doing justice to people requires attention to the specific voice(s) or language(s) in which they speak and to what they are saying" (p. 778). The claims I have made about Eileen's sexuality have been based on heterocentric notions of lesbian life (e.g., a woman who is not with a man must be a lesbian). In addition, these claims have been fueled by my own assumptions about the quality of heterosexual relationships: if Eileen wants depth, companionship, passion, and mutuality, she will find it with a woman, not a man. A universalized conclusion.

Recently, I began to appreciate the significance of what I once thought were harmless musings about Eileen. If Eileen had not trusted my recognition of my lesbianism, I would have felt betrayed, hurt, and angry. Yet, for some reason, I have not trusted her recognition of her heterosexuality. At first I was disappointed in myself for assigning a label to Eileen that she herself did not embrace. I felt that I must not be listening to her or giving due weight to the context of her life and the wants and needs that she has expressed. However, after some thought, I realized I derived a subtle sense of satisfaction from expecting Eileen to convince me that she is heterosexual. Although I see the danger in falling prey to stereotypic views of what it means to be a lesbian, I enjoy not taking Eileen's heterosexuality for granted. I like that I could ask her the kinds of questions typically posed to lesbians and gay men: "When did you first realize you were attracted to men?" "If you have sex with only one man, does that mean you are heterosexual?" "How do you know this is not just a phase you are going through?" Although my questions are raised somewhat tongue in cheek, I do believe that there is merit in examining the choices our friends have made about their lives, particularly choices regarding lifestyle and community affiliations. Moreover, questioning the nature of Eileen's "compulsory" heterosexuality (Rich, 1980) helps to demystify the conservative heterosexual agenda that has deemed lesbianism an anomaly (Phelan, 1993).

Yet, I fear that I may be guilty of the same identity bashing that I have fought so hard to withstand. To a certain degree, I have adopted the practice of labeling something as deviant (Eileen's heterosexuality) simply because it transgresses some arbitrary definition of "normal." On the other hand, I do believe there is a significant sociopolitical difference between questioning someone's heterosexuality and questioning someone's lesbianism. In questioning Eileen's heterosexuality, I was hoping to initiate a *broader* examination of her sexual identity by presenting lesbianism as a valid life choice. In contrast, when others have questioned my lesbianism they have initiated a limited examination of my sexual identity by denying the validity of my choice.

Still, by doubting Eileen's choice to live a heterosexual life I have challenged the person who has extended to me her unshakable trust and devotion. Clearly, what was once a seemingly apolitical friendship has grown into a friendship replete with ideological and philosophical questions, not the least of which is, would I feel closer to Eileen if she were lesbian? Perhaps my tendency to question Eileen's heterosexuality has come from my own need to feel that we are part of the same community.

June 26, 1994 was the twenty-fifth anniversary of the Stonewall riots in New York City. I asked Eileen if she would like to march with me in the parade commemorating this historical event. She accepted. We marched together down Fifth Avenue, proudly displaying our "Stonewall 25" flag, hissing at the Fundamentalist Christians who were waving signs that read "Faggots!" and "Homosexuality is an abomination." The day after the march Eileen asked me if I had a good time. She also asked if I thought I would have had a better time had I attended the march with a lesbian friend instead of with her. I think, in her own way, Eileen was asking me if I would feel closer to her if she were lesbian.

I was stunned by her question and offered a hasty response about not knowing how I would have felt had I marched with a lesbian friend. Looking back, I realize that this was a cowardly response. At moments during the march I did find myself wanting the company of my lesbian friends. I loved being there with Eileen, but somehow I did not feel the passion of the day that I imagined I would have felt had I been marching with other lesbians.

Perhaps it makes sense that I did not feel completely fulfilled by attending the march with Eileen, my heterosexual friend. How could she possibly understand the depth of my oppression as a lesbian? The Stonewall celebration was meant to symbolize the progress lesbians and gays have made during the last twenty-five years, yet I still cannot hold my lover's hand in public without the fear of being glared at or physically harmed. Eileen has not felt this humiliation. Eileen has not known the sorrow that comes from people making false assumptions about who you are, who you are partnered with, and the community you have chosen to identify with. Nonetheless, I was surprised by my dissatisfaction. Somehow, I had fashioned in my mind an image of Eileen and me at the march engaging equally in the meaning of the day. When that did not occur, I felt myself wanting the company of my lesbian friends.

I called Eileen last night. I wanted to talk with her about how sad I had been feeling about my endless job search and how hard it has been to maintain my sense of self-worth while receiving one polite rejection after another. As usual, Eileen provided the self-esteem boost I needed. We also talked about the Stonewall march, and Eileen expressed how impressed she was with the crowd and with the way we all handled the Fundamentalist Christians mocking us in the street. Although our verbal retorts served an important purpose, our strongest message came from our unwillingness to stop marching. We never stopped moving forward. It was during that conversation that I realized that Eileen and I did share equally in the Stonewall festivities. Clearly, we did not have identical experiences, but it struck me that Eileen was greatly responsible for my being at the march in the first place. Had Eileen not been the ally that I needed during the early years of my coming out, I may never have had the strength or courage to keep moving forward with my own process of embracing a lesbian identity. Risks are not nearly as scary when you have a portable safety net. I am not saying that my coming out was pain-free. Far from it. But knowing that Eileen was providing a reliable stronghold made taking some giant steps a little bit easier.

So, would I feel even closer to Eileen if she were a lesbian? I believe that as long as Eileen and I continue to share ourselves with each other we will get closer. This may sound easy, but in actuality the matters confronting our relationship get more and more challenging. In recent years, we have discussed our different opinions about financial matters, child rearing (even though neither of us has children), work priorities, professional ethics, safer-sex practices, partnerships, careers, etc. I am certain that we would talk about these matters, and probably still have different views about them, regardless of Eileen's sexual orientation.

In my view, we have yet to face our ultimate challenge: What will come of us if and when Eileen has a steady male partner in her life? I believe the presence of a man in *our* puzzle will make the political, social, and economic differences between us even more apparent. How will he react? Will we all appear on an episode of "Oprah" discussing "Husbands Who Can't Cope with Their Wives' Lesbian Friends?" In my heart, I know that Eileen would never get romantically involved with a man who was blatantly homophobic. But wouldn't many heterosexual men have some twinge about my sexuality and my friendship with Eileen? How will Eileen handle this? Can our friendship withstand the potential pain?

As much as lesbian friends have to cope with new partners coming and going, there remains a sense, often unacknowledged, of lesbian community and culture. Eileen and I have not been enclosed by this shared boundary. But, since my lovers have all been women, the threats to our friendship have involved factors that have so far been easily negotiated, like the amount of time we spend together. However, once a man enters the picture, I expect we will be confronted by factors that are not so easily negotiated, like the status and privilege that come from being a heterosexual woman partnered with a heterosexual man—a privilege which, in my experience, is even more powerful than any privilege granted to single heterosexual women. Our relationship may (will?) change. Worst case scenario: Eileen meets a man, falls in love, lives for nobody else but him, has three children, moves to the lovely Long Island suburbs, and calls me once a year, for my birthday. Yikes! Okay, so maybe I am overreacting. Maybe I am blowing things out of proportion. But privilege can be a powerful intruder, especially when you least expect its influence.

Would I feel closer to Eileen if she were a lesbian? I don't think so. Eileen's involvement with a lesbian would bring its own dilemmas: there would be another woman in her life. I wonder if I would be able to handle the "competition" is as well as she has? Realistically, I have no idea what the future will bring, regardless of Eileen's partner of choice. What I do know is that the quality and longevity of our friendship rests on the honesty, integrity, and history that we bring to it.

There has been much written in the lesbian and feminist press about the importance of "building bridges" and constructing alliances within and across race, gender, ethnicity, sexual orientation, etc. (e.g., hooks, 1984; Phelan, 1993; Pheterson, 1990). As much as I support and often participate in these community-building events, my relationship with Eileen has taught me that nothing can take the place of history. I know that we have some struggles ahead, but I have no doubt that we will grow old together. In fact, every time Eileen and I see elderly women at the movies, or shopping, or telling secrets over tea and muffins, we glance at one another knowingly, laugh, and talk about how that will be us one day. We also argue about who is going to die first, because neither one of us wants to be left without the other. Would my friendship with Eileen be any different if she were a lesbian? Of course. Would I feel closer to Eileen if she were a lesbian? Not necessarily.

REFERENCES

Blasius, M. 1992. An ethos of lesbian and gay existence. *Political Theory* 20: 642–71.
Ferguson, A. 1990. Is there a lesbian culture? In J. Allen, ed., *Lesbian philosophies and cultures*, pp. 63–88. New York: State University of New York Press.

Frye, M. 1990. Lesbian "sex." In J. Allen, ed., *Lesbian philosophies and cultures,* pp. 305–15. New York: State University of New York Press.

Hall, M. 1993. "Why limit me to ecstasy?" Toward a positive model of genital incidentalism among friends and other lovers. In E. D. Rothblum and K. A. Brehony, eds., *Boston marriages: Romantic but asexual relationships among contemporary lesbians,* pp. 43–61. Amherst: University of Massachusetts Press.

Hochman, A. 1994. *Everyday acts and small subversions: Women reinventing family, community, and home.* Portland, OR: Eighth Mountain Press.

hooks, b. 1984. Sisterhood: Political solidarity between women. In b. hooks, ed., *Feminist theory: From margin to center,* pp. 43–65. Boston: South End Press.

Money, J. 1993. Sin, sickness, or status? Homosexual gender identity and psychoneuroendocrinology. In L. D. Garnets and D. C. Kimmel, eds., *Psychological perspectives on lesbian and gay male experiences,* pp. 130–67. New York: Columbia University Press.

Morris, J. F. 1994. Lesbian coming out as a multidimensional process. Manuscript, University of Vermont, Burlington.

Phelan, S. 1993. (Be)coming out: Lesbian identity and politics. *Signs* 18: 765–90.

Pheterson, G. 1990. Alliances between women: Overcoming internalized oppression and internalized domination. In L. Albrecht and R. M. Brewer, eds., *Bridges of power: Women's multicultural alliances,* pp. 34–48. Philadelphia: New Society Publishers.

Rich, A. 1980. Compulsory heterosexuality and lesbian existence. *Signs* 5: 631–60.

Rothblum, E. D., and K. A. Brehony. 1993. Introduction: Why focus on romantic but asexual relationships among lesbians? In E. D. Rothblum and K. A. Brehony, eds., *Boston marriages: Romantic but asexual relationships among contemporary lesbians,* pp. 3–13. Amherst: University of Massachusetts Press.

FOURTEEN

Negotiating Difference: The Friendship of a Lesbian-Identified Woman and a Heterosexual Man

KAREN CONNER AND MARK COHAN

Friendship takes many forms. Popular culture is filled with the images and scenarios of the friendships of adolescent boys and preteen girls. Friendships among adults have also found a place on television and in feature films, including friendships between heterosexual women (e.g., *Cagney and Lacey, Kate and Allie, Thelma and Louise*), between heterosexual men (e.g., *Full House, Lethal Weapon*), between heterosexual women and heterosexual men (e.g., *Seinfeld, The Big Chill*), and even between heterosexual women and gay men (e.g, *Threesome, Victor/Victoria, Melrose Place*). Another, perhaps less-acknowledged, form a friendship can take is the type we have: a friendship between a lesbian-identified woman and a heterosexual man.

Although we would not presume to say how common or uncommon are friendships between lesbian women and heterosexual men, few would argue with the notion that they tend to be less visible than other types of friendships (e.g., those between heterosexual men). This virtual invisibility of friendships such as ours was one of the important factors that motivated us to tell our story. We feel it is important for people to recognize that gay women and straight men can and do form strong, lasting friendships. Though our friendship is relatively young (spanning just over three years), our experiences have required us to confront a number of concerns relating to our differing sexual orientations, concerns about the salience of sexual orientation per se, about sexual tension between friends, about how a gay-straight friendship fits into each individual's circle of friends, and about how our differing sexual orientation may lead to experiential gulfs between friends.

As we began planning this paper, we were both adamant that we wanted to present our relationship as we experience it, as an equal partnership. With that goal in mind, we wrote the majority of the text of this contribution together and in one voice. To begin with, however, we felt we should each first tell something of ourselves as individuals.

KAREN: I am a twenty-six-year-old native of Texas and a doctoral candidate in the counseling psychology program at the University of Florida. I have been "out" as a lesbian for approximately six years and "out" as a lesbian-identified bisexual for one of those six years. I suppose I include my year of bisexual identification within my six years of lesbian identification because I feel very "lesbian" and it would be dishonest to imply that I no longer identify as such. It seems I currently identify as both "lesbian" and "lesbian-identified bisexual."

MARK: I am twenty-six years old and have just begun my second year of graduate work in sociology at the University of Florida. My goal is to get my Ph.D. and pursue an academic career that will include both teaching and research. While I was working on my undergraduate degree and during several subsequent years when I was out of academia, I was a part-time political activist. Most of my activism during those years was in support of abortion rights and on behalf of local campaigns to combat violence against women. In the past two years, my community activism has shifted from political work to volunteer work.

Every relationship has its own special flavor and tenor. Our friendship is decidedly cerebral. Many a night we have sat across the dining room table with a couple of glasses of wine, just talking for hours.

We would talk about life in general and share intimate sides of ourselves. We would often talk about (read "analyze") how larger forces, like social norms and others' expectations of us, have affected our lives. In many instances, these conversations would hinge on how our respective sexual orientations have made us both very similar and very different.

In sharing our friendship with the readers of this volume, we wanted to try to capture a little of both the flavor and the substance of our everyday interactions—their chatty, one-to-one feel and their emphasis on topics both intellectual and personal. To do this, we decided to actually "let everyone in" on our discussions, give them a chance to sample our friendship experientially. To achieve this end, portions of transcriptions of conversations between us form the core of this paper. Consistent with the focus of this book, our discussions, conducted on three different evenings, centered on four broad topics related to how our differing sexual orientations are salient to our friendship. These topics were: (1) Karen's frustration with Mark "not getting it," that is, not getting how certain issues impact her personally and the lesbian, gay, and bisexual community in general; (2) Mark worrying about saying "the wrong thing" in situations related to Karen's sexual orientation; (3) other people's perceptions of our friendship; and (4) issues of sexuality and the emergence of physical attraction between us. For each topic, we provide a brief introduction of relevant concerns and history, then allow our friendship to "speak for itself," with lengthy excerpts from our conversations. While we don't want to detract from the naturalistic goal of this approach, we both felt moved to reflect briefly on the discussion at the end of the chapter.

We began our first evening of conversation with the intent of focusing on two of the areas where sexual orientation becomes especially salient for us: other people's perceptions of our friendship and Mark's concern about "saying the wrong thing" with regard to Karen's sexual orientation. The conversation weaved itself around and among these focal points and honed in on how each of us fits into the other's social circle.

MARK: My way of looking at other people's perceptions of us revolves around times when you and I would go out with other
friends of mine. Afterwards, my conversations with my other
friends would usually be like this:

"Karen. You know, you met Karen."

"Yeah. She's gay, right? She's your friend that's gay, right?"

Virtually all, if not all, of my friends have no problem with
homosexuality. But that doesn't necessarily mean that they're as
comfortable being around new people whom they perceive first
and foremost as gay, as I am. So what happens, I guess, is that I
play this whole scenario out in my head, and then probably there's
a lot of presumption on my part about how certain people might
react. Is everybody involved going to be able to handle this?
Should it just be *us* (and not include Karen), so everybody's comfortable? It's not as conscious as all that, but I want to go out and
enjoy my day and be absolutely comfortable; even though there's
probably not going to be *any* problem, I don't want to worry my
head over even the remote risk. There's a lot of vaguely insulting
ideas embedded in all that, but I think that's a pretty fair display
of what goes on. Well, I'm curious about a reaction.

KAREN: Well, what strikes me most is that it sounds like you're really
concerned with how *they* are going to be affected by my sexual
orientation, when other people might take the same situation and
think, "Am I going to invite Karen? Is *she* going to be made to feel
uncomfortable by my friends who aren't as knowledgeable?" I'm
mostly struck by the fact that you're much more the flip side of that.

Later in the conversation, we shifted gears and discussed how Mark
fits into Karen's social circle. One issue this topic raised was how our
friendship is similar to and different from stereotypical images of
gay-straight friendship, like "fag hag," that is, a straight woman who
hangs around a group of gay men, and "dyke daddy," that is, a
straight man who hangs around a group of lesbian women.

KAREN: It seems like when gay and lesbian people, friends of mine
that I know are around and *we,* you and I, are out together, they
have to integrate you somehow. Like at the party the other night:

people assumed that you lived here because you were pointing people out to the refreshments and things. It just makes me think that people must be thinking a lot on how to rationalize our involvement, other than just a friendship, because we happen to enjoy each other's company. Somehow it needs to be rationalized that you're actually gay and you need to come out, or you're bi and you need to come out, or you're my roommate, or you're a relative, or—you know? It can't just be "friend," because that experience isn't as common. You know, it's really a lot more common for gay men to have straight fag hags, female friends. Although what we call dyke daddies are actually pretty common on the whole, but I haven't necessarily seen a lot around Gainesville here or in general.

MARK: I'm not getting off on the community, I'm enjoying the friendship. In fact, my involvement in the community has been through friends, to be with friends—and occasionally I have political convictions.

KAREN: That's true. That's a good point. You have political convictions that de facto make you an ally, quite a bit, especially with the lesbian community.

MARK: I think that, when it gets right down to it, the primary reason that I think I get things like "your gay friend, Karen" is that there is still a sense that if you are spending this much time with a woman—your age, attractive, you enjoy her company—something must be going on. There must be some romantic involvement, and if there isn't, "What's wrong with you?" (What's wrong with me?) "Even though you're saying you're straight, are you gay? What's going on?" And I don't get those explicit questions about *my* sexuality asked to me, but I do get a sense of, "That's strange." They really don't know where to place that. I wish I could give an explicit example.

KAREN: Do you think they question *my* orientation?

MARK: No. No, I don't.

Two other topics we addressed in our first session were Mark's concern about the "propriety" of revealing Karen's sexual orientation to friends and acquaintances, and the saliency of Mark's sexual orientation in the circles of the lesbian, gay, and bisexual community that Karen moves in. We then concluded the discussion (and the first session) with some thoughts on how our experiences of negotiating the social "fallout" of our differing sexual orientations may relate to the broader social context.

KAREN: My sexual orientation *is* a big part of who *I* am. And your sexuality is a big part of who you are. Your sexuality may not necessarily be perceived as a big part of who *you* are, Mark, because you're heterosexual in a predominantly heterosexual culture. I really feel like the culture has made my sexual orientation—all minority sexual orientations—very salient to people. Sometimes I think about your sexual orientation when I'm talking about you to our mutual friends, Melissa and Katherine.[1] With them I'm a lot more aware of the fact that I have a straight male friend than I am with other people in my life.

MARK: How does it play out?

KAREN: Well, I'm not exactly sure. You just don't fit very naturally into that picture. So anytime I mention you it becomes very figurish, very bold.

MARK: That seems like a real nice way of putting it. I can relate to that experience. I think that's what happens for me. If the orientation comes up.

KAREN: You said people say, "Oh, Karen, your *gay* friend." I don't think that really happens with you. People don't say, "Oh, Mark, your straight friend." That's probably because we are a minority sexual orientation and you just don't talk about things like "Mark, your straight friend" very much, unless you're absolutely immersed in the gay subculture, and you don't know anybody who's not gay. Then maybe it would become more of an issue but, you know, most people I know are not that exclusively tied to their subcultures.

MARK: It's really interesting, over the course of this whole conversation—one of the things that *I'm* seeing is that—How much do we represent lesbian women in general and straight men in general?

KAREN: Yeah, right. We're not intending to be role models.

MARK: What is overarching—coming across in the picture to me—is that we're sort of mirroring the culture, in the sense that heterosexuality is sort of the understood, "unquestioned" orientation, while homosexuality sticks out like a sore thumb. You know, when I talk about feeling uncomfortable about these things coming up in my thoughts or in my planning or whatever, I think, "Damn, why did I learn to think that way?" But I think it's not even just learning to think that way, it's constantly being reinforced to think that way. And, in fact, I had a friend one time, and we were talking about race relations. And she said, "I don't think about it. And if you don't think about it, that's the only way we're ever going to get to treating people as equals and get beyond prejudice—to not think about it." And to me that was totally ridiculous. Of course you think about it. And if you don't think about it, you're trying to negate the difference.

The springboard for our second evening of taped conversation was a period in our relationship, about two years ago, when we found our friendship evolving into a romantic relationship sustained by subtle but persistent sexual energy. At that time, we found ourselves wrestling with perplexing sexual signals, painful revelations, and personal transformations. In the following excerpt, we talk about this time in our friendship and our attraction for one another—how it came up, how we reacted to it, emotionally and intellectually, how we dealt with it, and the changes it brought to our friendship.

MARK: Two years ago, in our conversations, we started to get a sense that, although we had a strong friendship, there was some point of rupture going on. There was some "leakage," I guess is the word we're coming up against. The issue of sexuality as a *personal* issue, not just as an orientation issue.

KAREN: Well, I remember it was maybe two years ago we were spending a *lot* of time together. It was at a time when it seems to me both of us were spending a lot of personal time with each other primarily, and other people were more secondary. We were more isolating ourselves—in general just being very affirming of each other. We were both frustrated with the local life, anyway.

MARK: I was feeling like that part of myself was being affirmed in our conversations. I remember each of us saying that "Well, you know, I find you attractive; I think you're an attractive person."

KAREN: I think a lot of people, especially women, over time will tend to sexualize their friends in some ways. If you spend a significant amount of time with a person, they become attractive to you. You see certain qualities about them you like or even physical qualities, as well as personality kinds of things that you like. You like the way they move their hand or laugh or whatever; it's physical.

MARK: Yeah. I remember specific experiences of that. I remember how astonished I was. I would be with somebody who was a friend of mine, and they were just a friend, they weren't anything more than that. The way that I tend to experience it is that I just wake up one day and I'm with them again like I was yesterday, but suddenly I'm thinking all these different thoughts. I'm seeing the way they move their hand, the way they laugh, you know, just the way they sit or something, and I remember thinking, She's very attractive, or, He's attractive, you know.

KAREN: This is kind of a trickier issue we've got, though: attraction between a lesbian-identified woman and a straight man. How to define yourself and how to understand what's going on, and what to do about it, if anything—what's worth it and what's not.

MARK: I think it tends to get portrayed as this sort of malicious thing that men do—that they just can't control themselves, and they always want sex—and it's not. It's just like you said: it's what happens when people spend a lot of time together and enjoy each other's company. Because of our orientations, it's a little bit trickier.

KAREN: Was it surprising to you because you hadn't really had that experience a lot before with women, or was it surprising to you because I was a lesbian, and you didn't really expect it?

MARK: Well, certainly not the first. The experience had come up many many times, and I was slowly trying to learn to deal with it. It wasn't primarily because you were a lesbian, it was primarily because I thought of us as friends. But I think your being a lesbian had something to do with it, because I realized, "Well, this is certainly not someone who is putting vibes out to me."

KAREN: It's really important for me to be honest and talk about things because my experience with you, especially—not so much the physical side of it as much as what you said, the verbal and cognitive processing and the talking through all of it that we allowed ourselves to do—really helped me come to a fuller understanding of my sexual orientation. I now, for the sake of explaining things to others, say "lesbian-identified bisexual." Really, I'm much more lesbian than I am heterosexual or bisexual. I think my relationship with you—as well as kind of paying more attention to my own reactions and processes and things around men and around women—helped me understand more who I am and what my sexual orientation really is and how it fits into things and how I can be attracted to a man or to men and still be a lesbian.

MARK: But the whole point is that it's not either/or.

KAREN: Yeah, to me that's a big part of the whole point of things. And that doesn't mean, or even imply, that our friendship works because I'm not completely lesbian or that the friendship is really based very heavily on some kind of sexual dynamic back and forth; that's not really true at all. It's simply a part of the relationship that became a very important part of the relationship for a time and has since receded.

MARK: That's interesting, because I don't think you've ever mentioned that to me before, making that link between our experiences and the evolution in your sexual orientation identity. Thinking of it from the standpoint of somebody reading about this, I can envision somebody saying, "So you had sex with Mark and that kind of delesbianized you." You see what I'm saying? How would you respond to that?

KAREN: No, that's not really what happened. It was the emotion surrounding the whole thing that helped me reconceptualize or reexperience my orientation. It wasn't a process of delesbianizing me; it was more allowing myself to be more emotionally honest about men and the space that men could occupy in my life, so to speak.

MARK: I was kind of playing devil's advocate there. I could see it being perceived that way, but I didn't think that was how you experienced it. It struck me when you were talking about how the emotional side of it affected you. I thought throughout most of it, since it was all very natural, we didn't anticipate any kind of attraction emerging between us. But in our discussions there was the sense that there was attraction on both sides. It occurs to me that the way that we dealt with it—that one night in particular— was such a botched thing, particularly on my part. To force the issue based on my own needs and purely on my own needs and not doing it in a very sensitive manner to begin with. It strikes me in hearing you say that there were some things going on that, while not exactly easy for you to deal with, were predominantly positive, because it was natural and it was pleasant and we were attracted to each other—and all of a sudden, this thing. And it was just a horror for some time and separated us for some time.

KAREN: I don't put all of the responsibility on you for that. I think I do agree that you really were motivated by your own needs that particular night and forced the moment to its crisis before it was ready. I think what happened, really unfortunately for us, is that, afterwards, I ended up feeling tired and old, and this was what I always did with men and I didn't like it, and why did I do it, and why did I let us do that, and it just wasn't right, it wasn't right for us, it wasn't right then. I felt all that. I was upset for myself, and I was upset for you, that it should have been much better for you. I think I ended up leaving and going—leaving in a more metaphorical sense—feeling like, "Well, that put the lid on that! I like men fine as friends; I don't want anything else" is kind of what it did for me. I really backed off and processed for a little while—not a real long time but a little while—and then I started being more open again and the process starting flowing back along. Now I'm at a point where I feel like I'm much more capable of being sexually and emotionally honest with a man that I might get involved with. I feel much more capable of stating, "Here's where I'm at, here's where I'm coming from. I like you as a person and I'm attracted to you and I would like to go out with you, etc., but you should know that it comes with this package sort of thing." In a not so guarded way, in a not so "What is this going to mean to me as a lesbian?" way, which was what I was doing before.

MARK: One of the things I really walked away with was the sense that I'm just not the kind of person that can separate sexuality and romanticism. That was part of what was so painful for you, from the way I experienced your reaction, that here we were in a very close friendship, and I was doing a lot of separating. I think maybe some of it was to try to protect your identity as a lesbian, so it was, "We're just doing this to do it." There was a part of me that felt like that was the way you were really wanting it to happen, and I was real wrong about that in some ways. That was part of the experience there, just between us. In the overall picture, I walked away feeling that I wasn't capable of, and it was wrong to even try, to separate the two.

KAREN: I ran up against a brick wall, because I really did not expect it. I had been, like, out of town or something—

MARK: No, *you* had picked *me* up at the airport.

KAREN: Oh, was that what it was? Okay. And it was like, "Oh, good, now we're going to get to talk," spending an evening talking and catching up on stuff. So I was looking forward to that. The way you presented sexualizing the relationship was very—I mean you tried to be like, "Let's just do this thing," but you also lit candles and made dinner. They were confusing messages.

MARK: Yeah, which reflected a lot about how confused I was about the whole thing. In some sense it's funny because it's like "Okay, I'm going to try to seduce a lesbian." [*Laughs*] How do you do that?

KAREN: [*Laughs*] So you kind of tried both ways at once!

MARK: "Well, okay, we could just do the sex thing, or we could have a nice dinner."

In our third and final evening of conversation for this chapter, we discussed the interplay between political action and sexual orientation, as we both work for lesbian, gay, and bisexual civil rights.

Early in the conversation, we made repeated reference to a particular period in local politics. During this time, the lesbian, gay, and bisexual community and the liberal activist community were working together to elect two contenders to seats on the *city* commission. The lesbian, gay, bisexual, and liberal activists working on these campaigns considered the incumbents who held these seats to be particularly homophobic. At the same time, our *county* commission was being asked to consider an amendment that would add *sexual orientation* to the county's antidiscrimination ordinance; however, the commissioners' slow progress (the county commission chose on several occasions to delay consideration of the amendment) seemed to indicate a degree of ambivalence about the amendment.

KAREN: The gay, lesbian, and bi community was working for Jill Whiting and Stan Wilson. (Frankly, we were a lot more excited about Jill Whiting than we were about Stan Wilson.) We had a big local issue going on about our county ordinance prohibiting discrimination on the basis of sexual orientation, or adding that clause into its general antidiscrimination thing, which includes race, gender, religion, and so on. I didn't agree that the community would have been better served to put that energy into the Stan Wilson campaign. I thought that the energy was very well served and very appropriate right where it was at. And if I remember right, you kind of agreed that it could have been more useful going into Stan Wilson's campaign.

MARK: Well, I don't think anybody felt like a whole lot of energy was worth putting into Stan Wilson's campaign, generally. But my sense was that we had a chance, as a community, to win two city commission seats, one with Whiting and one with Wilson. I don't know whether I'm right or wrong, but it's a political strategy thing as I was looking at it.

KAREN: Yeah. What really stood out for me, and continues to stand out for me about this whole thing, is you're much more rational and much calmer about it, whereas I feel very wrapped up and very, like, "Fuck them! Hell, yeah, we're going to ring the court-house!" I certainly haven't had the history of being the political activist that you have been. And I tend not to be very in-people's-face about things. But this was a demonstration that I definitely was for. And I remember feeling at the time when this difference between our positions was brought to light, my feelings were hurt. I felt misunderstood. And I felt like, "Oh, man, Mark, you can't even get that this was very upsetting, and that we as a community needed to have a mass demonstration. This was important for *us*." And to analyze it in political terms was, for me, somehow devalu-ing the human spirit that was tromped upon and subsequently invigorated by the action. I don't usually feel that way with you. Usually we agree on a lot of this kind of stuff.

MARK: The way that you present that just now makes me think of it in terms of sort of a broader perspective of looking over all my years of activism and how that plays out because I am a heterosex-ual white male. All of my activism has been for other minority groups or for an oppressed group that I'm not a part of. And my thinking has developed along the lines of, "We're all connected by this. When our local community discriminates against gays and lesbians and bisexuals, and when we have a climate in the commu-nity that's very accepting of rape, those are the kinds of things, those things affect *me*." (And also, they make white, heterosexual men look like hell, and our image is bad enough as it is.) And so sometimes I'm very aware of trying to present a different image of what a man can be, in some sense. But, at the same time, some-times I don't connect with the emotion of what's going on.

KAREN: So it kind of brings to light, when we get involved in these "in the moment" situations, so to speak, and away from the "idea world," where we spend a lot of our time, that we have some fundamental differences about how we're motivated and how we think and feel about things that are very relevant to our differing orientations. In some sense we're both reacting against what our "givens" are. My given of a minority sexual orientation and consequently being on the outside of society. And your given of being very much on the inside track of society.

MARK: Yeah, what you're bringing up is really complex and really difficult to pin down. If those differences come up, how much of it is "We're different people," and how much of it is "We're different *classes* of people"?

KAREN: Right. But I'm sure some of it is particular to orientation. I mean, if I were a male, the only difference would be sexual orientation. But the differences that we do have are *gender* and sexual orientation, which are *huge* differences, really. But we have *huge* similarities in terms of our place in society and our race and everything that kind of goes along with that.

MARK: And in more personal things, you know, we're very similar in terms of things that we want in our lives, at least in some respects. And in terms of the high value—in some cases maybe excessive value—we put on academics and education. Or, to put it less tritely, how cerebral we are and how much we're interested in what's going on "up here" and ideas.

KAREN: You feel like you're trying to help and do good, and you're having to worry about not offending as you're trying to help.

MARK: I think people have to recognize that it can be a real minefield for an outsider trying to be sensitive to the concerns of an oppressed group.

KAREN: Yeah. It can be a real minefield *within* the oppressed group, too!

Reflections

MARK: Reviewing the transcriptions of these conversations gave me a rare opportunity to hear or "see" myself, to reflect on the things I said with the benefit of at least a little distance and hindsight. Unfortunately, one of the most prominent reflections that I see in these conversations is one I find difficult to face. When Karen and I discussed how she fits into my circle of friends, I thought I was very sensibly explaining how my concern that people get along sometimes prompts me to resist bringing certain people together. Reading and rereading that portion of the conversation forced me to recognize that, for all my talk of social graces, what I was describing (and acting in response to) was homophobia. I was hiding Karen from some of my friends and from my family because she is a lesbian, and I was actively maintaining rationalizations that convinced me that that was okay.

I am not so naive as to think that recognizing my own homophobia has made it go away, but I hope that this act of recognition will be my first step in acknowledging and, ultimately, transcending long-hidden fears and biases.

Another somewhat troubling aspect of my friendship with Karen that is reflected in our conversations is what she called the "experiential gulf" that sometimes divides us when we look at particular social or political issues. For example, when I disagreed with the decision of lesbian, gay, and bisexual activists to interrupt campaign work to conduct a protest action, Karen experienced this as my "not getting" how important, emotionally, the action was for the gay community. She was, I think, particularly disturbed by what my lack of sensitivity in this and other cases might imply about the relationship between sympathetic outsiders and members of oppressed groups. Her sense was that if, I—a person who is *trying* to understand and assist the political and personal struggles of lesbians, gays, and bisexuals—don't feel homophobia and its effects as gay people do, how can she expect less sympathetic outsiders to ever see beyond their own homophobia?

I understand this concern, and I share it, to some degree. I don't want these experiential gulfs to separate gay and straight friends. It is difficult for me to see my friends' pain and anger, and yet not share it—even if I feel I *should* share it. My sense, however, is that my "not getting it" does not necessarily point to a broader problem. I think the situation is more indicative of my personal interactional style than of an inherent distance between homosexuals and heterosexuals. Other "sympathetic outsiders" may "connect" with the emotional struggles of members of oppressed groups more easily than I do. They may not confront the experiential gulf that Karen has encountered with me and that I have felt in other activist work I have done.

Finally, though the conversations presented here reveal much about our friendship, they also miss quite a bit. What seems most conspicuous in its absence, to me, is the fun. We have not talked about how enjoyable we find these night-long, anything-goes conversations of ours, nor have we mentioned comparing notes on what we find most attractive in women (a particularly intriguing pastime for a lesbian woman and a straight man!) or the various and sordid ways we have gotten into trouble together.

KAREN: In reading back over our conversations, several themes are salient to me: Mark and I talking in stereotypes about fag hags and dyke daddies, Mark's turmoil around introducing me into his network of friends, the fallout of our failed sexual relationship, and my hurt at seeing us disagree on what seem to me to be fundamental issues.

I found myself feeling uncomfortable while reading back over our first evening of conversations. Mark and I were using the derogatory labeling language of "fag hags" and "dyke daddies." Neither of those terms is comfortable to me, and I don't tend to use them in everyday language. It is interesting that Mark and I fell into that language pattern fairly early in our conversation, and that I did not make clear that I do not feel comfortable with those terms. In retrospect, it seems that while Mark and I were talking about how other people struggle to define our relationship, we ourselves were struggling even harder to determine whether or not our relationship was consistent with the "dyke daddy" stereotype.

I will admit that I am uncomfortable with the realization that Mark thinks about how *I*, being lesbian, will fit in with his friends, rather than about whether or not *his* friends will make *me* feel welcome. My feelings were hurt during the conversation itself when this first came up. Since then I have thought about Mark's desire for *all* of his friends to feel comfortable, and I acknowledge that this is an appropriate concern. Nevertheless, I still feel a twinge of hurt at realizing my "outsider" status, even with my close friend Mark. The admission that Mark feels his sexual orientation is called into question when his friends attempt to rationalize our involvement again highlights the "bold" status of my sexual orientation.

While I feel vulnerable at making the more personal aspects of my relationship with Mark public in this volume, I definitely feel they have been a focal point for my coming to a more complete understanding of my sexual orientation. Now, with the distance of time, I can see even more clearly how our attempt at sexualizing our relationship was a mistake. A mistake which caused a rift between us that lasted for several months. I don't think Mark and I even talked to each other, during those months, about our last encounter, or anything else. As for my sexual orientation, the experience with Mark "derailed" me for a period of time, in terms of acknowledging that I do have moderate sexual feelings for men. But ultimately the experience helped me to determine my degree of attraction to men and what that may (or may not) mean for my sexual orientation.

That Mark and I disagree over political action really does feel like the tip of a proverbial iceberg of experientially based difference between us. I still feel frustrated about our disagreement concerning the demonstration. More recently, Mark and I disagreed over the homophobic stereotypes that seemed evident to me in a recently released movie. We went around and around about this one, and still we disagree. Mark just does not experience the movie as particularly homophobic, while I experience it as *very* hurtful and homophobic. Mark has since told me that he feels I think he is "wrong" when it comes to these points of contention, that there is something "wrong" with him. I certainly did not intend to create such a feeling and tried instead to explain *why* the stereotypes I saw in the movie were so hurtful to me. This, I think, created somewhat of an affective bridge between the two of us on this issue, but the fundamental disagreement still remains, and that is very unsettling to me. Ultimately, I must find some measure of comfort in allowing us to diverge on what are for me fundamental issues around sexual orientation; I must not try to argue him out of his view or try to force him to understand mine.

NOTE

Except for those of the authors, all personal names in this chapter are pseudonyms.

Anndee Hochman (front, in pink hat), Rachael Silverman (left), and John Duke (right), in Portland, Oregon, December 1990. The photo was taken the day the three moved together to a house owned by Rachael and John.

FIFTEEN

Uncommon Kin

ANNDEE HOCHMAN

Every real friendship is a sort of secession, even a rebellion. Each therefore is a pocket of potential resistance. —C. S. Lewis, *The Four Loves*

Only the intrepid visit the Oregon coast in January. Rachael Silverman and I trudged over sand the texture of concrete under skies the color of oatmeal, our jacket hoods up, rain needling our faces.

I knew this was going to be a Serious Talk, the kind that required a long stroll with no particular destination. Rachael didn't waste much time with a preamble. "John and I have been talking about living together. And we want you to live with us. What do you think?"

Rachael was my best friend, as well as my housemate. Six months earlier, one woman had left the house I shared with five other people, and Rachael showed up in response to our classified ad. I came out to her, obliquely, within the first minutes we met, when I showed her my room and saw her eyes settle briefly on my poster of Tee Corinne's famous *Sinister Wisdom* cover, a solarized photograph of two women making love.

That first summer, Rachael and I roamed the area together— Saturday afternoons at the coast, evenings back in Portland at the Barley Mill pub, sipping Ruby Tuesday raspberry ale. With our coarse, dark hair and olive complexions, we easily passed for sisters—and sometimes took advantage of the resemblance, lying extravagantly to strangers with tales about Gypsy origins or shipwrecked Greek grandparents.

We danced at the Primary Domain, a women's bar, where my

friends flirted boldly with Rachael. And we danced at the neighbor-hood pub, a straight bar, where a goofy, harmless, very drunk Irish-man once followed us home at two o'clock in the morning. Wednes-day nights were for grocery shopping at the twenty-four-hour Safeway, followed by frozen yogurt and reports on our love lives: my affair with a woman seventeen years older than me and Rachael's crush on a man with "the most intense eyes."

John Duke, possessor of those eyes, was a bill collector by day, a musician by night, and the coordinator of volunteer escorts at the Feminist Women's Health Center, where Rachael worked. He stood tall and rangy, with a dark ponytail, and he loved Raymond Carver stories as much as she did. Once they began dating, I saw less of Rachael, and I missed her. But the prospect of living with both of them made me uneasy. Would I feel excluded, as a single lesbian in a house with a straight couple? Where would I go when they had a fight? What if their relationship didn't last?

I had separatist friends who wouldn't attend parties where men were present, much less consider living with one. Would my lesbian credentials be suspect if I moved in with Rachael and John? Would the Arbiters of Queer Culture take away my lavender card? And did I want to share a home with a relative stranger, even if my best friend was in love with him?

Shortly after that walk at the coast, Rachael, John, and I went out together—a sort of dry run to see how we functioned as a threesome. It was a John McCutcheon concert, a benefit for the local radical newspaper. Someone was hawking raffle tickets at the door, so we pooled our money and bought five of them.

During intermission, a man began calling the numbers. The first ticket pulled was one of ours! John ran up to claim the prize and came back with a couple of concert passes. A few minutes later, my number won: a set of bells from Cameroon. The people behind us started muttering; surely this raffle must be fixed. As we were playing with the bells, which made a hollow "klung" sound, another of our tickets was called. We'd won the grand prize, too: one night at a hot-springs retreat in central Oregon.

A lucky omen? Perhaps. Also an ironic one: our prizes, like so much else in this paired-up culture, came in increments of two. How would the three of us share two concert tickets, or a night—for two, naturally—at the hot-springs retreat?

In the giddiness of winning, I pushed those questions aside. By then, I'd already made my decision about where I wanted to live. As an only child, I'd spent much of my life in households of three, starting with my original family. I loved Rachael and wanted to continue living with her. I was willing to take my chances with John.

After that, everything moved fast: classified ads, rental applications, and, suddenly, a blue clapboard house with a front porch facing west, just three blocks from the place where Rachael and I currently lived. One night, before we'd hauled a single piece of furniture, the three of us walked through the new house. I looked at the vacant rectangle that would be my bedroom and writing studio, at the long cavern below the kitchen that John planned to insulate with egg cartons, so he and Rachael could play music there without disturbing our neighbors. We followed each other from basement to upstairs bathroom, smudging each doorway with a bundle of sage incense. John beat a drum in all the corners. Then, seated on the living-room rug, we each contributed an object for a "special shelf"—Rachael's wooden truck, John's small drum, my vial of dried lavender. We talked about our hopes for the house, what we wanted from our lives there, separately and together.

Simply performing that ritual made our friendship deliberate and distinct. To me, it felt like a consecration, an elevation of our bond above other friendships in my life. Most friends find each other by accident, by circumstance: Rachael and I were brought together by a classified ad, Rachael and John by a feminist health clinic. But in choosing to live together, in speaking our intention out loud and making a ceremony of it, we nudged our friendship past the circumstantial conjunction and into a wide, uneasy future.

Choosing to live together in this way meant we would develop expectations of each other, make demands, ask for mutuality. Perhaps we would borrow money, take care of each other when we had the flu, learn each other's secrets and ambitions, rely on one another in daily, constant ways. It was unmarked territory we were entering, and our ceremony that night felt like a commitment—but to what, precisely, I could not say.

Rachael and John talked of feeling nervous and happy to be living together as lovers. I said that I planned to quit my part-time job in the spring and write five days a week. For the first time, John would have his music studio and living quarters in the same place. "When I drum, I feel like something's breaking apart inside me," he told us. Sitting there on the mustard-yellow carpet, I felt that crackle, too. Under my ribs, an old pattern fractured into pieces.

Gradually, we set up house. John brought a futon couch, armchairs, heavy enamel pots, and about forty plants. I contributed my used piano and two cartons of kitchen utensils. Rachael, out of college for less than a year, owned books and a nonstick skillet. John's grandmother bought him a washing machine; Rachael and I each pitched in twenty-five dollars for a used dryer.

Our decorating habits were unorthodox. In lieu of a dining-room table, we propped an old door on cinder blocks and arranged John's plants on top of it. We added extra hooks to the inside of the bathroom door, put all three names on the answering machine. On the wall outside the kitchen, we hung a framed portrait of each of us.

If my friendship with Rachael was immediate, fierce, competitive, and intimate, my tie with John was the opposite—tentative, polite, and slow. I had other male friends, both gay and straight: a cadre of wry, cynical soulmates from high school and college, now scattered from Los Angeles to Washington, D.C. But those friendships all predated my coming out; most of my male buddies, in fact, were former lovers. Sexual energy had fueled those bonds, helped propel us through the awkward small-talk stage. Now I was a lesbian, making friends with a man. For weeks John and I tracked careful paths around each other, like creatures of different species.

Gradually our shyness abated, and our time together eased. John was fired from his bill-collecting job and cobbled together various part-time stints, working nights at a shelter for mentally ill adults, booking a friend's band, and helping to find lodging for Japanese exchange students. I wrote monthly profiles for the gay and lesbian newspaper and occasional features for the mainstream press; I was perpetually broke and didn't yet feel like a "real" writer.

That first summer in the new house, we both had too much time and too little work. In the morning, John drummed for several hours, while I made phone calls in an attempt to dredge up story ideas. Then we had brunch. On a good day, that could occupy us until two-thirty. By four, it was time to start making dinner.

While we procrastinated in the kitchen, sautéing eggplant or slicing potatoes, we began to divulge bits of our pasts. I talked about the trials I'd covered as a metro reporter for the *Washington Post*. I described my first powerful attraction to a close woman friend and the anguish, later, of coming out to my parents. John told me about his months teaching English in China; his drum teacher's enigmatic counsel; his first year in Oregon, when he was so poor that both he and his dog ate lentils the last week of each month.

Then we began to show each other our creative work—my first, uncertain pieces of short fiction, his quirky, ironic stories written for performance with a drum accompaniment. We sat in the kitchen late at night, offering critique, trading ideas. We joked uneasily about Rachael, with her $4.50-an-hour job at the health center, being our family's chief breadwinner.

By the end of that year, the three of us not only lived, but worked, together. John and I arranged to job-share (he worked four days; I worked one) at a social service agency, doing crisis counseling with homeless teenagers. Then Rachael was hired to run the agency's needle-exchange program for IV drug users. Our public and private worlds, work and home, overlapped. At dinner, "shop talk" about a fight in the drop-in center would segue into discussions of home-lessness, teen pregnancy, homophobia, the Meaning of It All.

Rachael, John, and I gave each other rides to and from down-town, packed each other's lunches and folded notes into the bags: "This lunch was inspected by No. 36492." We spent a vacation together, bicycling in the Canadian Gulf Islands, joined a grocery co-op as a household and took turns working there on Tuesday mornings. Our birthday tradition began that year; we celebrated with fancy dinners followed by homemade gifts—a painted lunchbox for Rachael, a short story for John, a cactus terrarium for me.

There were other routines: summer dinners on the front porch in the lavender twilight; February nights huddled on the living-room futon, watching videos and eating Haagen-Dazs bars, bickering about whose turn it was to sit in the middle; nightly hugs before bed. When one of us left for a trip, we turned John's small stuffed tiger, a souvenir from China, to face out the window for good luck.

Around that time, a friend dubbed us the "RAJ Mahal," the acronym made of our three initials. But not everyone was so eager to recognize our bond. When Rachael first told her parents of our plans to live together, her father was dubious: "Why would she want to live with you?" he asked. "Don't lesbians usually want to live with each other?" John's grandmother assumed I'd move out if I ever "met Mr. Right." My own parents worried aloud about my "situation"; it seemed further from the norm, even harder to comprehend, than my lesbianism.

With gay friends, I felt slightly traitorous when I described my household: Yes, I lived with a man. No, he wasn't gay. Yes, Rachael and John were my best friends. Sometimes the doubts crept under my own skin: what kind of weird arrangement was this, anyway?

Here's what I knew: Sexual orientation was a trait that divided Rachael and John from me, but there were plenty of other traits that both joined and split the three of us in various ways. Rachael and I were Jewish; John was raised Protestant. He and Rachael composed music, sang, and performed as a duo, while I could barely match a pitch. John and I, through our job-sharing arrangement, conferred about workday details that excluded Rachael. Whatever our three-way alliance was, it was not simple.

With heterosexual housemates, it was easier for me to pass than if I'd lived with a female lover. I sometimes hid behind the privilege, even allowed John's male friends to flirt with me, rather than take the risk of coming out. Other times, I resented the assumption that I was "straight until proven otherwise." On the surface, we looked like a single woman and a couple, sharing a house; the truth was more complicated and harder to describe.

I wasn't even sure what we ought to call each other. "Friend" had a generic, all-purpose connotation; Rachael and John surely didn't belong in the same category with someone I'd known since childhood but hadn't seen in nine years, or with the colleagues I chatted with at writers' meetings once a month. I'd read about the notion of "found kin," and that seemed an accurate description. *Sister, brother,* I'd think to myself, looking at Rachael and John.

As an only child, I had no personal reference points for those relationships, but I soon realized, watching Rachael and John with their actual siblings, that the simile fell short. While John and Rachael didn't share daily life with their blood siblings, they did possess years of family history, inside jokes, physical resemblance, and a certainty that their relationships were irrevocable. Even death would not negate the bond; a "late" sister is still a sister.

In contrast, our friendship felt vulnerable, equipped with no such guarantees. A million things less drastic than death could damage or end it: Rachael and John might marry; I might meet someone, fall in love, and move out of our cozy RAJ Mahal. We might stumble over "irreconcilable differences." If that happened, how hard would we try to overcome them? How much support would we get for efforts to mend a hurting friendship?

I had a history of remaining connected with people who had once been intimate in my life, both ex-lovers and longtime friends. But I could also think of some who had once been close and were not any longer, friendships that fizzled or burned out, connections snapped or simply allowed to drift until they disappeared. How could I be sure that wouldn't happen to the three of us? Perhaps if I used the language of family to name our relationships, they would take on that same sustaining power.

I had other questions. It was clear that our friendship triangle was not an equilateral one. Rachael and John, as lovers and partners, shared an intimacy that was quite different from the loving, intense bonds I had with each of them. Besides the physical and sexual relationship, their expectations of each other stretched far; to each, the other was becoming primary, the main source of companionship, love, emotional sustenance, practical help. They actively imagined a future together—a future that might or might not include me.

So perhaps that was the difference between friends and family.

Friendships occupy the present, subject to changing proclivity and circumstance, while family relationships arch over time—either backward to childhood, as with siblings, or forward toward old age, as with life-partners and children. But I wasn't satisfied with that arbitrary dividing line; it didn't account for the ways Rachael, John, and I *did* plan together, or for our expectation, spoken and unspoken, that we would always inhabit each other's lives.

True, there were nights I felt bereft, when I sat writing long after dinner in the living-room armchair and heard the soft mingling of John's and Rachael's voices upstairs. But usually I relished the variety of my life—to have company or be alone, to stay home and eat granola for dinner or go dancing as a threesome on a Saturday night. Our friendship thrummed with a different quality than any other I'd experienced; it was raw and deep, strenuous and complicated.

Over time, our dailiness had given way to uncommon intimacy. Rachael and John were privy to things no one else knew about me: that I like to read magazines on the toilet, that I suffer anxiety attacks in restaurants, that letters from my parents sometimes make me cry. I was living in the midst of a social invention—more than friendship, different from family, a relationship that refused all my efforts to tame it with a label.

I remember one summertime dinner. We lingered at the dining-room table, eating tempeh Reuben sandwiches and discussing how women in films always seemed to be punished for sexual assertiveness. Rachael got up to answer a knock at the door.

"Is there a man in the house?" I heard a stranger's voice say, and then Rachael, sharply: "Yes, but is there some way I can help you?"

The man's truck had broken down, and he needed a jump-start. I hurried up from the table, pulled my Datsun into the middle of the street, and jumped his car three times before it started with a wheeze. Rachael watched from the porch, smirking. John did the dishes.

I liked the way our household challenged expectations—other people's, my own. Every day I tripped on old beliefs, so carefully instilled: that only blood family endures, that lesbians can't live with heterosexual friends, that three is an unsteady number. I worked to silence those cautionary voices and listen instead to my own.

In that house, my writing flourished. After dinner, I sat at the computer in my room, while the sounds of John's African drums and Rachael's singing floated up from the basement. I began to compose opinion columns and personal essays, as well as short stories, stretching beyond the journalism I'd always done. The solidity of our household buoyed my desire to rebel, and my prose grew stronger, more opinionated. I felt safe enough at home to take risks in the world.

One year, two years, three . . . Time wove us together with simple repetition and unexpected crises. John's favorite great-aunt became seriously ill. A friend of Rachael's was raped. My father was in Candlestick Park during the 1989 San Francisco earthquake; Rachael and John wrapped me in blankets and fed me tea as I shivered for hours on the couch, watching the news and waiting for the phone to ring.

Valentine's Day marked the anniversary of our household: two years, three, four . . . We still had no language for what we three meant to each other. On days when I felt fragile and craved definition, I chopped onions fiendishly at 4 p.m., sizzled them in olive oil. The kitchen filled with smells of cumin and cornbread. I ladled up three bowls of soup at 7, reassured that we were, at least for that good moment, linked.

Then John's great-aunt died, and we became even more tightly, unexpectedly, wound together. I'd never met Julia; my image of her comes from a few anecdotes, a single telephone call, and one long story, the one that made John's eyes glisten all the way back from Julia's funeral. At least, that was how I imagined it, later. I pictured him telling the story to himself, driving in the rain up Interstate 5, murmuring it on the ferry to Salt Spring Island, where Rachael and I had started our vacation.

He would not tell us, though, until after dinner. So we ate in silence. The scallops tasted sweet. I looked out the window, while the sky closed down like a lid over St. Mary's Lake.

I knew John had come across Julia late in his life, and that she was the kind of relative you feel lucky to find in your late teens or early twenties, when it seems outrageous that the rest of your family is actually connected to you. She lived alone in a town near the Oregon coast and had never married. When she got sick, John drove three hours to the hospital every Sunday. He sat in Julia's room and talked to her, fed her soup by slow teaspoons, listened while she groped for breath.

Finally we finished dinner and John nudged his chair back from the table.

"About a week ago, when we were talking about bank accounts and bills, Julia told me about a green carton that was full of old check stubs. She told me to burn it. After the funeral, I found the box, but there were no check stubs. Well, there were some—maybe a year's worth. The rest of the box was filled with pictures.

"I started opening the envelopes, going through them one at a time. Finally I got to an envelope marked 'Germany' and one that said, 'Mostly Mary and Willi.' I'd never heard of them. I was pretty sure they weren't relatives.

"There were pictures of a cabin kind of place; maybe they'd rented it for the weekend, a cabin like this one. There was one picture of Julia leaning out of a second-story window. Her hair was shoulder-length and wavy. She was laughing. Then there were pictures of two other women. They all wore what looked like men's pleated wool pants.

"The pictures were different from all the others in the box. Careful. I mean, really *nice* pictures. And their expressions—kind of laughing, joking at the camera, glancing sideways, sort of mischievous.

"There was a picture of the taller woman dressed up like Charlie Chaplin, with a man's shirt and suspenders. Across her top lip, someone had drawn a pencil-thin moustache. And there was one of Julia and her sitting at a table on a balcony, leaning forward with their arms on the table, their arms really close together, almost touching.

"I think she might have been Julia's lover."

No one spoke for a few minutes after that. I could feel my cheeks flush, and my eyes got teary. I was thinking of family stories and the truths they withheld, and of links between our lives, glassy threads spun out across a dark place. For days afterward, I conjured images of Julia and her lover. I imagined conversations with them, the nods of understanding we'd exchange.

A few weeks later, John brought the carton of pictures back from Julia's house so Rachael and I could see them. We carried the box into the kitchen late one evening and pulled up three chairs.

Actually, they weren't very good pictures, just small, grayed snapshots hinged together with yellow tape. In the Charlie Chaplin photo, the woman's pencil-thin moustache was so faint I had to squint to see it, and I thought Julia's eyes seemed more distracted than mischievous. But we looked at those pictures for a long time, passing them carefully back and forth, leaning toward each other in the dim light over our own white kitchen table, almost touching.

The Julia story made me feel intricately connected to John, as if his having a lesbian aunt affirmed our kinship. The knowledge gave new resonance to our household's political gestures—such as the "No on 9" lawn sign we posted when a right-wing ballot measure threatened to label Oregon gays and lesbians "wrong, abnormal, unnatural, and perverse." Or the Gay and Lesbian Pride parades in which we all marched. When the statewide coalition fighting the antigay ballot measure spoke of the need for straight allies, I felt pleased, almost smug. I not only believed passionately in such alliances, I lived in one.

Then, on one summer solstice evening, Rachael and John became engaged. It was no surprise, by then, but I wept with loneliness and frustration. What about me? I wanted to shout. Where do I fit into all this, as a single person and a lesbian, as your best friend? Would I now become the invisible member of the household? Would I have to move out?

Their engagement skewed our unequal triangle even more, weighted their end of it with the baggage of tradition, the fanfare of marriage. I felt isolated, singular, unsure what my place would be in our changing trio. During the months before their wedding, we talked endlessly about marriage and heterosexual privilege, about details of the ceremony, about their hopes of buying a house afterward and what that would mean for all of us. I felt thin-skinned, sensitive to any hints of exclusion.

On one long winter car trip, Rachael and John squabbled in the front seats through an endless traffic jam, while I browsed through their library copy of *The New Jewish Wedding*. The author wrote of the "mitzvah" of marriage, describing it as each Jew's personal fulfillment of the faith's commandments. I closed the book and sobbed as John steered us over snowy highways back to Portland.

Closer to the wedding date, Rachael and I shopped for dresses together. I could feel salespeople sizing us up: Bride and Her Sister. Wrong. Bride and Maid of Honor. Wrong again. Already ornery, I tried on a green washed-silk dress, soft as rain, that I knew was far out of my price range, then berated myself for not being able to afford it. Clerks hovered around Rachael, while I sulked in dressing rooms. "What do you have for the Lesbian Friend of the Bride and Groom?" I wanted to ask. "Preferably in the low-income rack."

Eventually, I wore blue and stood up with John and Rachael at the wedding, held on the summer solstice in an Ohio synagogue. The three of us posed for a portrait, overruling the photographer's objections; he was flustered by the assymetry and kept trying to plug the "best man" into the picture, too. I felt proud of our refusal to cave in, one small rebellion against the rule that every person belongs in a pair.

I even spoke as part of the ceremony—at Rachael and John's invitation and with the rabbi's reluctant approval ("No more than three minutes," he'd cautioned). I quoted from Andrea Carlisle's book, *The Riverhouse Stories,* in which Lazy and Pubah, two women, discuss whether to get married. I described marriage as a privilege denied to some because of money, custom, or prejudice.

I also talked that day about the importance of witnessing each others' lives. In the years Rachael, John, and I had lived together, we'd watched each other falter and recover our balance. We all remembered John's stunned relief when he was fired from a job he hated, my fear and exhilaration about beginning a book, Rachael's doubts and pride about entering graduate school. We were each other's witnesses during a crucial period, when we all crept a bit more boldly toward our adult lives.

After the wedding, I continued to live with Rachael and John, even moved with them into the Victorian house they bought, a place so badly in need of repair that we lived for months amid plaster and sheetrock, in unpainted rooms with half-built closets. The objects from our "special shelf" got scattered in the move. Rachael's wooden truck sat in a downstairs cabinet. My vial of lavender ended up in a kitchen drawer. Bugs had taken up residence in John's drum, and he had to throw it out.

By then, I was dating Elissa, who had been my good friend for two years. I often felt pulled: Was I still part of a tight-knit, three-person household, or was I one half of an emerging couple? I was reluctant to let go of the sustaining patterns in my life; the first December Elissa and I were together, I debated for weeks about whether to accompany Rachael and John to visit his parents and sisters for the holidays, as I'd done before, or to go with Elissa and some women friends for a long weekend at the coast. We argued and wept; I defended my loyalty to the RAJ extended family.

At the last minute, I decided that what I really wanted was to stay at home, alone. I spent the holiday painting my room, eating Chinese take-out, and watching videos, my isolation confirming the uneasy limbo I felt, tethered to two families yet fully present in neither one.

In a photograph from the day we moved, Rachael, John, and I are sitting on the steps of the new house, grimy and disheveled, our arms looped around each other's shoulders. What I remember is that Elissa stood just out of the camera's range, and I watched her watching us, my focus half in and half out of the frame.

That house, a concrete symbol of Rachael and John's conjoined future, also became a source of painful arguments among us. I lived and worked there, but it was not *my* house in the same way it was theirs. I didn't share their enthusiasm about new cupboard latches or their willingness to spend whole weekends rolling paint on ceilings. I "helped," with varying degrees of good humor, resistance, and complaint, growing impatient as I waited for a heating grate to be installed in my chilly bedroom. I felt alternately resentful and jealous of their involvement in the house; at the same time, I was relieved to escape it several nights a week for Elissa's small, warm, finished apartment.

Did "family" mean you bought big things together? Rachael,

John, and I had made joint purchases—a dryer, a lawn mower, a bicycle rack—and I knew people, unrelated by blood or marriage, who had become co-owners of houses and cars. Again, I resisted the arbitrary dividing line. But I could see how that house, which Rachael and John were working day and night to make over according to their dreams, became an apt emblem of our changing lives. I spent less and less time there as my attention shifted to Elissa and our relationship, as the beloved threesome stretched awkwardly to make room for a fourth.

Eventually I moved into Elissa's apartment, though I continued to rent a room in Rachael and John's house as my daytime office. Over time, we abandoned old rituals and began new ones; the four of us shared a subscription to the Sunday *New York Times*, dividing the sections each Sunday and trading mid-week. We celebrated all four of our birthdays together and tried to schedule two "family" dinners each month—one a leisurely Shabbes feast with challah and wine, the other a more casual meal. My parents continued to send presents to Rachael and John; their grandparents asked about me.

Certain occasions left me feeling pulled between competing loyalties. On Valentine's Day, while Elissa and I celebrated with a candlelight dinner, I felt a tug of sadness and longing for the day, five years earlier, when Rachael, John, and I moved into that first house. My life is layered with these patterns, a fabric in flux.

I still feel angry sometimes that Rachael and John married, that they took advantage of a privilege Elissa and I are denied. As I watch them accrue the symbols of a settled life—the house, a new truck, dog and cat, raspberry bushes—I see myself growing ever more marginal by contrast. Elissa and I now live in an apartment in Philadelphia, stretching student loans and erratic freelance income from month to month. Three thousand miles separate us from John and Rachael. In my fragile moments, I fear our lives will grow apart as well, cleaving along some invisible but inevitable faultline.

I comfort myself with fantasies that the four of us might someday live in the same city, sharing a large duplex or buying houses on the same block. I miss living with Rachael and John, especially when being in a couple feels too confining and tidy. At the same time, I know our triad could last only as long as I remained single; add a fourth point, and the figure must change shape.

Rachael and John still occupy that vast unnamed territory between "friends" and "family." I wish there were a word for the place where these concepts collide, for the friends who, because of their intimacy, long-lasting presence and commitment, are "more than friends." Yet they are different from "family" as well—most significantly because, lacking the framework of established categories, we must continually create our relationships with them.

"Every real friendship is a sort of secession, even a rebellion," C.S. Lewis wrote. I rebel against the rigid, confining definitions of "family" and "friends." Perhaps what's needed is not a new term but a conscious expansion of the words we already have. We need to recognize that people unrelated by blood or marriage can create the deep, time-spanning links of love and obligation we think of as reserved for relatives. We need to remember that "friend" is not a second-best bond, but can describe a relationship of the most intimate and precious nature.

Besides the people we are born to and those we choose as primary partners are the ones we gravitate toward for some other, more mysterious purpose. What we create with them is profoundly important. These found kin, these more-than-friends, demonstrate the enormous reach of human originality, stubbornness, and love.

Today, seven years after we first moved in together, Rachael and John and I continue to bear witness, in cards and letters, in phone calls and visits, insisting on our places in each other's lives. "Missing you with the force of 5000 H-bombs," John writes on a postcard of Mt. St. Helen's exploding. "I love you," Rachael and I say at the end of late-night, long-distance talks. The legacy of that household still flourishes in me; it shapes my faith in the unnamed and the untried.

NOTE

Portions of this essay were adapted from Anndee Hochman's *Everyday Acts and Small Subversions: Women Reinventing Family, Community, and Home,* published in 1994 by The Eighth Mountain Press.

SIXTEEN

Friendships between Lesbian and Heterosexual Women

CHERIE G. O'BOYLE AND MARIE D. THOMAS

We are two psychologists, one lesbian and the other heterosexual.[1] During the process of becoming friends, we developed a shared interest in the topic of women's friendships, especially friendships between heterosexual and lesbian women. Our reading revealed that there is little scientific or popular literature on the topic of friendships in general (Pogrebin, 1987), less on women's friendships in particular (Eichenbaum and Orbach, 1988; O'Connor, 1992), and virtually nothing on friendships between lesbian and heterosexual women. To begin closing this knowledge gap, we have initiated a multi-year investigation of unexplored issues in women's friendships. In this larger project we will focus particularly on friendships between women who differ on important life dimensions, such as age, race, and sexual/affectional orientation.

This chapter reports findings from the first phase of our project: a study of friendships between heterosexual and lesbian women. As this first effort was exploratory—an attempt to generate a large number of issues to develop further in later phases of the project— we used focus groups as our data-gathering tool. Four groups were conducted, two composed entirely of lesbians and two entirely of heterosexual women. Within each focus group, participants discussed several topics related to friendships between lesbian and heterosexual women. We focused solely on intact friendships and did not discuss

240

relationships that ended because of the revelation that one friend was a lesbian. We acknowledge the importance of this issue and will explore it in the larger project.

The groups were semistructured: we posed a question and let the discussion develop freely. When the group had exhausted one topic, we raised another. The questions discussed in the groups developed over time; unexpected issues raised in one group might then be explored with the next. Each session was audiotaped. Participants were assured that their comments were confidential.

The participants were recruited primarily from our own friendship and social networks; in addition, some heterosexual women were suggested by their lesbian friends. Eighty-five percent of the women were European-American, while the rest were of Asian-, Native-, or Mexican-American descent. Caution should be exercised when generalizing from the experiences of our focus group sample to all lesbian-heterosexual friendships. The participants were primarily middle-class Caucasian women and, therefore, we cannot draw conclusions about women in other racial/ethnic and socioeconomic groups. Our sample was also limited to women in young and middle adulthood. Women in these generations have probably been strongly influenced by the feminist and gay rights movements. Both social movements have affected the nature of women's friendships in general and lesbian-heterosexual women's friendships in particular; differences might be expected in lesbian-heterosexual friendships found among younger and older women than those in our sample.

Likelihood of Having a Lesbian-Heterosexual Women's Friendship

We found evidence that lesbians are far more likely to have friendships with heterosexual women than heterosexual women are to have friendships with lesbians (as one would expect given the prevalence of heterosexuality in our society). When we recruited participants for our first two discussion groups (one lesbian and one heterosexual), we had no information about the types of friendships that the women had. It turned out that all of the lesbians in the first group had (at that time or in the past) at least one close heterosexual woman friend. In fact, only one of these women did not have a close heterosexual friend at the time the discussion was held. In contrast, fewer than half of the first group of heterosexual women had lesbian friends, either currently or in the past. This was a surprise to us, because this group of women consisted of self-identified and active feminists, they were all employed in the fields of psychology or mental health, and many had lesbian clients or associates. We assumed erroneously that at some time in their lives they would have lesbian friends.

Because so many women in our first heterosexual group did not have personal experiences with lesbian friends to discuss, the participants in our second group of heterosexual women were selected specifically because they had close lesbian friends. We asked the women in this second heterosexual group how likely it was for other heterosexual women they knew to have lesbian friends. According to these women, in their experience it was unusual for heterosexual women to have lesbian friends. In fact, some felt that there was a stigma attached to such a friendship. For example, one woman said that some of her heterosexual friends have trouble understanding her support for the "gay world," so she has stopped discussing her feelings with them. Thus, interestingly, we find that because heterosexual women may not feel free to discuss their friendships with lesbians with their heterosexual friends, a friendship with a lesbian puts some heterosexual women into their own personal "closet."

How Friendships between Lesbian and Heterosexual Women Begin

Most of us probably do not think much about where and how friendships start. As is true of all friendships, lesbian-heterosexual women's friendships can begin at different times of life. Two women might be friends from childhood, and later in life, after the relationship is well established, one of them reveals or discovers herself to be a lesbian. In fact, several of the lesbians in our groups reported that their "shared history" relationships with heterosexual women were the closest friendships they had. However, our lesbian participants agreed that part of the definition of close friendship must include being "out" with the heterosexual friend. In some instances, the lesbian friend did not feel comfortable sharing this information about herself, or the heterosexual friend was unable to accept her friend's new lesbian identity. In both of these cases, the friendship suffered.

Other friendships begin in adulthood. The lesbian friend might come out at the beginning of the friendship. In other relationships, the lesbian friend does not come out until later in the friendship, either because she does not discover she is a lesbian until later or because she is uncomfortable revealing this information until the friendship has reached a certain level of intimacy. In each of these situations, though, the lesbian risks losing the friendship (or derailing its development) when she comes out to a heterosexual woman.

Through the focus group discussions we are beginning to realize that friendships between two lesbians often begin in very different ways than other kinds of friendships. Friendships between lesbians are more likely to begin through intentionally constructed situations rather than through chance encounters. That is, for lesbians to have lesbian friends they generally must put themselves in places where they are most likely to meet other lesbians. Lesbians typically make lesbian friends through mutual acquaintances, at private parties, women's dances, gay rights events, bars, and other settings where lesbians congregate. The lesbians in our groups were unlikely to begin friendships with other lesbians through chance encounters for a couple of important reasons. First, lesbians do not typically recognize one another in the neighborhood, at work or school, or in nonlesbian social settings. Contrary to the opinions of some, homosexuals are as unlikely as heterosexuals to be able to accurately identify the romantic/sexual preference of unfamiliar adults (Berger, Hank, Rauzi, and Simkins, 1987). Second, many lesbians actively disguise themselves as heterosexual when outside lesbian settings, making it even more unlikely that they will be recognized by other lesbians. For example, a coworker of one of our lesbian participants repeatedly referred to her romantic partner as "he" in casual conversations. At one point several months into the acquaintance the coworker referred to our participant's partner as "he." When our discussant (a bolder lesbian than many) corrected her by saying, "My partner is a woman," the co-worker (after regaining her composure) acknowledged, "Mine too."

Nature of Lesbian-Heterosexual Women's Friendships

We asked the participants of our first two groups to give us their definition of a "close friend." The answers from heterosexual and lesbian women were strikingly similar. Some close friends are people with whom we share a history; a deep and special bond exists, even though the two friends may be far apart geographically. Shared values are also an important aspect of close friendships. Our participants spoke about intimacy, acceptance, respect, and regard. Significantly, for lesbians a close friend is someone who knows their "true nature" and with whom they can really "be myself" with "no pretending."

Given that their definitions of "close friendship" were so similar, we wondered if lesbians viewed their friendships with heterosexual women in the same way that heterosexual women viewed their friendships with lesbians.

Heterosexual Women Discuss Their Friendships with Lesbians

As mentioned previously, less than half of the women in the first focus group of heterosexual women ever had a close lesbian friend. Some women discussed how lesbians were "different" from heterosexual women: in their sexuality, level of political activism, focus on women, life experiences, and the importance of men in their lives. For some of these women, the beliefs they held about lesbians were barriers to establishing close friendships.

In contrast, the heterosexual women in the second group were chosen specifically because they had close lesbian friends. These women had difficulties coming up with differences between friendships with lesbians and friendships with other heterosexual women. But these women did differ in the levels of personal disclosure they experienced within their friendships with lesbians. One woman said that she discusses more intimate relationship issues with her heterosexual friends; she holds back with her lesbian friends, and they also hold back. Many discussions between heterosexual women friends focus on the problems and joys of their relationships with men. This is not a priority that lesbian and heterosexual friends share. We discussed the stereotype that "lesbians hate men" with the heterosexual participants in the second group and then asked how much they talked about men with their lesbian friends. One woman said that she used to think that lesbians hated men, but now that she has lesbian friends, she knows differently. Another woman believes that her lesbian friends are more tolerant of men than she is because they are more emotionally removed from men.

Lesbians Discuss Their Friendships with Heterosexual Women

The lesbians in our groups initially agreed that their level of personal disclosure in a friendship depended more on individual personalities than on whether their friend was heterosexual or lesbian. But as the discussion developed, a different perspective emerged. For some of the women, the common bond created by a shared sexual/affectional orientation became apparent as they talked about their social relationships with other lesbians. For example, one woman talked about feeling a sense of "kinship" with other lesbians, a sense that she is "with her own kind" and that those feelings increase the "comfort level" when she is with other lesbians.

This shared bond came up again as the discussion moved to questions about how much talk there is among friends about romantic relationships. Many of these lesbians expressed concern about discussing their own romantic relationships with their heterosexual women friends, and also about discussing the friends' romantic relationships. One woman feared that talking to heterosexual women about their romantic relationships with men would trigger the stereotype of lesbians as "man-haters." When asked about whether they talk with their heterosexual friends about romantic relationships, several lesbians brought up feminism as a necessary criterion in a friendship. That is, they were open to talking with a heterosexual woman friend about romantic relationships, but only if she had an identity separate from that of the man in her life. We found particularly interesting the lesbians' notion that if the heterosexual woman in question was a "feminist," she was better able to maintain a separate identity, even after marriage and children, and that her friendship with a lesbian was therefore more likely to survive.

Barriers to Lesbian-Heterosexual Friendships

At some point in these relationships, lesbian and heterosexual women are likely to face one or more potential barriers to the friendship. Some barriers must be overcome before a true friendship can begin. Others may be encountered after a degree of intimacy has been achieved. The discussion is primarily from the point of view of our lesbian participants, simply because they were much more conscious of the obstacles to lesbian-heterosexual women's friendships than were the heterosexual women in our groups. This is not surprising, since most (if not all) of the barriers we will discuss stem on some level from ingrained societal beliefs about homosexuality or gender roles.

Clearly the most significant barrier to the development of close friendships between lesbians and heterosexual women is the widespread hatred and oppression of lesbians in our society. In fact, this oppression hinders the development of these friendships in ways too numerous to even begin to discuss here. As long as lesbians must justifiably fear loss of jobs, family, personal safety, and in some parts of the world even their lives, if they reveal their sexual/affectional orientation, close friendships with heterosexual women are unlikely to develop as easily or as frequently as friendships among lesbians. This barrier to friendship is probably more significant than anyone realizes. It is probably true that when a fortuitous acquaintance does occur, the heterosexual woman is often completely unaware of the hidden part of her friend's identity, and a close friendship is unlikely to develop.

Several of the lesbians in our groups contended that, from early childhood, heterosexual women tend to be much more focused on traditional gender roles than are lesbians. This preoccupation interferes with the development of interests they might share with lesbians and, therefore, hinders the establishment of a friendship. Indeed, when previously single heterosexual women gain husbands and children, additional polarizing may occur in the friendship—as gender-typing may increase and time for the friendship decrease. Still, for others, these changes may bring lesbian and heterosexual women friends closer, especially if each friend is involved in a couple relationship as well as parenting.

One other barrier to friendship mentioned by several lesbians in the group was the concern that heterosexual women might be wary of their lesbian friends: "Are they going to cross the (sexual) line?" This may lead some lesbians to restrict physical intimacy or conversations that touch on sexuality or each other's sexual relationships.

In sum, in the focus groups we found that loving, rich, and mutually satisfying friendships exist between lesbian and heterosexual women. Friendships can survive (and thrive after) the disclosure that one of the friends is a lesbian. Such friendships flourish despite the many barriers that could derail the relationship's development. These obstacles cannot be discounted, however, because they probably prevent the establishment of many friendships between lesbian and heterosexual women. In a sense, in order for true, deep friendships to exist, both heterosexual and lesbian women must overcome the sense that the other is "different." For heterosexual women, this means challenging the homophobia and heterosexism that is so prevalent in our society. For lesbians, it means seeking out heterosexual women who share their goals, interests, and priorities. It may also mean trying to be more understanding about the changes that may occur in the lives of their heterosexual friends when they marry and/or have children. We will continue studying these issues.

There are many questions that are unanswered. What are the benefits of these friendships for the women involved? Why do some friendships not survive the disclosure that one friend is a lesbian? What happens when romantic or sexual feelings arise in such a friendship? These and many other issues will be explored in later research.

NOTE

1. Authors' names are listed in alphabetical order. They contributed equally to this project.

REFERENCES

Berger, G., L. Hank, T. Rauzi, and L. Simkins. 1987. Detection of sexual orientation by heterosexuals and homosexuals. *Journal of Homosexuality* 13: 83–100.

Eichenbaum, L., and S. Orbach. 1988. *Between women: Love, envy, and competition in women's friendships.* New York: Penguin Books.

O'Connor, P. 1992. *Friendship between women: A critical review.* New York: Guilford Press.

Pogrebin, L. C. 1987. *Among friends: Who we like, why we like them, and what we do with them.* New York: McGraw-Hill.

PART IV

Fixed Points in a Changing World: Personal and Political Dimensions of Friendship

Pat T. Bunny (Pat Schmatz, right) and Lynnepig (Lynn Wander, left) mining their special relationship for all it is worth. Photo by Joe Eisenberg.

SEVENTEEN

Pat T. Bunny Meets Lynnepig

PAT SCHMATZ

Pat T. Bunny was born in a rabbit burrow in a big, big field on the edge of a big, big forest. It was all very wild and beautiful, with tall things blowing and swaying in the warm spring breezes. Green and green and green. Fresh, bright smells, and dirt washed by hard-pounding rains, lighting up in thunder rumbles and sparkling the next morning in the pink-gray sunrise time.

Even though this bunny world was filled with magic beauty, Pat T. Bunny was afraid from the start. Mixed in among the wonder, there was evil lurking behind the bushes. Bad, wicked, nasty, evil things lived all over the field and forest, and P.T.B. managed to bump into a lot of them. Her mother was very busy counting clover, and her father was a big, rough rabbit who had a funny way of looking like a fox. Neither of them paid much attention to Pat T., other than to be sure that she knew how to count clover and groom herself properly.

Through a series of harrowing adventures and narrow escapes, Pat T. managed to travel far away from the wondrous and terrifying world where she was born. Bravely journeying across rivers and over the road, she found a barnyard. It was a large and busy barnyard, full of friendly and not-so-friendly creatures and machines. It was overwhelming but also interesting, so Pat T. Bunny found the ideal place for a rabbit hole and settled in. Pat T. soon began to mix with all the different kinds of animals in the barnyard. Among these animals, she found a most interesting new creature. It was a Lynnepig.

Pat T. Bunny liked this Lynnepig immediately, for three reasons: (1) She had a quick and clever mind. (2) She worked at a pizza place and was often inclined to give away free slices. (3) She was not afraid to say what she thought, even when it was different from what everyone else said and thought. Pat T. was also afraid of Lynnepig. This was partly because Pat T. was afraid of everyone, and partly because Lynnepig seemed Very Sure of Herself. P.T.B. liked animals who tiptoed around her and deferred to what she said and thought, and Lynnepig was not that sort of animal.

Days passed in the barnyard, and many busy things happened. For the most part, P.T.B stayed away from the interesting but somewhat scary Lynnepig.

Then, things being as they are and happening as they do, Pat T. Bunny received a small dose of Fear Remover in a dewdrop that she sucked off of a piece of clover. She was suddenly less afraid of Lynnepig, and so she approached her. At the same time, Lynnepig was drawing closer to P.T.B.'s world, and their ideas were becoming more alike. As they worked together in the barnyard one day, P.T.B discovered that Lynnepig was Funny, and a Good Story Teller. These were virtues that P.T.B. loved and admired, and she began to watch Lynnepig more closely, to see what other worthwhile things might emanate from her being. To her surprise, P.T.B. found that she genuinely liked Lynnepig.

Soon after, Lynnepig embarked upon a long journey and was gone for many days and nights. Pat T. Bunny discovered that Lynnepig wrote Amusing and Diverting Letters, and that she answered her mail promptly. Pat T. Bunny had a very special place in her rabbit heart for animals who answered letters, and she began to hope that Lynnepig would come back to the barnyard someday.

Eventually, Lynnepig did return, and she and Pat T. Bunny began to circle each other warily. Each was an extremely cautious animal in her own way, and each had a tendency toward being Sharp-Tongued and Defensive. So, they circled one another defensively. During this circling, P.T.B. noticed that Lynnepig was not always sure about everything, and that helped Pat T. relax enough to notice that Lynnepig was Thoughtful and Considerate and Usually on Time, and that she recognized What Was Important. Also, Lynnepig was Pragmatic and Not a Flake, and she knew some things that P.T.B. did not. All of these discoveries made P.T.B. feel safer and more interested, and slowly, slowly, she let down her bunny guard a notch or two. She found herself humming "Into the Mystic" as she began to examine things like acid and crystals and scared animals and The Talking Heads and kindness and The Good Thing from a Lynnepig Perspective. Pat T. found that when she examined these things from Lynnepig's point of view, she had New Insights. Being the sort of rabbit who treasured New Insights, she sidled up closer to Lynnepig and began to read any book that L.P. recommended.

Then, something bad happened. Lynnepig got hurt. She was very badly hurt on the inside, and it made her sigh a lot. Her tail stopped curling, and it hung limp and dragged behind her, leaving a trail in the barnyard dust. She didn't eat and she lost weight and she was very, very sad.

It was a Bad Thing, but it was also a Good Thing, because it changed the status quo. Lynnepig was forced to look at things differently, to reach out, and to become a more Open Pig. Pat T. Bunny found a measure of compassion inside of her when she saw Lynnepig hurting so badly, and she forgot more of her fear. She found that in addition to the already known assets, Lynnepig was Loyal and Courageous and Determined. She heard that Lynnepig was Sensitive and Articulate, and she found this to be true. Pat T. Bunny found herself wanting to help Lynnepig, and in the process she decided that Lynnepig was a Good Friend and a Wise Counselor.

Lynnepig went on another long journey, and Pat T. Bunny missed her dreadfully. When Lynnepig returned, with her tail beginning to show signs of curl, P.T.B. invited Lynnepig into her home and heart in a new way. Pat T. Bunny and Lynnepig made a solemn vow to Try Something New with one another. It was A Risk. For Pat T. Bunny, it meant a decision had to be made. The decision was that her relationship with Lynnepig was more important than her fear. This was a very hard decision for Pat T. Bunny, but she almost didn't notice it, because she was so busy.

She was learning more about Lynnepig. To her increasingly delighted surprise, she found Lynnepig to be Compassionate and Gentle and Emotionally Responsible. She also found that Lynnepig Listened Well and was Open to Change. Best of all, when she and Lynnepig both put their minds together and worked on something, they made Astounding New Discoveries about Life. Pat T. Bunny sometimes wondered if these things had been there in Lynnepig all along, or if they had appeared over time. Either way, she changed Lynnepig's status from Good Friend to Grand Friend.

Lynnepig's tail began to curl more tightly, and her snout stopped dragging in the dirt, and Pig and Bunny had fun together. They worked very hard. They wondered about The Mysteries. Sometimes when things were too hard to say, they wrote them instead. They learned to respect one another's Feelings and Tender Spots and to accept one another's Flaws. They acknowledged the differences between a Pig and a Bunny, and each worked at learning more about the other's experience. They poked around in frightening areas like Fears and Boundaries and Differences, Pride and Politics and even Anger and Hurt. Slowly, Pat T. Bunny found that she could trust Lynnepig to poke gently and with care. She found herself being gentle and careful as well, and she liked herself better. That made her value Lynnepig all the more.

It would be wonderful to say that Pat T. Bunny and Lynnepig lived happily ever after, but that isn't yet clear. For now, they are very warm and close animals who are practicing Important Things with each other for two reasons:

1. So they can continue to mine their special relationship for all of the joy and surprise and fun and comfort and healing and learning that they can find.

2. So they can spread what they learn throughout the Barnyard, touching other animals and making the Barnyard—and maybe even the countryside—a warmer and safer place for every kind of animal.

EIGHTEEN

Deeper than Biology

GAIL M. DOTTIN

For Dionne

Telling people around me that I love them while they're still here is real important to me. Which is why I tell Dionne that I love her as she sits down across from me in the booth at the diner. D is looking and feeling low today. No money. No job. She needs an angel. So we talk and I try to help her sort out her panicked mind. "Don't give up before the miracle," I say. "You've been here before. There's something to learn. You'll never be homeless. Too many people love you." I say this for both of us, actually. See, D and I are the same person, sistas. So I know what she's feeling. I know what she's going through. There's no doubt in my mind that she's going to make it, that she'll leave this world richer for her having been here. But sometimes she gets in her own way—like I do—and needs someone to show her the good stuff in her life. Tell her, "Don't give up before the miracle comes." So that's what I do, 'cause like I said, D and I are sistas, for real. Maybe not the same mother but sistas just the same. This goes deeper than biology.

Our lives run in opposing cycles. She's down, I'm up, and vice versa. Just two months ago, on New Year's Eve, I was about to jump out a window. I was through and tired. My girlfriend pulled me in and called D. D was there; she listened and preached to me. Told me I was smarter than that. Told me I wasn't a punk. Told me that our ancestors didn't endure firehoses, whippings, and other forms of degradation so that I could punk out like that. She told me she loved me.

Now, the girlfriend is gone. But I'm still here, with a new optimism and a new woman. And so is D. As it should be. So buying her a cup of coffee and uplifting her spirit wasn't nothing but returning the favor. 'Cause me and D are in this life together. She thanked me for the blessing but she didn't have to. That's my sista, for real.

Nancy Davidson (left) on the bay in Provincetown, Massachusetts (1977), where, as Nancy's story describes, Skinny "charmed a bluefish from a Portuguese fisherman." They then had a cookout on the beach with other friends, "and took pictures of our fine time." Photo by Dotti Shami.

NINETEEN

Portrait of Skinny and Me

NANCY S. DAVIDSON

I was wild about her from the moment I met her. This unknown woman had floated into the staff room of the rape crisis center and announced to whomever was present that she had just received the photography job of her dreams; it meant a lot of money and a four-day week. Who wasn't thrilled for her, even if we didn't know her? She was so tickled, thankful, and gracious all at once. I have liked her and loved her ever since. It has taken me many years to understand her influence upon me.

We were living in the contradictions of an era that for a few years went unnamed and undesigned until Calvin Klein bought the decade. It was the mid-1970s—that jumble between political upheaval and the "Me Decade"—when we came together. I was twenty-five and eager to make my identity. Skinny was a few years older and, for me, she made life seem like an endless bazaar of passionate experiences. Amidst the backdrop of the pressure of being "politically correct," Skinny danced the tightrope between having a good time and living with a political conscience.

We shared a coming of age together. We met at a time when the movement for gay and lesbian rights was taking off like wildfire. No matter what our chronological age, a second adolescence of gay and lesbian pride was infiltrating our adult identities. We wanted group identification, political power, and personal attractiveness. We wanted it all. Dressed in our white linens and Bogart hats, we took the champagne train to New York to be part of the one hundred

thousand that marched for gay and lesbian rights in 1976. Afterwards, we hit the gay bars. And when it was time to go home we
rebelled and charged a hotel room on Skinny's credit card. We
weren't through enjoying life yet.

Our talks were the best. We had important and "heady" questions
to answer, such as, "What is 'sleazy politics' versus the limitations of
applying ideals of perfection to an imperfect world?" Skinny opened
up ideas to me about feminism, politics, hard work, hedonism, style,
looking good and still being politically correct, gourmet food, and
design. Together we tried to understand the best and worst in human
nature, our painful family roots, and any other slice of life that
caught our eye. We were both TV fanatics who read books. We didn't
know what category that put us in—dumb intellectuals or interesting
morons?

I nicknamed her after my neighbor's cat. She was long and lanky,
like the kitty who learned to open my kitchen door and join an
already sleeping me for a nap. I'd wake up with "Skinny Kitty"
stretched out beside me. I loved that cat.

Skinny made events. I loved to have fun but Skinny's capacity to
organize was unsurpassed. Once, she charmed a bluefish from a
Portuguese fisherman in Provincetown and decided to make a cookout on the beach. She sent us off with instructions to get this and
that, and an hour later we ate broiled bluefish soaked in white wine
with fire-roasted vegetables. The sun set on the bay and we sat on the
seawall and took pictures of our fine time.

We had escapades. We even went undercover. Skinny got the idea
to do a documentary on psychics. So, dressed with a hidden camera,
we visited five palm readers in a row. We couldn't stop laughing at
the wholesale fraud: "You will marry and have three children." Yeah.
Sure.

There was something of the artiste in Skinny's approach to daily
life. I know of no one else who could pull off painting her apartment
a deep maroon and have it work. Then she added the icing to the
cake and draped colored cloths on the wall to create "fabric sculp-
ture." They hung like dancers.

We lived together for a time—Skinny, me, my lover, my cat, my lover's cat, and Skinny's fat cat, Emily. We lived in Skinny's big loft. Skinny shared her newfound wealth. Her career was zooming. I was an overeducated bartender and broke. She had a lot of money and we discussed our bourgeois guilt to death and then concluded, "Hey, we have to live somewhere." The cats never became as tight as their owners. They hissed into eternity. My cat kept beating up Emily. It was one hundred degrees that summer. I didn't have a dime, but I can honestly say I'd do it all over again.

Then there were the lesbian loft parties. We had a political and a personal life, but we needed a social life as well. For one of the parties, we sent out invitations to one hundred women. They came in droves. They came by Volvo, Subaru, Toyota, and any other "small is beautiful" car. We served hors d'oeuvres and danced all night to the new disco sounds of Donna Summer's "Love to Love Ya, Baby." One friend arrived and gushed out, "I've never seen so many beautiful women!" It was true, but it wasn't simply physical beauty; it was the glow and happiness of being together that radiated.

We were building and living a happy and proud lesbian lifestyle. We shared a zest for new experiences. We were always on the prowl for new and mysterious lovers. We were cool and we knew it, and if one of us momentarily forgot, the other one reminded her. We laughed at our vanity and consoled each other when, feeling fragile and loveless, we cried inside. We were friends, advisors, and family to each other.

It's so odd to be initially drawn to someone for the depth and essence of who they are, and then somehow, out of personal insecurities, start to see them as something *other* than who they are. It's like lovers who meet, fall in love, and then start to unravel the closeness. I did that to Skinny and me. I thought she changed, but that wasn't true. You see, Skinny was a shiny jewel for me. The smile would start in her forehead and move to her eyes, and then even before she said anything, playful thoughts would beam out and tickle me. I was in her spell, and I wanted to be. Even though I was already special to her, I guess I needed even more. Needing to be wanted and fearing not being wanted was a volatile combination for me.

Maybe if I knew what she saw in me, I could have calmed down.

It wasn't Skinny's fault, though: she paid me compliments, but I had no place to put the information. I was like an ill-equipped artist who, when asked to draw a composite sketch of herself, fills the page with extraneous limbs and unconnected joints. I had no overall sense of myself. I was as good as my last witticism.

One day I blew us up. At the time of my attack, I blamed it on a tumultuous new love affair: the woman of my dreams and I were disintegrating. Skinny and I had that in common. We didn't always pick lovers who were good for us. Back then, we picked women who were exciting. We picked women that played on our crazies. We spent a lot of time rebounding. Our styles were different. I would convert hurt into torpedoes and aim close to home. Skinny would just go inside until spring came round again.

With Skinny I had the fight I was too afraid to have with my new lover. I took out my disappointment and anger on Skinny. I remember it was a sunny winter day. We sat in the car. I called Skinny selfish, and somehow, in anger and in tears, I elaborated on my accusation for quite some time. Eventually, I calmed down and tried to patch us up. I thought I had. That summer, I moved to California. Skinny moved up the ladder. I thought San Francisco was what I should want: a gay oasis, beautiful and progressive. I found out that I was an East Coast kind of person. I thought, spoke, and walked fast. I liked structure in my life. I was on the wrong coast, and I felt like a failure. I called up Skinny and asked her if I was wrong to want to come back. She said, "You are trying to find an environment where you flourish best." "Thank you," I told her, and I moved back East. Skinny found me a place to live.

We continued our friendship, but something had shifted. The 80s weaseled in the Reagan years and served as a metaphor for the confusion I felt about Skinny and me: I kept trying to figure out what was real and what was not. Our lives flourished, and our relationship slipped away. The career-building years began. I entered a doctoral program in psychology. Skinny became an award-winning television producer. We each settled down into long-term commitments and saw each other infrequently. Monogamy and nesting, I rationalized, took up a lot of time.

We each continued bringing lesbian and gay issues into the fabric of mainstream culture. Skinny used her influence to produce television shows that focused on lesbian and gay issues. I "went after" homophobia in the field of psychology. I became an "out" lesbian therapist, teaching public and professional audiences about the damage done by homophobic and heterosexist attitudes.

The years came and went, and once in a while we would run into each other. There was an awkwardness between us. Sometimes I thought that Skinny believed that I wasn't good enough for her new, "upscale" friends. Other times, I concluded that I was acting like a jerk. One day, Skinny asked me out to lunch and told me she had never gotten over that rotten day in the car when I took my anger out on her. It was only after that lunch with Skinny that I came to understand that I had destroyed what I loved, and then—like a small child—pronounced it "broke." I finally understood the pain it had caused Skinny and the price of my anger.

After that lunch, our friendship experienced a renaissance. We became pals, advisors, and family again. We lunched, movied, and walked together. Our lives were moving at full speed. Fast, but we were still maintaining a healthy pace. Often at night, we would climb into our beds and call each other on the phone as we flipped through the channels with our new TV toy, the remote. Each of us had piled, by the side of the bed, endless amounts of books, newspapers, and magazines. We were still self-styled media critics, ever watchful for the decline of Western Civilization. One night the absurdities of the 80s hit me. I called Skinny and told her that I had, lying on my bed, the *Wall Street Journal, Mother Jones,* the *Lesbian Position,* the *Journal of Clinical Psychology,* and a book on Jewish mysticism. "Which identity do I attend to first?" I asked her.

Now—it's Stonewall's twenty fifth anniversary, 1994. It's twenty years later from where Skinny and I began. The growth and complexity of lesbian and gay visibility seems like a fabulous sci-fi story. The plot revolves around a group of oppressed drag queens who riot, motivating other homosexuals to fight mainstream culture. In some states we "come out" as congressmen and women, athletes, rock stars, schoolteachers, and cops. Public newsstands openly carry lesbian and gay magazines. Discrimination on the basis of sexual orientation is prohibited under the law. A gay and lesbian TV channel beams into our homes. Gay high schools have been established. The Gay Games fill Yankee Stadium. Some states allow gay and lesbian couples to legally register their domestic partnerships. Millions march on Washington for equal rights for lesbians, gays, and bisexuals. I win a scholarship for lesbians doing research on lesbian issues.

Twenty years ago, Skinny and I sat in the basement of a gay men's disco bar. We slouched at a card table with folding chairs, the lights bright enough to do a root canal by. Two drunk men and a butch standing at the bar, talking, drinking, and smoking. Harold Melvin and the Blue Notes pulsating at deafening decibels into the temporary territory of "lesbian space." It was Tuesday at the bar—"Women's Night."

How far our lesbian lives have come. How far our own ambitions and evolutions have led us. It's the 90s. We are still close, but we don't have the kind of time together we would like. Our lives are on fast forward; we are each overextended and committed to our creative pursuits. Skinny is finishing a documentary and book, and I'm completing my dissertation, writing, and doing my art projects. Sometimes we talk by cordless phone, Skinny on her treadmill, me on my Stairmaster. Mostly, we're exhausted.

I don't think it's only us. Life is more serious. The 90s are kind of like castor oil, and there's always one more global problem to swallow. We each do what we can in a world seeming more and more out of control. Skinny takes her camera and documents the pregnancy of everyday life. I work with survivors of abuse and trauma. Both of us belong to various groups that devote time and money to making the world somehow a better place.

Our adventures are quieter. We share homeowner secrets now. We discovered that appliances die in groups, so that if the refrigerator goes, expect the furnace and water heater to croak in solidarity. When I hit forty, I momentarily panicked. Skinny suggested we find women who are older and feel beautiful and happy. "Cool, I said, "Do we know any?" We thought for a while. We ruled out celebrities and women with money. We wanted to find our role models in everyday life. We began a prowl for older women role models.

We're older now, and we like ourselves. We check out vacation homes in gay hot spots. We fantasize about how, when we are really old, we are going to live in a lesbian retirement mansion by the sea. We do miss our hanging out days, when time was a patient friend who never left. Recently, I stopped wearing a watch. I told Skinny that I am happier without it. "I don't need reminders," I told her. "I know exactly what time it is."

Still, those moments of truth, when we allow each other a glimpse of our current lives, are like sinking into a piece of a favorite chocolate. I know I can't and won't eat as much as I used to, but when I taste the richness, I know it was worth the wait. I've always felt there was this richness about Skinny.

When Skinny got her car phone, she called me up from her red convertible and announced, laughing into my answering machine, "You're the first person I'm calling." The cars roared by. "I just want you to know," she yelled over the traffic, "You're one of the most important people in my life, on the planet." She laughed into the wind until my answering machine clicked off. I kept on laughing.

TWENTY

Cindy

CONNIE S. CHAN

If I hadn't found Cindy when I did, I would have spent much more time floundering. I desperately desired a friend like Cindy—a reflection of parts of myself in a bolder, sassier form. She was a feminist, an activist, a proud lover of women, a public spokesperson for battered women's groups, and she, like me, was Chinese American. While all of Cindy's identities were important to her and to me, it was the fact that she was a Chinese American lesbian who identified proudly as a woman of color that linked us as comrades and friends.

I had never known anyone who was both Asian American and a lesbian until I met Cindy. There she was, arguing passionately about the need for Asian American women to work with our Black and Latina sisters on common issues of reproductive rights, more battered women's services, and the like. I was captivated by her words, but even more by her determination and self-confidence. As a fledgling "baby dyke" who was just coming out, I watched this woman, and I knew, I just *knew*, I was meeting my first Asian American lesbian role model. Fresh as I was to lesbian life, my gay radar had zeroed in on Cindy squarely and all signs read "lesbian." I was, as the saying goes, "beside myself." I had to meet her. Putting aside my customary reserve, I boldly walked right up to her. As I recall, the conversation went like this:

"Hi, I agree with what you said, and I'm interested in working with you on the Asian women's caucus."

"Oh, great. Here, sign up on this list. We'll call you."

"Okay." Now what do I do? I stood there, unsure, refusing to miss my chance with this woman, this one single Asian American lesbian in my small world. "Cindy," I stammered, "can I call you? Maybe we could get together." I hoped I did not sound as desperate as I felt. To be young, gay, and convinced that the only other Asian American lesbian in town was standing a foot away from me was exhilarating and draining at the same time.

"Oh." She stopped her rapid chatter to study my face. Our eyes locked ever so slightly, and she pulled away. "Sure. I mean, okay. Here's my number."

She wrote it on a corner of the tablet, and I tore it off, stuffing it into my front jeans pocket. I called her the next day.

Years later, one of our friends asks me if I had been "interested" in Cindy when I first met her, if I had been so excited about her because I wanted to date her, to be lovers with her. Searching my memory, I'd have to say I honestly don't think so. I was just thrilled to meet someone like me; I didn't really fantasize or try to define the nature of our relationship. But I did know one thing from the beginning: I wanted to get to know her. I wanted to talk to her. I wanted Cindy to be my friend.

Our friendship lasted for ten years. The early years were full of excitement and discovery, laughter and sharing. We cooked Chinese food together, went to bars and danced, talked about our crushes on new women, went to the beach, and went to marches and rallies. Most of all, we shared "war stories" about our families, about how they didn't understand us, about the parts of Chinese American culture which were painful to me, and which I didn't have to explain to Cindy. In our relationship, I could be myself, Chinese cultural nuances and all. I didn't have to try to accommodate to the ways of American culture, to pretend, and to be gracious.

With Cindy, I could be indirect, as Chinese culture often is, in my communications, and she would know what I was saying without my having to say it. We knew when to push each other to be more open and when to allow for the privacy—the reserve in expressing feelings—that is the core of a Chinese woman's self. We became,

along with a few gay Asian brothers, the families we all had to some
degree lost.

Cindy and I were both fun-loving and loud, and we loved to laugh,
but we didn't look alike physically. Yet I would often be mistaken for
Cindy and she for me at meetings, at parties, and in the women's
community. This annoyed us no end, but even in our annoyance, we
made fun of it, and I convinced one or two of the truly gullible that
Cindy and I were lesbian sisters in a Chinese family of four gay
children.

There was no way, however, that we could have fooled either of
our *real* families, and family interactions were times when I deeply
appreciated my friendship with Cindy. Two stories come to mind:
The first is the time when Cindy is helping to start up a new battered
women's safe house, and we are moving furniture from her parents'
home to the shelter. Since we have several heavy items to move,
Cindy and I bring along two of our Asian gay brothers to supply the
brawn. We pull up in a huge rental van with the guys, both with
sculpted bodies and wearing earrings. Cindy's grandmother comes to
the door, takes one look at the four of us, and starts pulling us into
the living room to sit and have refreshments. She insists that Cindy
and Andrew sit on one couch and situates Larry and me on the other,
plying us with soft drinks and cookies. We are trying to be gracious,
but our minds are on all the furniture we've got to move, so Cindy
jumps up and charges down to the basement. The guys follow her
immediately, glad to be relieved of the anxiety of sitting in the living
room. "Popo," Cindy's grandmother, grabs my arm and whispers to
me in Cantonese. I start laughing and give her a big smile and a hug.
Popo chortles loudly and starts to sing. The others look at me with
wide eyes, but I just smile and shrug my shoulders. The furniture gets
moved into the van. Popo stands on the curb, signing and waving at
us. While we throw ourselves into our seats, Cindy yells at me, "All
right, what was so funny?" I burst into laughter. I can hardly speak.
"It was Popo. She told me that Larry and Andy were the cutest,
prettiest boys she had ever seen, and that you and I should stop
moving furniture with them and get home and make wontons for
their dinners. It's the quickest way to their hearts. And that they

would make great husbands, because they were clearly men of refinement. Look, they were even wearing earrings, a sign that they were looking for queens to marry." I tell them how I could only laugh and give her a hug. Then Popo had started singing a Chinese song about a young prince who finds a girl and makes her a queen one day. She doesn't know how right on the mark she is, with Andrew and Larry, about looking for queens! The boys loved this story and begged me to teach them the song, but I didn't really know it well enough. Cindy loved having me around to talk to her family in Cantonese and run interference at family gatherings. It is as comforting to have cultural and family quirks understood by a Chinese friend as it is not having to explain the little nuances of gay life to straight friends.

When I gave birth to my daughter, Cindy and our gay Asian family understood the importance of having a traditional one-month party. In Chinese tradition, when the baby is a month old, you hold a gathering, with special foods such as red eggs, pickled pigs feet, and "drunken chicken," to celebrate, and you introduce the baby to her extended family. Excited about the baby in our lives, my gay Asian family cooked a wonderful meal with all the special foods, and we had a joyous celebration. Still, at the end of the day, I was feeling some sadness at not having my blood relatives and family at this special occasion. It was a bittersweet event for me, and when we cleaned up at the end of the day, Cindy acknowledged the trade-offs she and I had made in the lives we had chosen. We had forged new family ties with our friends (and now with the baby, I had even started a family of my own), but Cindy and I had also pushed the limits, straining our ties with our families of origin.

As my daughter grew and my parenting responsibilities increased, my friendship with Cindy continued, but not with the same intensity. She, too, was busy: she was in a long-term relationship, and her time was filled with her new graduate studies. Once a month, when we could, we cooked our delicious wontons and caught up on each other's lives, but our visits were less frequent than before. We did save for each other our stories about the disappointment and conflict we were experiencing with our families. Indeed, we always felt nurtured when we talked about our families. It was the bond in our friendship, the place where Cindy and I found strength without having to explain, openness without loss of privacy.

After Cindy graduated, she moved to Virginia with her lover to accept a new job with wonderful potential. It was her first time away from her family, and from her many friends in the Boston area. I missed her a great deal. Slowly, over time, without our awareness, we reached a point where we saw each other only once or twice a year, catching up when we could, writing long messages on Christmas cards. Without regular contact, the strong bonds of our friendship were starting to fray. We were not putting in the time or paying enough attention to even notice points at which we still could have reinforced them.

Three years ago, I was in Virginia on business and called Cindy to see if we could get together for dinner. A friend answered, saying she was house-sitting for Cindy, who was up in New York for some medical tests. I called Cindy a week later, and the news was devastating: she had been diagnosed with liver cancer. It seemed as though it happened overnight, like a nightmare: first the diagnosis, then hospitalization, a "circling" of her family and closest friends, and unexpectedly quickly, she was gone. I spoke to her once and sent cards and letters, but she had already slipped away from me, and then, from all of us.

At the funeral service, I listened to Cindy's family and friends, grief-stricken, talk of what a loving, accomplished woman she had been, of her many political and work-related achievements. Although her lover and ex-lovers were all there, there was no direct reference to her being a lesbian, to being a proud, beautiful Asian American lesbian, one of the few I have ever met and the one whom I have loved as a friend, as a sister in our gay Asian family. I struggled with whether I should say something, to cross the line Cindy's friends were all carefully dancing around, all of us respecting her family's presence and silence. I remembered our many heartfelt talks about our struggles with our families, our disappointments, our trade-offs, our discomfort and silences at family gatherings. I thought of the role we had played in each other's lives, running interference with our families, talking to them in Cantonese, deflecting the issues. I swallowed the lump in my throat and remained silent. At the end of the service, I spoke to her parents and told them that Cindy had been a true friend to me, understanding without need of explanation, sharing of herself openly, and that she had loved, and had been loved by, many friends and lovers. I am fortunate to have been among them; I miss her friendship more than I can let myself feel.

"Significant friends" *and coeditors* of Lesbians at Midlife: The Creative Transition, *Joyce Warshow (left), Adrienne Smith (center), and Barbara Sang (right) are here shown together at the home of Joyce Warshow in East Hampton, Long Island. Photo by Robert Giard.*

TWENTY-ONE

A Significant Friend

JOYCE WARSHOW

Adrienne Smith was my friend. I met her in 1975 at the lesbian caucus of the Association of Gay Psychologists ("Lesbian" was added to the organization's name later). Adrienne drew me into her circle, where I met wonderful women, several of whom, in addition to Adrienne, became close friends.

We shared our personal musings and doings as well as our political hopes and fears. She would spin panel and workshop ideas to help us to formalize what we had been thinking and feeling. These presentations, and her participation in the creation of new organizations such as the Feminist Therapy Institute, were an effort to be proactive and to bring feminist therapists together so that they could nurture each other as well as educate others about the salience of gender in doing therapy with women. She was deeply committed to both the women's community and the lesbian and gay community.

In the early 70s Adrienne served the lesbian community by giving workshops for nongay therapists on how to work with lesbian clients. She was a role model for other lesbian and gay therapists, who often feared that their life's work was in jeopardy if they revealed who they were personally. She exemplified a basic mental health principle that we must be who we are and not who people want us to be. She was instrumental in the creation of the American Psychological Association (APA) Division 44 on Gay and Lesbian Studies and served as its president in 1990.

As a colleague, Adrienne had wonderfully creative suggestions and believed in the feasibility of all of them. These projects also involved bringing many people together. One such project was the book *Lesbians at Midlife* that Barbara Sang, Adrienne, and I coedited. Because Barbara and I live in New York and Adrienne lived in Chicago, we would always room together at conferences and "bounce ideas off each other." When someone once asked us if we were "significant others," we laughed and replied, "Yes, but not in the way you mean." We brought such different perspectives to these discussions and to our collaboration on the book. In true feminist fashion, we facilitated each other's work, each of us appreciating the other's contribution and receiving appreciation in return. One of Adrienne's contributions was her skill in editing and helping to clarify ideas.

What I liked best about Adrienne as a friend was her warmth, acceptance, and willingness to share her intelligence, insights, friends, and personal journeys. I loved to dance with Adrienne. As we shook our bodies at each other on the dance floor, her eyes would light up. She had always thought of herself as uncoordinated, but how we looked to others didn't bother either of us. It was simply an expression of our joy in being friends and in the work and purpose we shared. She particularly loved to be at the dances that were racially mixed and included both gays and straights, like the black women's annual fund-raising dance at APA.

Adrienne continued to be a role model in her effort to take control and fight for her life, which she did steadfastly and valiantly. She shared and received health information through networking with other women (including Audre Lorde, the black, lesbian, feminist poet laureate of New York State, who lost her own fourteen-year battle with cancer in November of 1992). When there was nothing further to do, she let go, as one friend commented, "surrounded by a sea of love."

Her effect on all those people whom she influenced and the effect they will have on others is her legacy. That effect was about letting women know they were valued and that what they had to say was important. It was also about the importance of community in our lives as a way of furthering the rich culture that develops when people have been disaffected and must come together to form their own ethos and affirm themselves. At the end, she also taught us how to die.

Even after her death from cancer, Adrienne got to educate the public about the lives of lesbians and gays by expressing who she was in a videotape made shortly before her death to say good-bye to her friends and colleagues. A writer for the *Washington Post* saw her video tape (shown posthumously after the Division 44 Presidential Address, delivered by Connie Chan) and wrote on it in his column about the APA conference. In this tape, Adrienne talks about how important it has been to her to be a member of Division 44 and before that to be one of the first openly lesbian psychologists and a founder of the Association of Lesbian and Gay Psychologists. In addition to the important work that was done by these organizations, they were places, as she said, "where my professional and personal lives could come together."

When I went to Chicago to say good-bye to Adrienne and to have a last visit with her, just before the APA conference in Washington, a heterosexual client of mine who discovered *Lesbians at Midlife* on her own said to me, "Please thank Adrienne for me." This client's readiness for self-disclosure seems to have vastly improved after reading the book. Her initial shock that I was a lesbian gave way to the lessening of her own sense of shame as she sought to work through the challenges in her own life. She said she wanted to thank Adrienne because she could see from my autobiographical sketch in the book that Adrienne had a profound effect on my "coming into my own as a lesbian," which she felt had a lot to do with my being "a wonderful therapist." (This woman has also since defended the acceptance of openly lesbian and gay clergy in the Presbyterian Church's recent dialogue on this issue).

Unfortunately, I arrived two hours too late to deliver the message and to play a wonderful Klezmer music tape I had brought for her. We had often shared our pleasure at being "doubly blessed" as Jews and as lesbians. However, one piece from the tape did become a part of her memorial at the Feminist Therapy Institute, an organization she helped to found.

I miss her deeply. In my own way, I will try to carry on our shared vision of an end to misogyny, racism, and homophobia.

"Celebrating Friends" is the message on the cake at this second annual gathering (1994) to celebrate friendship and Linda Strega's continued survival following her 1993 surgery for cancer. Pictured here, from left to right, are Linda, Bev Jo, Sylph, Lisa Hubbard, Karen Shepherd, Elizabeth Kristen, and Carol Cox.

TWENTY-TWO

A Lesbian Love Story

LINDA STREGA

On January 29, 1993, I found out I had cancer and needed surgery. I've had chronic fatigue immune dysfunction syndrome (CFIDS, also known as ME or myalgic encephalomyelitis) since 1981 and multiple chemical sensitivities (MCS) for almost as long. I couldn't imagine how I could survive the toxins, stresses, and exhaustion of surgery and hospitalization, never mind the cancer itself, and I wasn't sure I wanted to. My first reaction to the bad news was a nauseating terror about the prolonged pain, dependency, and death that might be in my near future. My next thoughts were, "I barely have the energy to get through each day as it is. How can I do all the things I'll need to do to prepare for surgery and then try to recover? And how am I going to pay for it all?"

There's no way I can adequately describe the life-saving, encompassing support given me since then by Lesbian friends—almost all Separatists—in my home community of Oakland, California, or the warm and generous support of over seventy Separatists and other Lesbians from the U.S., Canada, Aotearoa (New Zealand), Argentina, Japan, Australia, and Europe who sent me money, information, cards, letters, and notes of loving encouragement. Some of these wonderful Lesbians I've known for twenty years, some for less than a year, and some I've never met. Most are Separatists, but some have very different politics; still, almost all are activists.

I'm writing this to publicly thank them all, to share information that might be useful to other Lesbians in similar situations, and to share the good feelings and sense of hopefulness that an experience like this can give. Like any Lesbian, especially one who's been a Separatist for a long time, I've had my share of painful disappointments, betrayals, and alienation within Lesbian community, and it feels wonderfully healing to now be able to write about an experience where Lesbian friends and community embraced me and carried me through a life-threatening crisis. I could not have made it through surgery and hospitalization, or the times before and after, without the support I was given, and I'm not sure I would have even wanted to make it through. Having been chronically ill and socially limited for thirteen years, I was awfully low on energy, patience, and love of life. The love and support I got not only took care of my physical needs, it gave me a tremendous boost of relief and joy as well.

Fifteen months after my diagnosis I'm less tired than before surgery, and life has a renewed sweetness. I've been told that because I had an unusually aggressive type of cancer, my chances of having a recurrence and/or metastasis is up to 50 percent. But no matter how short or long the rest of my life is, I know without doubt that I am well loved, and I feel connected with more Lesbians, especially other Separatists, than ever before.

Friends in Action

My core support group of wonderful Lesbian Separatist friends did, and continues to do, the major day-to-day work of helping me survive. They are: Bev, my housemate and my best friend of twenty years, who also has CFIDS and MCS; Sylph, who is Bev's lover and my good friend and has lived in Oakland almost three years; and Elizabeth, Lisa, Karen, and Carol, who have all moved to Oakland within the past three and a half years. I want to describe some of what they did so other Lesbians can get an idea of what's needed in a situation like mine, and how much is possible.

As soon as I got the cancer diagnosis, Bev called all our friends and told them, and then began a series of stress-filled phone calls to doctors' offices to get information about which further tests and surgery I should have and to find a good female surgeon who accepts the state welfare health insurance and who practices at a reputable hospital. The information came in bits and pieces: much of it was contradictory; some we knew was wrong; many doctors' receptionists were cold and nasty. So Bev was making phone calls for hours every day for weeks. Bev also immediately took on most of my half of our usually shared household tasks. Being very sick herself, this work, added to her anxiety for me was very hard on her. In spite of this, she continues to give me the utmost ongoing emotional support as well as daily physical help.

Sylph also made phone calls for me in search of medical items and supplements I'd need, fixed meals for Bev and me, and wrote and mailed notices to Lesbian publications about my having cancer and needing money and information. Bev, Elizabeth, and Lisa also called Lesbians we all knew in the Bay Area to ask for donations of safe blood in case I needed transfusions during surgery. Elizabeth herself gave blood, and so did Louise and Mady. I did require a transfusion during surgery, and it's great to know I got safe, Lesbian blood.

Lisa and Elizabeth went to the Berkeley Women's Cancer Resource Center to find and photocopy needed medical information. They called SMASH (Separatist Mutual Aid Society, Hooray), Lavender LEAF (Lesbian Emergency Action Fund), and the Dykefund, so that I got donations through all three to help with medical bills not covered by the state insurance. (SMASH was organized by and for Separatists at the 1991 Separatist Conference; LEAF and the Dyke-fund were created locally by and for poverty-class and working-class Lesbians.) Lisa took on the frustrating job of applying for the state welfare medical insurance for me, which involved countless visits to the state agency and many phone calls, with all the usual waiting in lines and being given wrong information. It was Lisa's persistence that got me the insurance, just in time for the scheduled surgery. There was no way I could have done it myself without physically collapsing. The cruelty of the welfare system and the anxiety it put us through was one of the hardest things to live with during the weeks between diagnosis and surgery.

The money I've received from donations means I don't have to choose between medical care and food or other necessities. It also helps pay for herbs, vitamins, homeopathy, and Qi Gong/Tai Chi lessons, all of which are part of my alternative healing plan and which are doing me a lot of good. (My surgeon recommended radiation or chemotherapy to try and kill any remaining cancer cells, but I decided not to accept either one, because both methods kill healthy tissue as well and further damage the immune system and vital organs.) [1]

Lisa, Elizabeth, Karen, and Carol began cooking meals for Bev and me right away and brought us two meals a week for about a year, on a rotating schedule they arranged among themselves. They were great meals, too! They stopped only when Bev and I asked them to. They've also done our weekly grocery shopping for us, except for several months when Kate, a Lesbian volunteer from the Women's Cancer Resource Center, took over. That help alone has relieved me from a huge amount of fatigue and relapses of CFIDS and MCS symptoms, not just because shopping takes energy but because breathing in the toxins from other customers' perfumes and fabric softeners makes me a lot sicker. Carol picked up medical supplies and medical records I needed, often on short notice. Lisa drove Bev and me to my doctor appointments and presurgery tests and usually came into the doctor's office with us, to be a witness and to help us remember things. Elizabeth and Lisa bought Bev and me an answering machine to reduce the fatigue of dealing with so many extra calls. Bev sought out and brought me books about cancer, hysterectomy, and alternative healing.

Lisa, Elizabeth, Bev, and Sylph wrote a letter about my situation for all the Lesbians we know, and Lisa and Elizabeth typed, photocopied, and mailed it. An update was later written and mailed in the same way to all Lesbians who responded to the first mailing. Lisa acted as a conduit for donations and messages received.

Friends like Barbara Ruth and Jessica, who are themselves disabled by chronic illness and are disability rights activists, gave me wonderful support, always practical and encouraging, acknowledging both my strengths and vulnerabilities, understanding from their own lives just what I needed at any given time. They also showed deep and understanding concern for Bev. Jessica phoned Bev and me at the most significant times to find out how we were, giving us both a strong ongoing sense of her caring presence. Throughout the crisis, I could feel Lesbians' thoughts, concern, and love as an abiding strong and gentle presence, so that I seldom felt alone when I didn't want to be alone.

Barbara Ruth sent me essential information about how to educate the surgeon and anesthesiologist about chemical sensitivities, what to request from the hospital staff, and what to provide for myself, and she gave wonderful emotional support, telling me, "Trust your intuition, and don't let anyone railroad you into anything." She also sent me an MCS treasure: my own plastic oxygen tubing so I could wash and air it out myself a few weeks before going to the hospital. She put me in touch with Amanda, a nurse practitioner who shared information with me about her radical hysterectomy and hospitalization for cervical cancer, as well as valuable medical information my doctors didn't bother to tell me. Judith also described in detail her experiences with hysterectomy and hospital life. Both helped me prepare myself better for the surgery and saved me from some panic-creating surprises, like waking up with three tubes sticking out of my lower belly. Barbara Ruth also put me in touch with Ann, a Lesbian doctor who has MCS herself, who gave me a very helpful telephone consultation at a reduced fee.

Many friends who don't live near me, including my longtime Separatist friends Frances and Roxanna, sent emotional support, information, and money. Frances helped me in another way as well. Two years ago she generously gave me the money to have my mercury amalgam dental fillings replaced with safer ones, hoping that might reduce or eliminate my chronic illness. Though I still have CFIDS and MCS, getting the mercury out of my mouth relieved me of other debilitating symptoms of neurological damage connected with mercury poisoning. As a result, I got through my ordeal this year with less pain and lots more calm than I would have otherwise.

Even with all the help I got, I was busy with preparations all day every day right up to the day of surgery. There's no way I could have done it alone or even with the help of just one or two friends. At the very least, I would have been much sicker and weaker, I probably would have suffered toxic reactions in the hospital, I would have had no choices at all about which surgeon and which hospital to use, I might have been pressured into accepting harmful procedures, and my recovery would have been slower and more difficult. At worst, I might not have survived at all.

On the dreaded day of surgery, Bev, Sylph, Lisa, and Karen all came with me into the tiny curtained cubicle where the last preop interviews and preparations are done. Under the alert watchfulness of my four friends, every medical person who attended me was very careful and courteous. Then, while I was in surgery, my friends cleared as many toxic products out of my hospital room as possible and remade the bed with unscented cotton sheets brought from home. (Elizabeth had bought and given me a gift of four sets of new untreated cotton sheets—another treasure to a Lesbian with MCS— because my own sheets were too worn to bring to the hospital and, anyway, might have got ruined by permanently absorbing smells from the toxic disinfectants and cleaning products used there.) Then these sweethearts stayed at or near the hospital for the long hours that I was in surgery and the recovery room, and were there to get the surgeons' report about how things had gone. Their waiting for me when I was brought to my hospital room couldn't have been a more wonderful welcome.

Elizabeth came to spend that first night in the hospital room with me. She "slept" on the uncomfortable little fold-out chair provided by the hospital—except that there was no sleep that night, what with the male nurse constantly coming in to wake me and check my vital signs, and the frequent loud beeping announcing that one of my IV additives had run out, and the constant clack-clack of the contraption that squeezed my legs to prevent blood clots. Carol endured the same experience the next night. It was so reassuring to have a Lesbian friend with me who sat up or got up every time a nurse came in to tend me, making sure I was all right and that no harm was done to me. Without them, I think the nightmare feelings that hovered close to me those first few nights would have closed in and shaken me badly. Lisa, Carol, and Elizabeth had scheduled for one of them to stay with me every night, but by the third night I felt more confident and decided that from then on it was more important that they not lose sleep in the hospital, and I knew I'd need their help more in other ways.

I did need more help, and my friends came through each time. Elizabeth made an emergency trip to pick up and deliver a homeopathic remedy for me one night when she was already exhausted from work, and she didn't get cranky about it, either. She was downright sweet about it. Bev went to several natural food stores one exhausting afternoon to pick up and bring me an assortment of fruit juices and other liquid foods when I was finally taken off the IV and couldn't keep anything in my neglected stomach. I was in a San Francisco hospital, and trips over the San Francisco-Oakland Bay Bridge are not quick or easy.

I was impressed with my friends' abilities to put aside their own fears and insecurities while they were with me during the hardest times, so that I didn't feel as if I had to take care of them. I knew they went through some rough times, in doctors' offices, in the hospital, and when I talked about my own fears. It also couldn't have been easy to add this extra work to their already full lives, and some were going through hard times of their own.

After ten days in the hospital, I was suddenly told one morning that if I could keep breakfast down I had to be out by 2:30 P.M. So on that short notice I phoned Lisa and asked her if someone could come bring me home. She and Karen and Petra arrived just before 2:30. They did all the packing-up I hadn't been able to finish and brought me triumphantly home. We attracted a lot of stares and second looks from the heterosexuals in the hospital hallways and elevator—me, in my own Lesbian clothes and with an eleven-day beard, in the hospital wheelchair, a lilac blossom from home in my hand and happy tears in my eyes, accompanied by three dashing and obvious Lesbian friends. I was quite proud and happy.

Unexpected Friendship and Support

The outreach my core-group friends did to other Lesbians was what brought me most of the outpouring of warm messages and donations from Lesbians outside our home community and even outside our Separatist community. Many of the Lesbians who wrote to me had read *Dykes-Loving-Dykes*, which I coauthored (with Bev and Ruston), and the book had meant a great deal to them, so that had formed a connection I hadn't been aware of before. I learned that every single message, even a short note on a scrap of paper, means a lot during a crisis. I remembered the times when others were in crisis and I'd thought what I was able to give was so inadequate to the size of the crisis that it might only be annoying. Now I know better. I also learned how good it feels when someone is clear and specific about what she can do, with no unnecessary apologies about what she can't do, and I was impressed by how many Lesbians know how to do that.

I'm very touched by all the help I also got from Lesbians who didn't know me. Rowan happened to phone me the same day I got the cancer diagnosis, in answer to an ad I'd placed about a Lesbian support group. She offered help immediately and ended up sending me a large amount of money each month for three months, which made a huge difference in my life.

Hedda, Michi, and Barbara, three thoughtful and generous Lesbian Separatists from Austria who befriended Bev and me by mail after reading *Dykes-Loving-Dykes*, continue to send both of us extensive information about alternative healing, translated by Hedda into English, and many health aids that are hard to get in the U.S., all at their own expense. It's a wonderful proof of Lesbian friendship and commitment to receive such wholehearted support from Lesbians we've never met and who live in different parts of the world.

It was also heartening to get help from friends and acquaintances who don't socialize with me anymore but who said they still care about me. I even received some cards and donations from Lesbians I've had painful conflicts with in the past. It was a profoundly emotional and aware time in my life, and I felt these messages and gifts came from Lesbians who have a sense of us belonging with each other as Lesbians and as Separatists in ways that go beyond personal differences or discomforts with each other. Maybe life-and-death crises help remind us of the things we do like about each other.

A Caution about Professionals

In contrast to the support given me by other Lesbians, I was badly let down by one Lesbian doctor who is part of the wider local Lesbian and feminist community. Though she was my doctor for several years, during which time I had obvious symptoms of cancer, she failed to give me needed information about further testing and even falsely reassured me when I developed a copious watery discharge—a clear warning sign of advanced cancer—telling me it was an improvement over the previous bleeding. I'd been having annual checkups and Pap smears, which always showed negative for cancer, yet I had almost continual spotting and bleeding while going through menopause. When I asked her if I needed to go to a gynecologist, she said no.

This doctor didn't tell me about adenocarcinoma of the cervix, that it's usually not detected by a Pap smear until well advanced, and that it's been increasing in frequency to as much as 34 percent of cervical cancers. (The more common squamous cell cancer is usually easily detected in the early stages by a Pap smear.) When I asked about further testing, she told me I could be further examined by a cone biopsy, which means cutting out a piece of the cervix under general anesthesia and which causes heavy bleeding. I didn't feel safe having this done and asked if there were any less traumatic tests. The doctor said no and didn't tell me about the more appropriate tests—a colposcopy (to look more closely at the cervix) with cervical and endometrial biopsies—which are fast and relatively painless office procedures and which would likely detect adenocarcinoma at an earlier stage. (These biopsies are not 100 percent accurate either, and in some cases a D & C may be necessary.) In desperation, I finally did go to a gynecologist and later learned I had endometrial (uterine) cancer which had moved down into my cervical canal. My Lesbian doctor had told me that uterine cancer isn't a big killer, but it happened that I had a less common type—clear cell adenocarcinoma—which is very fast and invasive, metastasizes easily, and does not give as good a survival rate as the more common types. When I called this doctor and told her I had cancer, she said she was too busy to talk with me and never called me back.

I was also falsely reassured by two community herbalists/acupuncturists and told not to worry about cancer. This points up the need for Lesbians to share health information from our own personal experiences and to be cautious about relying too trustfully on professionals, even if they're Lesbians themselves or have a large Lesbian clientele.

There are wonderful, competent Lesbian professionals. I mention my experience only as a caution. For those of us lucky enough to find a Lesbian doctor or healer, our natural inclination is to put lots of trust in her and to be reluctant to change doctors or even get second opinions from other doctors, especially for gynecological problems. But sometimes we have to.

Putting Lesbians First

I want all Lesbians with chronic illnesses like chronic fatigue immune dysfunction syndrome, multiple chemical sensitivities, lupus, and multiple sclerosis to routinely receive the same kind of attention and care I did during my bout with cancer. I've shared sadness and frustration with some friends who also have CFIDS and/or MCS, because there are no organized support services for us. When Lesbians with CFIDS or MCS do receive any care at all, it's usually from a lover or from other Lesbians with CFIDS and MCS. Many Lesbians with cancer don't receive the kind of care I did, either. There are many reasons for this lack of support. Most Lesbians' time and energy is very limited, because our lives are not easy. But there are still lots of Lesbians giving their precious time and energy to taking care of gay men with AIDS, raising boys, working on heterosexual women's issues, and caring for heterosexual women physically and emotionally. What if all that energy was going toward Lesbians instead?

In January 1989, Jackie Winnow, a Lesbian activist who founded the Women's Cancer Resource Center in Berkeley, made an extremely important keynote speech at the Lesbian Caregivers and AIDS Epidemic Conference in San Francisco, in which she pointed out the severe lack of health care and support services for sick Lesbians, while large numbers of Lesbians are taking care of gay men with AIDS. Jackie's speech, later printed in *Out/Look*,[2] describes in eloquent detail many of the reasons for this situation and encourages Lesbians to care for Lesbians and women first. I would also add that because it is easier for men to ask for and get help from women and Lesbians, and easier for heterosexual and bisexual women to ask for and get help from Lesbians than it is for Lesbians to ask for or get help from *anyone,* we Lesbians need to take care of each other first.

Almost all of the Lesbians who are helping me through my crisis do put Lesbians first in their lives, and that is making all the difference in the quality of my life and in my ability to stay alive as long as possible. There is nothing theoretical about this: I feel the effects every minute of the day.

NOTES

1. The decision to accept or refuse chemotherapy and radiation is a very personal and difficult one. Because we can't rely on doctors to tell us all the risks involved, it's important to keep asking them questions and ask for help gathering as much information as possible from friends and acquaintances, Lesbians' and women's cancer resource centers, medical journals and books. An excellent, politically focused anthology is *1 in 3: Women with Cancer Confront an Epidemic,* ed. Judith Brady, published in 1991 by Cleis Press (P.O. Box 8933, Pittsburgh, PA 15221 and P.O. Box 14684, San Francisco, CA 94114).

2. Jackie Winnow, "Lesbians Working on AIDS: Assessing the Impact on Health Care for Women," *Out/Look* 5 (summer 1989). Edited versions were published as "Lesbians Evolving Health Care: Our Lives Depend on It," in *Cancer as a Women's Issue,* ed. Midge Stocker (Chicago: Third Side Press, 1991) and as "Lesbians Evolving Health Care: Cancer and AIDS," in *1 in 3: Women with Cancer Confront an Epidemic.* (Jackie Winnow died of cancer in 1991.)

TWENTY-THREE

Lesbian Friendships Create
Lesbian Community

BEV JO

Like Lesbians ourselves, Lesbian friendships are a magical thing, something that persists even when we're forbidden and not supposed to exist. In almost every part of the world, we Lesbians are hated and lied about. Yet we persist in surviving, in every culture and country, appearing where there are no others like us, coming from people who try their hardest to make us not be Lesbians. Most of us grew up without any truth or information about Lesbians. The misinformation that does exist describes us in pornographic terms or as perverted, pathetic, lonely, suicidal beings.

Lies and oppression do damage, and too often Lesbian-hating lies are absorbed by and damage us and our Lesbian friendships. Many of us naturally formed close friendships with other girls when we were growing up. Some of us even knew clearly that we loved other girls. But while close friendships between girls are sometimes tolerated if they're not too close, they are not supposed to be considered as important as any other connection. Families are always expected to come first. And no matter how close girls are to their girlfriends, even after a lifetime of friendship girls are expected to immediately abandon girlfriends (or at least lessen their closeness) as soon as they get boyfriends. The few who do not give up their girlfriends usually put their boyfriends first (even ones they hardly know). Those of us who stayed close with girlfriends and chose to never be heterosexual are very rare. Females are just not supposed to be that close or that loyal with other females.

I believe those rules still affect and limit our Lesbian friendships. Many of us have experienced that betrayal when Lesbian friends chose to become heterosexual or bisexual. Almost nowhere in the world are Lesbian friendships considered real, important, and valuable. In the twenty-three years (since 1971) that I have been part of a Lesbian community, I have watched and experienced how easily Lesbians end friendships, and how often friends are not valued. Too often Lesbians will abandon friends when they get a lover, yet will reappear when that relationship ends, expecting their friends to take care of them.

Sometimes friendships are permanently ended over political disagreements, but they are also ended because of inequalities. When Lesbians become upwardly mobile, they often don't want to be around poorer friends, and non-disabled Lesbians sometimes end relationships when friends become chronically ill or disabled in another way. Yet if family members become ill or disabled, most Lesbians will devote endless time and energy to them, even if these family members have been abusive, hate Lesbians, and would force their Lesbian relative to be heterosexual if they could. "Family" usually means being forced into relationships against your will with people you would never choose as friends. And, of course, the time and energy that Lesbians devote to their families means less time and energy for other Lesbians. Often Lesbians also choose to put men (including transsexuals) and heterosexual and bisexual women before Lesbians. (This is happening in most "Lesbian" social and political groups and organizations.) I believe lack of commitment to each other as friends and as Lesbians seriously limits how much of a community we can have. If most Lesbians decided to really try to work out problems and disagreements, including trying to not be oppressive of each other, it would transform our communities.

In spite of all the hostility and hatred against us, many Lesbian friendships, like Lesbians ourselves, continue to thrive and flourish. For twenty years now I have been best friends with Linda Strega. It feels very special to have shared so much of my life with her, to love her so deeply and to feel so loved by her. We became lovers in 1974, when she was thirty-two and I was twenty-three, and, even though we stopped being lovers two and a half years later, and we both have had other lovers since, we have always stayed close. I have been closer with Linda longer than with anyone else in my life. (I am lovers now with Sylph, whom I love deeply, but my friendship with Linda will never lessen, and Linda and Sylph are also good friends.)

Linda and I have shared a lot together. We are both Dyke Separatists and committed to building Lesbian community. We wrote *Dykes-Loving-Dykes* together, taught self-defense classes, and worked on Dyke Separatist projects over the years. We lived apart for five years and together for fifteen. I know I can always trust Linda and be safe with her; I trust her love, her caring, her commitment, and her wisdom. I trust how she thinks, feels, and acts.

Linda's and my friendship is also special because our connection with each other is purely our own choice. We are friends simply because we *want* to be. We are not linked by anything outside of ourselves, any rules that say we *should* be close. The ties of family, said to be the strongest of all, do not bind us. Being a friend is so much more than that. Some Lesbians try to reclaim the term "family" to describe close, loving, committed Lesbian friendships, but I think the word is too contaminated by the abuse in families, and what Lesbians create with each other is so much more real, deep, and intense—like nothing else that exists on earth.

I feel that Linda has literally helped me survive through some of the hardest times in my life. We have been there for each other through years of chronic illness and through times of fear and pain. A year and a half ago, Linda found out that she had a particularly fast-growing, dangerous kind of cancer. I felt so worried for her, and also for myself, because the thought of living without her in this world is unbearable. She is, we hope, free of cancer now, but the risk and fear of recurrence is still very much there. I and all her friends worry for her.

Lesbian friends create our own culture of love and closeness and commitment. For all the betrayal and losses of friends I have experienced, I am always amazed at the strength and depth of the Lesbian friendships I have and that other Lesbians have. And I believe the more Lesbians accept and value themselves as Lesbians, the more they will value and love other Lesbians. That extending and growing friendship network will create a Lesbian community across the world. That is what I've wanted my entire life and that is what I am beginning to experience. The help that Linda got from dear Lesbian friends and also from Lesbian acquaintances and even Lesbian strangers made such a difference for her and for me and for everyone who loves her. It was a tangible web of Lesbian friendship that we felt and continue to feel. It truly helped us to survive and to go through such a terrifying time feeling much safer and protected. I want that network to continue to grow, until it is wide enough to help all Lesbians who love and are committed to Lesbians.

PART V

Afterword

TWENTY-FOUR

Toward a Politics of Lesbian Friendship

CELIA KITZINGER

Among lesbians in my community, the question, "Are you in a relationship with her?" means "Do you have a sexual relationship with her?"—as though only "sex" makes a relationship real or worth commenting upon. I remember once having a long, intimate, and fairly detailed conversation with a lesbian friend about the difficulties I was experiencing in my "relationship" with another friend, someone we both knew, who was not (and never has been) my lover. I only learned some time afterward that throughout the course of the conversation, she had assumed—from my use of the term "relationship" and from the seriousness of my commitment to that "relationship"—that the two of us were lovers. Relationships between friends—at least among the lesbians I know—are considered somehow less interesting and less worthy of serious attention than are sexual relationships.

This book puts lesbian friendship firmly back on the agenda as a passionate, absorbing, and vital concern for lesbians today. It is a rare pleasure to read a text which prioritizes friendship among lesbians: most research and writing about friendship is resolutely heterosexist, and most research and writing about relationships between lesbians is heavily biased toward sexual relationships (see Kitzinger and Coyle, 1995). In comparison with the now vast literature on lesbian sexual relationships—lesbian dating, lesbian sex problems, lesbian couples' struggles with (non)monogamy, housework, children, boundary issues and so on—lesbian friendships are desperately underexplored and undertheorized. Often (certainly in work by lesbian psychologists) friendships are discussed only in terms of their impact on the lesbian couple relationship: "good" friendships are those that prop up or help to sustain lesbian couples; "bad" friendships are those which cause problems for, or pose dangers to, lesbian couples.

Many of the contributors to this book emphasize the vital importance of friendship in their lives and point out how the language we use often serves to trivialize and dismiss it. If a sexual relationship is a "primary relationship," does this mean that friendships are "secondary"? If a sexual partner is a "significant other," are friends "insignificant others"? And what about the question, "Are you two together, or are you just friends?" when we are both "together" and "friends" and there is no "just" about it. Bev Jo sees the trivialization and erasure of lesbian friendships as one way in which heteropatriarchal values have pervaded lesbian communities:

> No matter how close girls are to their girlfriends, even after a lifetime of friendship, girls are expected to immediately abandon girlfriends (or at least lessen their closeness) as soon as they get boyfriends. . . . I believe those rules still affect and limit our Lesbian friendships. . . . Too often Lesbians will abandon friends when they get a lover.

It can be surprisingly difficult, even in a lesbian context, to insist on the importance and centrality of friendship to our lives. Joyce Warshow writes about her friendship with Adrienne Smith: "When someone once asked us if we were 'significant others,' we laughed and replied, 'Yes, but not in the way you mean.'" As Anndee Hochman says, "We need to remember that 'friend' is not a second-best bond, but can describe a relationship of the most intimate and precious nature."

One of the strengths of this book is its refusal to romanticize or to glorify lesbian friendships. Although our friendships may often be vibrant and joyous, productive and supportive, intense and passionate, at the same time the problems are all too evident. In part, these seem to arise because it is relatively rare for friends to be explicit about their expectations of, or their feelings for, each other, and it is often unclear just what is involved in being a "friend." Jeanne Stanley describes difficulties that may arise from lesbians' different styles of friendship, with some wanting close contact with many friends and others wanting relatively few, and perhaps less intense, friendships. I was once deeply shocked to be told that now that I was someone's "friend" she expected me to want to phone her on a weekly basis with reports of my activities. My definition of friendship certainly didn't encompass this degree of involvement in each other's lives, but my sense of claustrophobia at her expectation was matched by her dismay at my apparent detachment. Friendships have to be negotiated, sometimes painfully, into being, and this can be especially true of friendships across racial boundaries (Ruth Hall and Suzanna Rose) or across other socially significant differences (Kris Morgan and Rebecca Nerison). Writing of the conflicts that arose in their friendship ("I was angry and hurt, and she didn't seem to care."), Kris Morgan says, "I had to learn the hard way that there are many ways to do friendship." Taking friendship seriously—as seriously as our relationships with lovers—would mean addressing the problems, seeking to better understand and to deal with obstacles to friendship, with ruptured or broken friendships, with waning friendships, and with open warfare between friends. As Andee Hochman asks, "How much support do we get for efforts to mend a hurting friendship?"

The distinction between "friends" and "lovers" is a conflicted issue for many lesbians. For many of us, our lover *is* our best friend. Some happily combine friendship and "uncommitted sex" and write of "celebrating wild erotic friendship" (Marcia Munson). Others find that sex and friendship don't mix so well (Lauren Crux). And in spite—or perhaps because—of the fact that many of the friendships described in this book (as elsewhere) are friendships between ex-lovers, many tensions between friends and lovers are apparent. Various contributors to the book address the struggle to maintain lesbian friendships through the early overwhelming experiences of falling in love (or in sex) with someone else, the jealousies, guilt, and antagonisms between a friend and a lover, and the difficulties of balancing commitments to various lesbians in one's life. Jeanne Stanley reports that lesbians share a common experience of feeling "abandoned, expendable, or replaced" when friends enter new sexual relationships. Shelagh Robinson describes how, when she and Karen became lovers, their (joint) best friend Shawna wept bitter tears at her exclusion. Jane Futcher's half of the story of her friendship with Catherine Hopkins offers a detailed account of such feelings over the course of many years. When Catherine first becomes involved with Joan, Jane tells her friend how "it was a blow when you told me that you two were looking for an apartment together, that you were ready to make a lifetime commitment, to create a home." Later she is thrilled to be able to go on holiday with Catherine and without Joan: "We won't need to worry about hurting Joan's feelings with our memories and jokes, with this old, deep bond that sometimes makes her angry and restless." Later still, Catherine has cancer, and while Joan is with her in the hospital where she has an emergency operation, Jane is at her own home: "I want to see you, but it would only confuse things. . . . And my presence, I know, would be a pressure Joan doesn't need."

My own position on lesbian friendships derives from my commitment to building radical lesbian feminist politics. I have described elsewhere my concern about the psychologization of friendship, with lesbians increasingly turning to therapy, recovery programs, twelve-step groups, and cocounseling as substitutes for friendship (see Kitzinger and Perkins, 1993). Friendship is "psychologized," too, when it is addressed solely as an individual issue—as though friendships are the personal property of the lesbians involved. Friendships (like relationships between lovers) are much more than simply individual, private affairs: they are the building blocks of lesbian communities and politics. In reading the contributions to this book, I began to think of ways in which lesbian friendship could be expanded—ways in which the concept of friendship could enable us to encompass more fully the political imperatives of lesbian feminism. As Claudia Card (1995, p. 105) says, "What lesbian communities need to foster is friendship among lesbians who have never been and may never be lovers and who may never even know many details of each other's lives." Linda Strega describes a concrete example of this kind of friendship and the way in which it functions to create "a sense of us belonging with each other as Lesbians and as Separatists in ways that go beyond personal differences or discomforts with each other." She tells how her friends ("Some . . . I'd known for twenty years, some for less than a year, and some I've never met") offered practical help when she was diagnosed as having cancer—help that included obtaining information, donating money and blood, assistance with shopping, housework, and transport. She describes these generally undervalued, relatively impersonal acts under the title, "A Lesbian Love Story," emphasizing them as acts of caring by lesbians for lesbians and so as building lesbian community.

In constructing lesbian feminist politics of friendship, we need to move beyond the constraints of psychological versions of what friendship is and how it works. Depsychologizing friendship means expanding the concept beyond individual personalities and personal likes and dislikes. Friendship does not always have to involve a sense of personal liking or emotional bonding: it can also encompass impersonal acts of care for other lesbians. Expanding our concept of friendship in this way to include the ethics and politics of lesbian community may serve to bring those communities into being and may enable us to realize a vision of what is possible for lesbians when we integrate the personal with the political.

REFERENCES

Card, C. 1995. *Lesbian choices*. New York: Columbia University Press.
Kitzinger, C., and A. Coyle. 1995. Lesbian and gay couples: Speaking of difference. *The Psychologist* 8: 64–68.
Kitzinger, C., and R. Perkins. 1993. *Changing our minds: Lesbian feminism and
  psychology*. New York: New York University Press.

Contributors

CONNIE S. CHAN, Ph.D., was born in Hong Kong and grew up in Honolulu, Hawaii. She is an associate professor of Human Services and codirector of the Institute for Asian American Studies at the University of Massachusetts at Boston. As a psychologist, her work focuses upon the interaction of culture, gender, and sexuality among complexities of emotions and relationships. She is particularly intrigued by cultural nuances and the ways in which families have become cross-cultural as well as intergenerational, including those built among friends.

MARK COHAN is a second-year doctoral student in the sociology program at the University of Florida. His interests include masculinity and social constructionism. He is currently preparing a paper with William Marsiglio entitled "Young Fathers and Child Development," to be published in *The Role of the Father in Child Development,* 3d ed., edited by Michael E. Lamb. In the near future, Mark plans to conduct a narrative study of men involved in antisexist activism.

KAREN CONNER is a fourth-year doctoral candidate in the counseling psychology program at the University of Florida. She is particularly interested in dissociation and the nature of consciousness, as well as personality and psychopathology. Karen looks forward to a career as a psychotherapist, educator, and research scientist, focusing specifically on these interests.

LAUREN CRUX, at any given moment, is a poet, photographer, art student, backpacker, cyclist, storyteller, and adventurer. Her poetry and prose have appeared in numerous journals and anthologies. She lives in Corona Del Mar, California.

NANCY S. DAVIDSON maintains a psychotherapy practice in Manhattan and New Haven, Connecticut. She has a doctorate in clinical psychology from Antioch/New England. In addition to intensive psychotherapy with individuals with abuse histories, Nancy works with couples, groups, and families. Most recently, she has begun focusing her work on providing career counseling geared to the particular needs of the gay/lesbian/bisexual community through classes, workshops, and individualized sessions. She researches and writes about how to heal internalized homophobia.

GAIL M. DOTTIN was born a poor black chi . . . (Wait a minute. Sorry, someone else's life). She was born a middle-class lesbian princess in Jamaica, Queens to Huxtable-family prototypes from Panama and the West Indies. (Her dad's sweaters weren't as cool as Bill's, though). She's a graduate of Sarah Lawrence College, where she supposedly studied creative writing and theatre but, generally, stayed up late ruminating about life and perfecting angst. (It is also the place that, according to her mom, she was brainwashed, in a Moonie-like fashion, into *that* lifestyle, by ill-meaning white people.) She has been writing since she could hold a crayon and discovered what they did to interior painted walls. She's studied, written, directed, and performed theatre for the past fourteen years including two of her own one-woman shows: *Double Stuff* and *The Questions and Other Observations about Growing Up Sane.* She was a member of the renowned WOW Cafe, where she was an actor and a techie for a whole bunch of shows, including her own *Disconnected Pieces,* a work in progress about oppression and hope. She has rearranged her entire life to edit and compile a book of coming out stories of people of Latin and/or African descent, tentatively entitled *Brothas y Hermanas.* The book will be a tremendous gift to her community and those curious about it, reflecting upon the roles of race and spirituality in the process of sexual discovery. Gail thanks her Creator for leading her to Unity Fellowship Church, showing her that the bigots aren't right; being gay and Christian is not an oxymoron.

Someday, she hopes to produce a grunge album with Whitney Houston.

DIANE M. FELICIO, Ph.D. was born and raised in Queens, New York. She is the youngest and only daughter in a white, middle-class, Italian American family. She was raised Catholic and, to the dismay of many of her friends, had mostly positive experiences within the Church. Although she does not support the politics of the Catholic Church, she still considers herself a practicing Catholic. "It is how I know God." Diane holds a Ph.D. in social psychology from the University of Vermont. Her research on the experiences of women in medical school was recently published in the journal *Basic and Applied Social Psychology*. Diane currently teaches psychology and feminist studies as a faculty member at Goddard College in Plainfield, Vermont. When she is not working, she is usually on the telephone with Eileen, riding her bicycle, baking, or discovering the "joys" of first-time homeowning with her partner, Jan, in Burlington, Vermont.

JANE FUTCHER and Catherine Hopkins met and fell in love when they were working at Harper and Row Publishers in New York in 1974. Jane is the author of two novels, *Crush* and *Promise Not to Tell*, and of *Marin: The Place, the People*. Her essays, short fiction, and poems have appeared in the following anthologies: *Bushfire, Afterglow, Hotlicks, The Next Step, Dyke Life, Lesbian Adventure Stories, A Loving Testimony*, and *The Poetry of Sex*. She is a masseuse, an ESL teacher, and an editorial writer for a daily newspaper. She lives in Novato, California, with her partner, Erin Carney, who is a home-birth midwife.

RUTH HALL, Ph.D., is an assistant professor in the Department of Psychology at Trenton State College. Her research interests focus on racial identity development in women and athletes. Dr. Hall currently is completing a master's degree in sports psychology. She also is a licensed clinical psychologist in private practice and a consultant to agencies and organizations concerning issues affecting people of color, women, and athletes. She is the 1995 recipient of the Christine Ladd-Franklin Award of the Association for Women in Psychology for her outstanding service to feminist psychology. Her interest in friendships derives from her own rich and vibrant congregration of fictive kin and the strength and love that they engender in each other.

ANNDEE HOCHMAN is a freelance writer of articles, book reviews, profiles, essays, and short stories that have appeared in *Ms.*, the *New York Times Book Review,* the *Philadelphia Inquirer, Philadelphia Magazine,* the *Oregonian, Glimmer Train Stories,* and other magazines, journals, and anthologies. Her first book, *Everyday Acts & Small Subversions: Women Reinventing Family, Community, and Home,* was published in 1994 by the Eighth Mountain Press. For nearly five years, she thrived in Portland, Oregon, with Rachael Silverman and John Duke, her allies and accomplices. The three occupied a series of houses in which they played music, wrote stories, watched Bette Davis movies, argued, laughed, and ate blackened-tofu sandwiches.

CATHERINE HOPKINS was an art director for Doubleday and Harper & Row before she became a freelance graphic designer and photographer. She has had photography shows both locally and nationally. At the time of this writing, she was living in Catskill, New York, with the novelist Joan Alden; they are the coauthors of the children's book *A Boy's Best Friend* (Alyson Publications). Catherine passed away on January 4, 1996.

BEV JO is working-class, disabled (chronically ill with myalgic encephalomyelitis/chronic fatigue immune dysfunction syndrome since 1981), ex-Catholic, and of Irish, English, German, and French ancestry. She was born in 1950. She's never been heterosexual and has been a Lesbian from her earliest memories. She became lovers with her first lover in 1968 and became a Dyke Separatist in 1972. She cowrote (with Linda Strega and Ruston) *Dykes-Loving-Dykes: Dyke Separatist Politics for Lesbians Only.*

KATHLEEN M. JONES is a twenty-five-year-old black woman and a lesbian. She has completed a master's degree in guidance and counseling. In her spare time she likes to read, go horseback riding, write poetry and short stories. Kathleen is planning to become an educational psychologist and work with language impaired children.

CAREY KAPLAN, Ph.D., is director of Gender Studies and professor of English at Saint Michael's College in Colchester, Vermont. Carey has published books on the modern British writer, Doris Lessing. Her most recent book, written with Ellen Cronan Rose, is *The Canon and the Common Reader*, a feminist analysis of the current curriculum debates.

CELIA KITZINGER, Ph.D., director of Women's Studies at Loughborough University, U.K., is the author of *The Social Construction of Lesbianism* (Sage, 1987), and coauthor of *Changing Our Minds: Lesbian Feminism and Psychology* (New York University Press, 1993). Her edited books include *Heterosexuality* (Sage, 1993) and *Feminism and Discourse* (Sage, 1995), both with Sue Wilkinson.

HILARY LAPSLEY, Ph.D., is a senior lecturer in women's studies at the University of Waikato, Hamilton, New Zealand. She is a psychologist who has mainly worked on tough topics such as sexual abuse of children, pornography, woman battering, and mental health services. To keep her sanity she turned to studying psychological growth instead of psychological damage. Her interest in Margaret Mead and Ruth Benedict's friendship began when she researched them for a case study of women and mentoring. She was fascinated by their story, and now she is at work on a full-length biography of the pair, to be published by University of Massachusetts Press.

KRIS S. MORGAN, Ph.D., collects rocks and ceramic fish and loves television as well as novels written for teenagers. She lives with her partner of fifteen years and two furries. Now in her mid-thirties, graduate school behind her, her life feels more comfortable all the time. She loves her work as a counseling psychologist in private practice in Seattle, Washington.

MARCIA MUNSON, forty-four, has been a grass-roots lesbian community organizer and feminist activist since the early 1970s.

Her projects have included founding the Astoria Women's Resource Center, the Oregon Women's Land Trust, and the Women's Wilderness Institute Northwest; leading consciousness-raising groups for San Francisco NOW; and passing a gay rights ordinance in her hometown, Boulder, Colorado. She has worked as a wilderness guide, a forest fire fighter, and a mail carrier. She currently works seasonally as a white-collar bureaucrat for the federal government, and does sex-education workshops at lesbian events. She spends her free time backpacking, hiking, and cross-country skiing.

REBECCA M. NERISON, Ph.D., ever the explorer, has made Cape Cod her latest home. When she's not reading, writing, painting, beachcombing, or enjoying domesticity, she works as a psychologist.

CHERIE G. O'BOYLE has lived and worked most of her life in northern California. Before entering graduate school in 1987, she was a carpenter and licensed general building contractor for sixteen years, a planning commissioner for the County of Sacramento, and a feminist political activist. She received her Ph.D. in psychology from the University of Oregon, Eugene, in 1991. She is currently an assistant professor at California State University, San Marcos, where she teaches developmental psychology and the psychology of women, and conducts research on emotional and social development in infancy and attachment across the lifespan. Cherie is single, and the mother of a grown daughter.

TERRI DE LA PEÑA has written about lesbian friendships in her novels, *Margins* and *Latin Satins* (Seal Press, 1992, 1994). In her forthcoming collection, *Territories* (Third Woman Press), she also includes stories about friendships between women and between lesbians and gay men. She is on the editorial boards of the *Lesbian Review of Books* and *Conmocion: Revista de Lesbianas Latinas*. She lives in her hometown, Santa Monica, California, where she is writing her third novel.

SHELAGH ROBINSON, twenty-eight, is currently pursuing doctoral studies in educational psychology in Montreal, Canada, and she continues to share food fantasies with Karen and Shawna. Her goals include counseling lesbian and gay youth, adults, and couples and entering into private practice and opening a bed and breakfast in the Okanagen. Although she feels that shedonistic spontaneity is one of her greatest attributes, she does recognize the karmic ramifications of her behaviors and is striving to move away from the center of the universe. She will one day acquire a life for herself, a partner, and a well-stocked fridge, on the beaches of Gili Trawangan.

ELLEN CRONAN ROSE, Ph.D., is director of Women's Studies and professor of history at the University of Nevada at Las Vegas. She has published books and articles on the modern British writers Doris Lessing and Margaret Drabble. Her most recent book, written with Carey Kaplan, is *The Canon and the Common Reader,* a feminist analysis of the current curriculum debates.

SUZANNA ROSE, Ph.D., is associate professor of psychology and of the Institute for Women's and Gender Studies at the University of Missouri-St. Louis. Her research is in the area of personal relationships, focusing primarily on how gender, sexual orientation, and race affect friendships, romantic relationships, and sexuality. She has a special interest in lesbian dating and relationship development. Dr. Rose also is founder and director of the St. Louis Lesbian and Gay Anti-Violence Project, which documents homophobic hate crimes and provides counseling and referrals to victims.

ESTHER D. ROTHBLUM is a professor in the Department of Psychology, University of Vermont. Her research and writing have focused on lesbian mental health, and she is former chair of the Committee on Lesbian and Gay Concerns of the American Psychological Association. She received the Distinguished Scientific Contribution Award from the Society for the Psychological Study of Lesbian and Gay Issues. Esther has edited the books *Loving Boldly: Issues Facing Lesbians* (Haworth Press, 1989) and *Boston Marriages: Romantic But Asexual Relationships among Contemporary Lesbians* (University of Massachusetts Press, 1993). She is currently working on two edited books, one on lesbians in academia (Routledge), and the other on the prevention of heterosexism and homophobia (Sage).

PAT SCHMATZ is a thirty-two-year-old middle-class lesbian. She grew up in a Christian family in rural Wisconsin and came out as a lesbian in 1981 in Lansing, Michigan. She moved to the Bay Area in 1984, where she met Lynnepig, quit drinking, and started writing. She currently works in inventory control for a computer software company, where she has great fun driving the forklift and counting things.

JEANNE L. STANLEY, Ph.D., grew up in Towson, Maryland and is currently living in Philadelphia, Pennsylvania. She is the coordinator of the master's program in psychological services at the University of Pennsylvania, where she also teaches courses in the psychology of women, psychological interventions, and sociocultural diversity. Dr. Stanley also has a private practice as a therapist, working predominantly with the lesbian, gay, bisexual, and transgendered community. Her interest in lesbian friendships culminated in her 1993 dissertation, entitled "The Partnered Lesbian and Her Friends: The Impact of Friendship on Self-Esteem and Relationship Satisfaction." When she is not teaching, counseling, or conducting research, she is enjoying the company of her partner and, not surprisingly, her friends.

LINDA STREGA is a working-class, ex-Catholic Lesbian Separatist of Italian descent, born in an East Coast U.S. factory town in 1941. She's been a Lesbian since 1972 and a Separatist since 1973. She cowrote *Dykes-Loving-Dykes: Dyke Separatist Politics for Lesbians Only* with Bev Jo and Ruston, published in 1990 and available through Battleaxe, P.O. Box 9806, Oakland, CA 94613.

MARIE D. THOMAS is a native New Yorker who received her Ph.D. in psychology from Fordham University, New York City in 1981. After eight years of full-time teaching at the College of Mount St. Vincent in New York, she moved to San Diego to work on gender and multicultural issues with the U.S. Navy. She is currently an assistant professor at California State University, San Marcos, where she teaches psychological testing and statistics. She is the regional coordinator for the San Diego chapter of the Association for Women in Psychology. Marie lives with her life partner and has no children.

JOYCE WARSHOW, along with Adrienne Smith and Barbara Sang, coedited *Lesbians at Midlife: The Creative Transition.* Joyce has been on the steering committee of the Feminist Therapy Institute and is president of the Women's Psychotherapy Referral Service in New York. She is now turning her attention to video portraits of older lesbian activists, who have been activists all their lives and who link their own civil rights issues with other civil rights movements. At the age of fifty-eight, she's delighted to be learning new skills which she hopes to use to educate the public and benefit our community at the same time.

JACQUELINE S. WEINSTOCK is an assistant professor in the Human Development and Family Studies Program at the University of Vermont. Her research and writing have focused on friendships, especially the roles they play in the development of individuals and communities confronting various forms of oppression. Jackie is coauthor with Mary Field Belenky and Lynne Bond of the forthcoming book *A Tradition That Has No Name: Public Homeplaces and the Development of People, Families, and Communities.* She is currently at work on an investigation of the friendship experiences and expectations of lesbian, gay, bisexual, and transgender individuals.